Building & Tuning High

ELECTRONIC FUEL INJECTION

Custom Engine Management Systems for Domestic and Import 4, 6, and 8-Cylinder Engines

BEN STRADER

CarTech®

Copyright © 2004 by Ben Strader

All rights reserved. All text and photographs in this publication are the property of the author, unless otherwise noted or credited. It is unlawful to reproduce – or copy in any way – resell, or redistribute this information without the express written permission of the publisher.

All text, photographs, drawings, and other artwork (hereafter referred to as information) contained in this publication is sold without any warranty as to its usability or performance. In all cases, original manufacturer's recommendations, procedures, and instructions supersede and take precedence over descriptions herein. Specific component design and mechanical procedures – and the qualifications of individual readers – are beyond the control of the publisher, therefore the publisher disclaims all liability, either expressed or implied, for use of the information in this publication. All risk for its use is entirely assumed by the purchaser/user. In no event will Cartech®, Inc., or the author be liable for any indirect, special, or consequential damages, including but not limited to personal injury or any other damages, arising out of the use or misuse of any information in this publication.

This book is an independent publication, and the author(s) and/or publisher thereof are not in any way associated with, and are not authorized to act on behalf of any of the manufacturers included in this book. All registered trademarks are the property of their owners. The publisher reserves the right to revise this publication or change its content from time to time without obligation to notify any persons of such revisions or changes.

Edited By: Travis Thompson

Layout By: Bruce Leckie

ISBN-13 978-1-884089-79-4
ISBN-10 1-884089-79-8

Printed in China

CarTech®
39966 Grand Avenue
North Branch, MN 55056
Telephone (651) 277-1200 • (800) 551-4754 • Fax: (651) 277-1203
www.cartechbooks.com

OVERSEAS DISTRIBUTION BY:

Brooklands Books Ltd.
P.O. Box 146, Cobham, Surrey, KT11 1LG, England
Telephone 01932 865051 • Fax 01932 868803
www.brooklands-books.com

Brooklands Books Aus.
3/37-39 Green Street, Banksmeadow, NSW 2019, Australia
Telephone 2 9695 7055 • Fax 2 9695 7355

Front Cover, Main: **This 3.5-liter Acura V6 powers a sand rail owned by Mike Dean. Induction consists of twin turbos feeding a custom EFI system that includes a custom plenum, six individual throttle bodies, and Autronic controls. With 18 pounds of boost, this engine produced 456 horsepower** *at the wheels.* **Wiring and installation were done by Dino Dobbins; the system was tuned by the author.**

Front Cover, Inset: **The easiest way to really tune your car, either with your laptop or with a hand-held programmer, is on a chassis dyno. Plus, it's much safer than doing it on the street.**

Back Cover, Upper Right: **MoTeC is viewed by many as the king of the hill when it comes to flexibility and reliability in a fuel-injection system. MoTeC's desire to be the industry leader in fuel-injection technology has driven it to stay on top of all the latest technology. Chances are — if you have an engine, MoTeC can control it.**

Back Cover, Upper Left: **Some fuel injection kits, including this one from ACCEL, come with everything you need to get going — including the intake manifold, throttle body, sensors, fuel pump, and air filter.**

Back Cover, Lower: **Tuning a sophisticated induction system, like this one featuring individual throttle bodies, is easier to accomplish with computer control. Fuel injection can help you have good idle quality, great wide-open throttle performance, and excellent throttle response throughout.**

TABLE OF CONTENTS

Dedication		 5
About the Author		 5
Preface		 6
Introduction		 7
Chapter 1	**Carburetors vs. Fuel Injection**	 10
	Carburetor Operation	 11
Chapter 2	**The Basics of Electronics**	 17
	Voltage	 18
	Amperes	 18
	Resistance	 19
	Catch a Wave	 19
	ECU Output Control	 21
Chapter 3	**Tools and Equipment**	 23
	DVOM	 23
	Test Light	 24
	Powered Test Light	 25
	Vacuum Pump	 25
	Fuel Pressure Gauge	 25
	Oscilloscope	 26
	Dynamometers	 26
	Air/Fuel Ratio Monitor	 28
Chapter 4	**ECU Inputs**	 30
	MAP Sensor	 30
	MAF Sensor	 33
	Throttle Position Sensor	 34
	Coolant Temperature Sensor	 35
	Intake Air Temperature Sensor	 35
	Engine Speed	 36
	Camshaft Position Sensor	 36
	Knock Sensor	 37
	Oxygen Sensor	 37
	Exhaust Gas Temperature Sensor	 38
Chapter 5	**ECU Outputs**	 39
	Ignition Outputs	 39
	Fan Relays	 40
	Air Conditioning Relays	 40
	Injectors	 41
	Matching Injectors to the Engine	 42

Table of Contents

Chapter 6	**Tuning Maps and Basic Engine Calibration**	45
	Base Fuel Map	45
	Base Ignition Map	47
	Idle Spark Map	48
	Coolant Temp Correction	49
	Air Temp Correction	49
	Altitude Correction	50
	Acceleration Enrichment	50
	Deceleration Enleanment	50
	Basic Engine Calibration	51
	Idle Fuel Requirements	52
	Part-Throttle Requirements	52
	Full-Throttle Requirements	53
	Understanding Ignition Timing	55
	Correction Maps	56
Introduction to Part 2		57
Chapter 7	ACCEL/DFI	58
Chapter 8	AEM Plug & Play	65
Chapter 9	Autronic	70
Chapter 10	Edelbrock Pro-Flo and Advanced Programmable Fuel-Injection Systems	77
Chapter 11	EFI Technology	83
Chapter 12	Electromotive	88
Chapter 13	F.A.S.T	95
Chapter 14	Haltech	103
Chapter 15	Holley Commander 950	109
Chapter 16	MoTeC	114
Chapter 17	Simple Digital Systems (SDS)	120
Appendix A	EFI Manufacturers	126
Appendix B	Fun Formulas	127

Dedication

I would like to dedicate this book to my dad, Robert, whom I've always strived to make proud of me. He always believed that I could do anything I wanted and he had a gentle way of relaying that message to me. Growing up as a kid, I always thought that there was nothing my dad couldn't do, and I wanted to be just like that when I grew up.

Thanks dad, I hope you are as proud of me as I am of you.

About the Author

Ben Strader was born and raised in northwest Indiana. He grew up with a passion for all things mechanical and often daydreamed about racecars and what it would be like to build and tune race engines. He began his racing career at age 17 by helping out a friend who owned and raced a stock car at the local circle track. It was the nights when the track was rained out that he actually loved the most — that's when everyone would sit around and "bench race," retelling the stories of the glory days. He knew then that his only possible career could be in racing.

Strader was a fire fighter and welder with the US Navy, where he also studied engineering. After the service, he landed a job with Protomotive Engineering in Southern California building and tuning high-powered Porsche engines using turbochargers and electronic fuel injection. That's where he gained the valuable experience he would later need when he operated his own engine building and dyno tuning shop in Southern California.

The shop had an engine dyno, chassis dyno, cylinder head flowbench, and a first class cylinder-head machine shop. Strader regularly worked on building, testing, and development for all types of engines — four cylinders, V-6s and V-8s, using carburetors, EFI, nitrous, superchargers, and turbochargers. He built and tuned engines for street and show cars along with projects for race teams in circle track, drag racing, road racing, off-road racing, and even a few marine-racing engines.

Strader spent literally thousands of hours learning the ropes of testing and calibrating a wide variety of engines, and became familiar with most all the EFI systems available on the market today. He also traveled across the country to tune race engines on contract; this gave him first-hand experience on many different engine and chassis dynos, along with exposing him to many other philosophies of engine tuning.

In 2003, Ben sold his shop and founded EFI University in Southern California, which offers seminars on building and tuning high-performance EFI systems (www.efi101.com). EFI University travels all over the world, and it is now a place where Strader can share his knowledge by teaching others how to build and tune EFI systems and engines.

PREFACE

I never started out to write this or any book. I actually began compiling this information to give technical seminars, so that I could share my passion for fuel injection with others, and pass on my knowledge to those wanting to learn more about building electronic fuel injection (EFI) systems. I figured it was a good way to have fun and promote my business of building custom EFI systems at the same time.

Somewhere along the way though, through encouragement from John Baechtel of Westech Performance, my friend and fellow enthusiast who has written many books on various automotive subjects, I was introduced to the wonderful staff of editors at CarTech and S-A Design. We decided that this was a good opportunity to broaden our horizons and really get this information out there so that you, the readers, could access easy-to-understand information about how to go about building and tuning your own custom EFI system.

Writing this book has been a long project and a tremendous learning experience that has introduced me to some of the most experienced and friendliest people in the fuel-injection industry. Hopefully, you will enjoy reading this book as much as I enjoyed researching and writing it.

Eventually, I did turn part of this project into not just a technical seminar, but a thriving educational institution called EFI University. This is the first and only school of its kind, designed to teach everyone from novice to veteran about building, setting up, tuning, and troubleshooting a modern engine management system. I owe the success of my company to all those who have helped me along the way in this book project, in my own career, and in my personal life.

I hope that this book will serve as a textbook-like manual for you to follow as you progress through your own projects whether as a hobby, or as a career. Have fun along the way. Be creative in your projects, and always remember that there are many other people in this industry who you can count on for help when you need it! Good Luck!

On a special note, I would like to thank Lawrence "Chip" Latshaw for all of his help with the photography for this book.

INTRODUCTION

The advent of electronic fuel injection (EFI) has allowed performance enthusiasts access to a whole new world of engine tuning. Modern electronic engine management components are available that can be much easier to tune than carburetors and distributors.

Modern engine bays are very complex compared to those of the hot rods of yesteryear — this one from a Chrysler Sebring. Can you count the fuel-injection and ignition sensors in this picture?

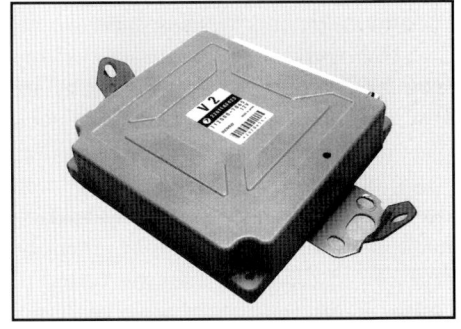

Factory ECUs do a fine job of controlling OEM (stock) engines. However, due to their proprietary nature and the complicated equipment and procedures necessary for modification, recalibrating them is beyond the scope of the average hot-rodder.

Since the internal combustion engine was invented, men have tried to find ways of making it more efficient. It seems like by now every possible avenue should have been explored, and it shouldn't be possible to progress any farther than what we already have. Still, the spirit of the hot-rodder lives on and we constantly find new and innovative ways to make our engines more powerful and more efficient.

For those of us who dare to strive for only the best in performance and efficiency, we have the major auto manufacturers to thank for giving us electronic fuel injection (EFI). At first we feared EFI, thinking that they had taken away our ability to modify and tune our performance engines, but then the fear of the unknown gave way to the challenge of learning and understanding how these "black boxes"

Building and Tuning High-Performance Fuel Injection

Introduction

worked, and better yet — how to modify them.

Before long, companies started to market their ability to modify the factory computers to enable them to control aftermarket parts and engines.

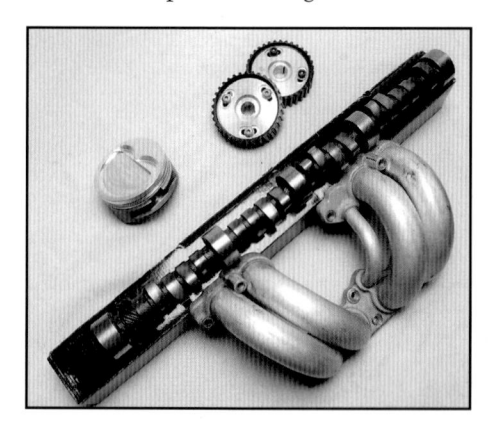

Custom engine management systems enable tuners to get the most from aftermarket performance parts such as camshafts, intake manifolds, high-compression pistons, and modified cylinder heads. The factory ECU will not be able to keep up with these serious modifications.

Modifying factory computers, however effective, is limited by several factors. First, it can be very slow and tedious because of the nature by which it occurs. The process usually requires a fair bit of specialized equipment, mounds of knowledge about computer programming, and lots of labor removing and replacing EPROMs or chips, which can, in some cases, only be used once.

The operator must remove the chip from the computer, place it in a device that can extract its information, decipher this information, decide which parts of the program to change, and then program this new information back into the chip. It may then be replaced in the computer and tested to see if the desired results were achieved. This method of tuning, like any other, can require lots of trial-and-error before the perfect combination is reached. That means that each time, the entire process must be repeated. This method was very effective, but the average hot-rodder was still very much in the dark about any of this computer

The EPROM is the heart of the factory ECU. The information stored in it is changed during the recalibration process. To do this with an OEM ECU requires sophisticated equipment and complicated procedures.

Aftermarket ECUs have made engine tuning more accessible to the average hot-rodder. They are user friendly, easy to interface, and most are infinitely adjustable to suit different engine configurations.

language mumbo-jumbo and was forced to rely on the skills of others to make their projects work. This simply did not conform to the do-it-yourself mentality of most enthusiasts, and so the marketplace for a better way to mate rowdy performance engines with sophisticated computer control was born.

Enter the aftermarket programmable fuel-injection system. These stand-alone engine management computers

Hot-rodders can purchase and install custom electronic fuel-injection systems and program them for unique engine applications. Enthusiasts can street-tune these systems or enlist the help of professional tuners and dynamometers. Don't be afraid to get help from someone with experience.

Building and Tuning High-Performance Fuel Injection

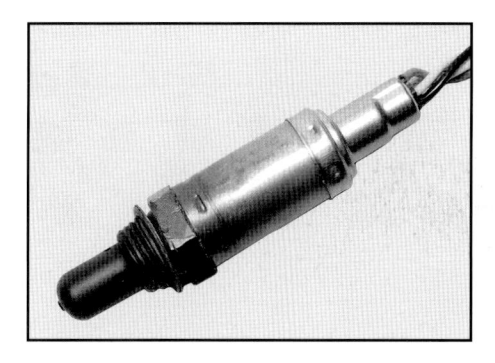

Introduction

Oxygen (O2) sensors provide feedback about air/fuel ratios, enabling tuners to quickly reach performance goals. The O2 sensor produces an electrical signal proportional to the engine's air/fuel ratio by sampling the amount of oxygen and hydrocarbons in the exhaust stream.

Tuning the engine's fuel curve with a carburetor requires properly sizing the main jets to match the airflow over a range of engine speeds. The power valve adds extra fuel under heavy engine loads.

Tuning engines with mechanical devices such as distributors and carburetors is a lengthy trial-and-error process. Tuning the distributor's advance curve relative to engine speed requires altering the weights in the centrifugal advance mechanism and the tension of the springs holding the weights in place.

can be configured to control a variety of engine functions and, with easy to understand and use interface software, can be finely tuned by most anyone who can turn on a laptop computer.

Now the average enthusiast can plop down his money and take home a user-friendly black box that he can use to tune his own engine in real time, without having to remove and replace any cumbersome chips and without the expensive and complex equipment required to reprogram them. Not to mention the fact that no special programming language is required to understand how to use these systems.

In addition to the ability to make changes to the engine's fuel and spark curves, engine tuners now had helpful tools such as the oxygen sensor to aid in feedback information to give them a sense of how well their program is working.

This is much easier than the lengthy trial-and-error process that was required when they were dialing in their carburetor jets and distributor weights.

PURPOSE

The purpose of this book is to allow the reader to get to the next level of automotive performance by providing a thorough investigation of the theory and operation of electronic fuel injection. It is aimed at all levels of enthusiasts from the novice hot-rodder to the experienced professional engine builder who is currently tuning carburetors.

This book will help you first to understand what it is that an engine needs in order for it to perform in a given manner, and then how to get there using computer control. For instance, you will learn how to tune an engine for great part-throttle economy, yet have lightning fast response and brute power when you put your foot down. You will also learn several techniques for tuning that will allow you to quickly and efficiently extract the desired performance from your engine.

The goal is not to try and make you an overnight expert EFI tuner, but to arm you with the basic knowledge and information required to set up and tune an engine using modern aftermarket programmable fuel-injection systems.

It is our intention to cover the basics of how these systems work, along with the general principles of electronics that operate under the surface of every computer-controlled engine management system. We will then cover in depth the different brands and models of aftermarket systems available for you to choose from.

Once you have read and understand this book, it will serve as a resource for you to call upon when trying to decide which system will fit your needs, and how to use and understand the features of that particular system.

No matter how bold the engine project, stand-alone programmable EFI systems can help it reach maximum performance. Modern aftermarket EFI systems can control supercharged, turbocharged, nitrous-oxide injected, or naturally aspirated engines with ease.

Building and Tuning High-Performance Fuel Injection

Chapter 1

Carburetors vs. Fuel Injection

The debate in recent years throughout the performance community over whether or not carburetors are as good as EFI has been a heated one at times, but a close look at the capabilities of the two systems will reveal many shortcomings of the carburetor that can be easily overcome with computer control.

EFI and carburetors have been tested against each other many times and in many different configurations to see which one makes more power, but in my opinion, few of these tests have been properly performed. This may sound whiny at first, but know that I completely understand the difficulties involved in making any testing program accurate and consistent. Facing the challenges involved in trying to accurately compare two such diverse animals is a monumental, if not impossible task.

The problem is that the two are not designed to do the same things, yet we always want to try and make them compete in an arena they were not intended to be in. For instance, a manifold that was originally designed for a carburetor must deal with complex issues of a wet-flow environment where air and fuel must exist together before they reach the combustion chamber. On the other hand, a manifold designed for the air-only requirements of EFI can have a very different shape that is much more inclined to maintain high air velocity without sacrificing volume of flow. The two are not the same, and are required to perform entirely different functions, and therefore it is difficult to compare them on an even playing field. When carburetors and fuel injectors are tested on the same kind of intake manifold, one or the other would always have an advantage. This because each system is designed to make the most efficient use of a certain type of manifold, and testing either sys-

In recent years, electronic fuel injection has become increasingly popular with the street-rodder sect because it allows the use of radical intake manifold configurations, yet still provides very docile engine operation for street driving.

The carburetor is the traditional method for delivering air and fuel into internal combustion engines. This model is a 750-cfm 4-barrel Road Demon manufactured by Demon Carburetion.

10 Building and Tuning High-Performance Fuel Injection

Carburetors vs. Fuel Injection

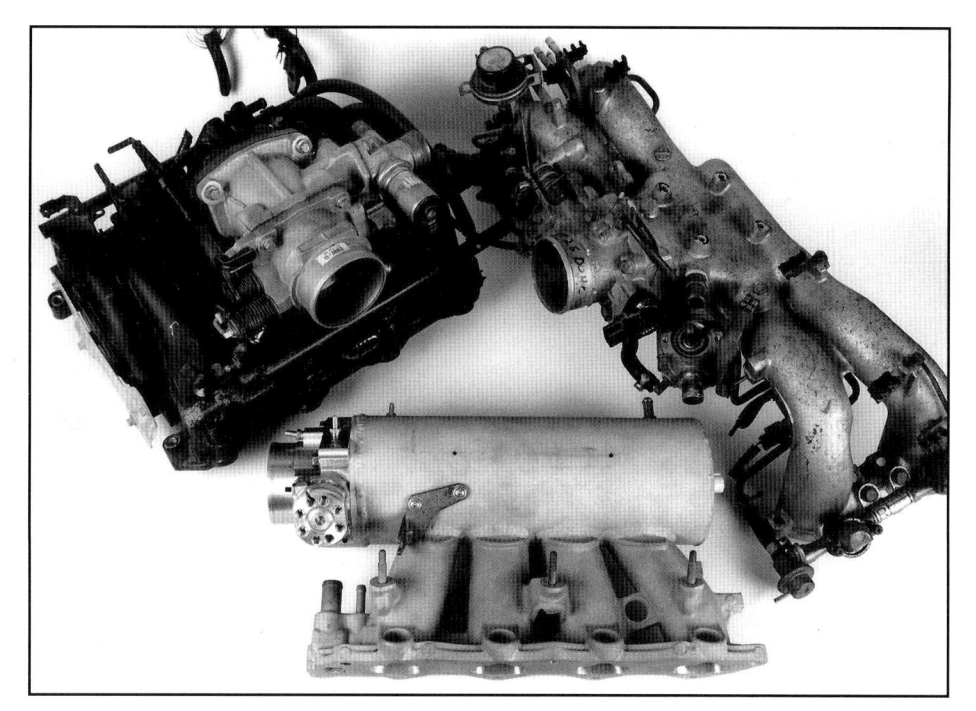

Complex manifold shapes are possible in the air-only environment of an EFI system. Carbureted manifold systems must deal with air and fuel mixed together. In this environment, fuel can sometimes puddle in the intake causing uneven fuel distribution to the cylinders. This happens because fuel is heavier than air.

Typically, manufacturers have used 4-barrel carburetors (right) in applications requiring higher power, and 2-barrel carburetors (left) when fuel efficiency is the primary goal.

This early model Holley carburetor shows just how simple of a device the carburetor was in the beginning. It was designed mostly through trial and error to achieve the correct ratio of fuel and air delivery over a very narrow range of engine speed. It may look crude, but it got the job done!

tem on any other manifold would skew any results heavily to one side.

As an example, say we took a mid-1980s Chevrolet 350-ci engine and placed it on the dynamometer and tested two systems on the same engine: a carburetor on top of a manifold designed for flowing air and wet fuel, and a fuel injection system with a dry type manifold designed for flowing only air.

Theoretically, if both engines were tuned properly and both could have the same amount of airflow at a given engine speed, they would produce similar power outputs. The problem arises when we try and test both systems on the same manifold. Imagine if we took the carburetor and placed it on top of a long-runner Chevy tuned-port manifold. The manifold was never designed with shapes and sizes in mind for flowing fuel through it. The fuel would easily fall out of the air-stream and form puddles, which would greatly affect the fuel distribution at low engine speeds.

Conversely, if we test a fuel-injection system on a wet-style manifold, we would be giving up the low-speed torque advantage these systems are designed for because of the fact that their manifolds were designed specifically to have good fuel distribution and very high-speed airflow to each cylinder at low engine speeds. In the end, if either system were tested on the other's manifold type, the results would be heavily in favor of one or the other.

However, an engine is ultimately an air pump, and its power output is generally dictated by the amount of airflow that can be obtained at a given engine speed. Therefore either system can be capable of quite comparable peak power outputs.

I believe though, that regardless of peak output numbers, the fuel-injected engine will outperform the carbureted engine in overall power due to the fact that it can be tuned to correctly control the engine's fuel curve over a vastly wider power band than the carburetor can. Let's take a look at why this is true.

Carburetor Operation

Hopefully by this stage in your engine-tuning career, you have a basic understanding of what an engine needs to perform. In fact, you may have successfully tuned one or many carburetors to accomplish this task.

Having said that, it is assumed that you already know how a carburetor works, but at the risk of seeming rather academic, I'll briefly explain the basic operation.

A carburetor uses a round tube, which is narrower in the middle than at the ends. This tube is called a venturi. Being narrower in the middle creates a restriction as air tries to pass through this section of the tube. Bernoulli's law dictates that as air flows through this venturi, it must pick up speed, and also, that there is a corresponding drop in pressure at that same point. This drop in pressure can be viewed as a vacuum.

Building and Tuning High-Performance Fuel Injection

Bernoulli's Principle

Well before carburetors were ever invented, a man named Daniel Bernoulli described a mathematical equation that laid the foundation for what would become the world's most common method of supplying fuel to automotive engines in the twentieth century.

Daniel Bernoulli was born on February 8, 1700, in Groningen, Netherlands. He studied medicine at several famous universities before he became interested in mathematics. He published more than 70 papers dealing with physics and applications of probability theory before he died in 1782. The paper we are most concerned with deals with pressure and velocity.

Daniel imagined what would happen if a fluid passed though a tube that was smaller in the middle section than at the ends. Through careful evaluation he realized two things about the dynamics of fluid behavior.

First, he found that if his tube were compared to a tube of the same length and diameter, but without the restriction in the middle, and an equal amount of fluid were passed through each tube over an equal amount of time, that the liquid in the first tube would have to increase and then decrease its speed at some point.

Second, he realized that in order for the fluid to increase its speed, there must be a corresponding increase in pressure to force the fluid to move more quickly, and that there must also be corresponding decrease in pressure when the fluid slows down again. Thus, the pressure and velocity of the fluid in question are interrelated.

If you look at the venturi in a carburetor, you will discover that it is just such a tube. Also, you will see that with the increase in speed that the air sees as it passes through the venturi, there is a corresponding drop in pressure just below the venturi. It is this low-pressure area, or vacuum, that causes fuel to be drawn out of the fuel bowls and into the air stream.

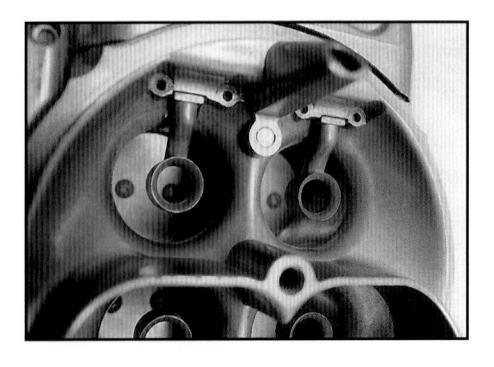

Carburetor venturis operate based on the Bernoulli principle. As air passes through the venturi, it speeds up, which causes a decrease in pressure. This decrease in pressure, or vacuum, draws fuel out of the fuel bowl and into the airstream.

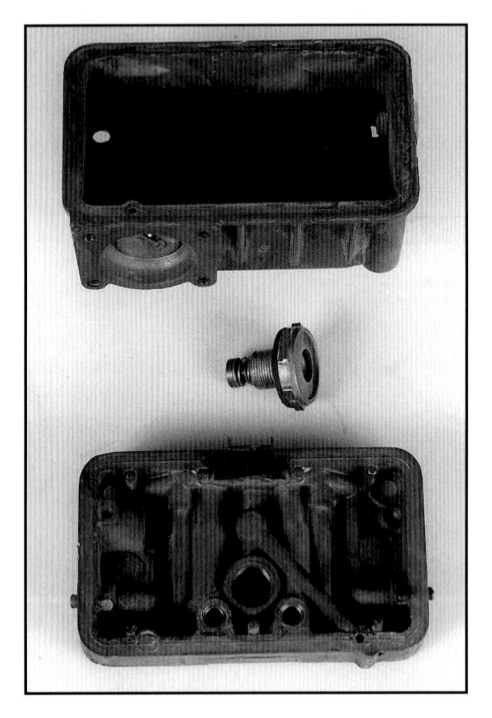

The carburetor's fuel delivery components consist of a fuel bowl, power valve, metering block, and jets. The fuel bowl holds the fuel, the power valve adds extra fuel under heavy acceleration, the metering block directs the fuel to the proper circuit, and the main jets determine the overall fuel calibration.

The small port that connects this high-speed, low-pressure area to a fuel source is normally referred to as the bowl. The bowl receives this vacuum signal and allows fuel to be drawn out into the fast-moving airstream through

The idle mixture screw allows the tuner to match the fuel delivery to the engine's fuel requirements at idle. Turning the screw in or out delivers more or less fuel to the engine under idle conditions. Once the throttle is opened, this circuit is no longer used.

a metered orifice called a jet. Here the fuel will be finely atomized and will travel along with the air on its way to the combustion chamber. Atomization takes place when the liquid fuel breaks down into smaller parts and mixes with the airstream.

If our engine were to always operate under the exact same conditions, then this would be a fairly acceptable way of metering fuel. Unfortunately though, an engine rarely operates in such a steady environment. Changes in engine speed, engine load, and atmospheric conditions can have a dramatic effect on the required amount of fuel the engine needs to continue operating effectively. Thus, we must find ways to supplement our single venturi.

Idle Circuit

When an engine is at idle, the throttle plates are closed and therefore present a large restriction to airflow. Again, this restriction creates a corresponding vacuum signal that is transferred to the fuel bowl. The trouble is that even though there is a powerful vacuum signal to our fuel bowl, there is not a very large quantity of air actually making it into the engine. Therefore it is necessary to create a way for a small amount of air to bypass the throttle plates to even out the ratio of fuel and air going into the

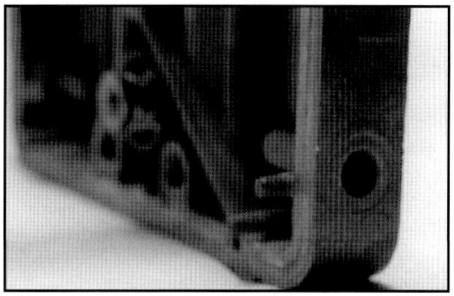

Carburetors vs. Fuel Injection

The idle mixture screw is located on the metering block behind the fuel bowl. Some 4-barrel carbs use an idle screw at all four corners, while others use only two on the front two venturis.

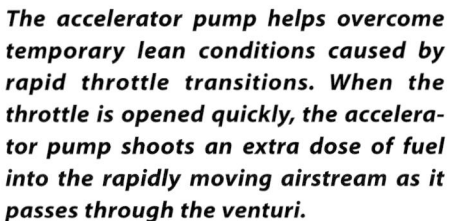

The accelerator pump helps overcome temporary lean conditions caused by rapid throttle transitions. When the throttle is opened quickly, the accelerator pump shoots an extra dose of fuel into the rapidly moving airstream as it passes through the venturi.

This early Holley carburetor was the first to use an acceleration enrichment lever to squirt extra fuel into the engine during rapid throttle changes. This design was so effective that its variants are still used today in high-performance carburetors.

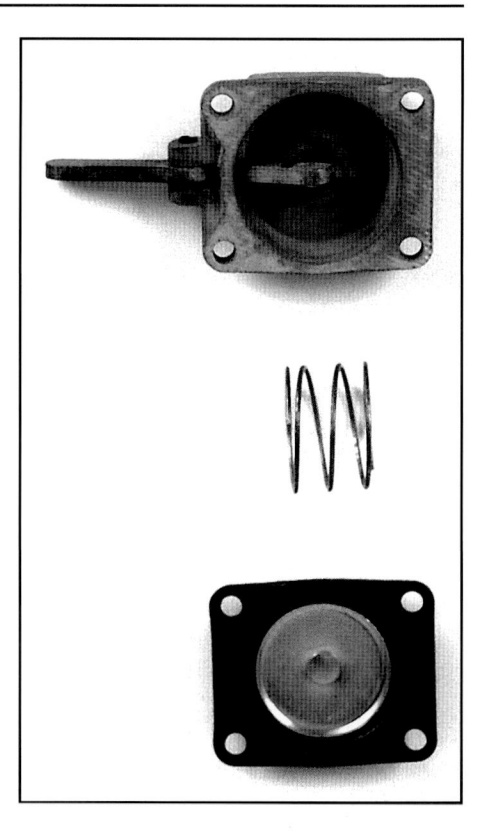

This is an exploded view of an accelerator pump. The throttle linkage is connected to the pump lever (top). The lever compresses the diaphragm, which pushes fuel through the metering block and into the venturi. When the throttle is released, the spring (center) causes the diaphragm to return to its normal position.

engine. This is normally accomplished by having a passage that circumvents the throttle plates and also has an adjustable diameter so that it can be fine-tuned. Typically, a tapered screw is used to move into or out of the passage to regulate the airflow getting past the throttle plates. This setup is called an idle circuit.

Acceleration Circuit

Once we have our engine idling smoothly, we have to deal with the next situation that occurs when we want to transition from idle to an open throttle position. Since air is so much lighter than fuel, it can accelerate much faster. This means that when we open the throttle plates rapidly and remove the restriction to airflow, the air can rush in very quickly, while it takes a moment for the fuel to catch up. This temporarily creates a lean mixture that will cause the engine to stumble and sometimes even stall.

This issue was overcome by adding a mechanical pump to the accelerator linkage that will push a small amount of fuel into the air stream anytime the throttle is rapidly opened. This compensates for the increase in airflow until the venturi has enough time to produce a strong enough signal to pull fuel from the bowls and through the main jets.

Carburetor Problems

As you can see, for every problem a carburetor faces, we can find a way to mask the problem with an acceptable fix, but since this book is about EFI, it is outside of the scope of this book to continue any farther in the discussion of general carburetor theory. Instead we'll focus on why carburetors have trouble keeping up with the many requirements the engine places on them.

Because of these inherent compromises that must be made to get the engine to operate under a wide range of speeds there are several problems with the carburetor as a method of fuel delivery.

First, since the carburetor meters fuel based solely on airspeed, it is lacking in the ability to determine the actu-

Building and Tuning High-Performance Fuel Injection

Chapter 1

Eventually carburetors became very complex instruments for fuel delivery. Just look at the one shown here. For every hurdle the engineers needed to cross, a "fix" was added to the carburetor. As you can see, this one is outfitted with an accelerator pump, a choke for cold operation, and even an idle circuit!

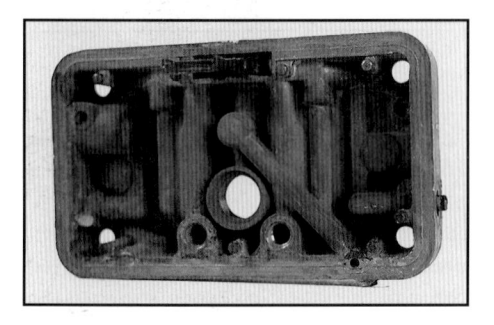

All fuel passes through the calibration circuits in the metering block before entering the airstream. The metering block contains the idle circuit, the main fuel circuit, and the power-enrichment circuit.

al amount of air entering the engine because the velocity of the air passing the venturi is not always proportional to the density of the air, which can change dramatically with changes in atmospheric conditions or geographical location.

Since the carburetor uses airspeed for its primary input to meter fuel, it is rather difficult to achieve wide swings in the air fuel ratios in order to suit every different engine condition. The calibration is normally set to provide optimum performance under a few certain operating conditions and then be just close enough to provide a reasonable air-to-fuel ratio under all other conditions.

What is Air Density?

When talking about the amount of air an engine is using, it is helpful to know the air density. When we say that an engine is using 500 cfm, we mean that a volume of 500 cubic feet of air is moving through the engine over a period of one minute.

While helpful, this doesn't exactly tell us how much air there is inside the engine. For any given volume of air, or any substance for that matter, the actual mass of air inside of our volume container can vary drastically. This is because the mass of substance inside any container of a constant volume is related directly to the density of the substance inside of it.

The reason we are concerned with the density of the air, is because density is directly related to the actual mass of air entering the engine. In simple terms, density is the weight of a given volume of material. For example, a gallon of water weighs more than a gallon of air. The two substances have equal volumes of one gallon, but the fact that the volume of water weighs more than the same volume of air shows that the water is denser than the air. So, knowing this, we can surmise that when a carburetor is calibrated to deliver a specific quantity of fuel for any given airspeed, the actual ratio of air-to-fuel can vary dramatically as the air changes its density, and the poor carburetor has no means of compensating for this change automatically, and we must manually recalibrate for the new density.

Since air density is affected by many outside forces such as altitude, temperature, and barometric pressure, it is important to check and measure the air density when calculating the actual amount of air an engine is consuming.

If we have a carburetor, we must continually adjust the fuel mixture to compensate for changes in air density. This usually involves some amount of carburetor disassembly and changing the size of the jets. Not only can this be time consuming, but at times, it can also be very messy.

By using a computer to constantly monitor and adjust the fuel curve, we can avoid the hassle of constantly working on our carburetor.

Carburetors are acceptable fuel metering devices for steady-state engines like this portable irrigation pump. Because steady-state engines do not require a wide range of air/fuel ratios, carburetors are well suited to meet their fuel-supplying demands.

As it turns out though, engines normally require vastly different air-to-fuel ratios under different operating conditions to obtain optimum performance throughout the range of engine speeds and loads. It is not uncommon to see ratios as lean as 15 or 16 to 1 or leaner under certain lightly loaded conditions, and as rich as 11.5 to 1 for specially built high-powered racing engines! The old carburetor is just simply not up to the task when it comes to such large differences in fuel requirements.

With electronic control, we can tailor the exact ratio of air and fuel that the engine requires for peak performance at any given engine condition. This is possible because we use many different inputs for calculating the fuel demands and to determine the actual mass of the air entering the engine, rather than just depending on airspeed by itself. We'll get to that later in the book.

14 Building and Tuning High-Performance Fuel Injection

Carburetors vs. Fuel Injection

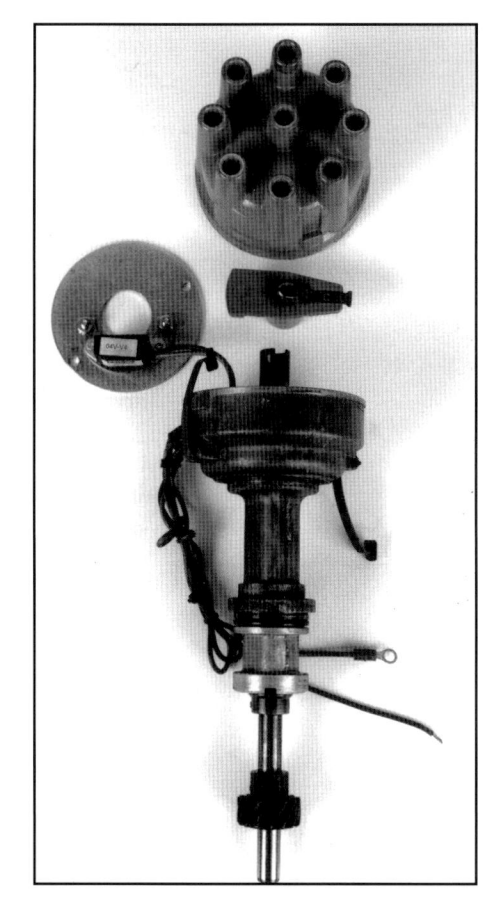

Some high-powered racing engines will require air/fuel ratios as rich as 11.5 to 1. It is this extra fuel in the combustion chamber that helps keep the exhaust gas temperature within reason.

Although reliable, the distributor is not the most efficient means of delivering spark to the plugs. With a distributor, the ignition timing is based only on engine speed. In modern EFI systems, timing is based on many factors including engine speed, engine load, air temperature, engine temperature, and many others.

Under lightly loaded conditions, engines can use lean air/fuel ratios to conserve fuel. OEM ECUs have different air/fuel ratios preset at the factory. But if, like the owner of this Corvette, you have plans for performance beyond what the factory intended, you may have to take matters into your own hands.

Weights and springs in the distributor provide additional ignition advance based on engine speed. As engine speed increases, the centrifugal force pulls the weights outward, which rotates the distributor housing and advances the timing. The springs draw the weights back in and the timing returns to normal as the engine speed drops.

Ignition

Now we will quickly take a look at why the distributor is also a compromised part of modern engine tuning. The venerable old distributed spark system has been around nearly as long as the internal combustion engine itself, and it does a magnificent job of getting a spark transferred to the spark plugs.

The problem with using this type of ignition system though, is not unlike the ones facing our carburetor. It uses only one variable to calculate the engine's spark requirements — engine speed. The weights in the distributor and the tension required of the springs needed to retain them are all calibrated only against the speed of the engine. Unfortunately, the engine has vastly different ignition requirements under various operating conditions.

Most engines using a distributor start with a certain amount of advance called the base timing and then add progressively more timing as the engine speed increases. Again, we end up with many compromises that give us the optimum performance under only a few operating conditions and enough timing to just get by under all other circumstances. For example, most small-block Chevrolet engines require about 34-38 degrees of advance under full load, high-speed operation.

This is fairly common knowledge, but what many do not know is that under certain lightly loaded conditions, at high engine speeds, it is possible to find peak engine performance with as much as 50 degrees of timing or more!

Again, we are limited by what we can achieve with our distributor, because of its mechanical operation and the fact that it uses only one variable to calculate required amounts of ignition advance.

With modern computer control, we can dial in exactly the right amount of ignition advance required for any situation, sometimes within 1/2 degree of accuracy! Later in the book we will talk about how our computer does this and we will also take a look at how it calculates optimum advance.

Building and Tuning High-Performance Fuel Injection

Chapter 1

Why DIS ?

Most engines using a distributor start with a certain amount of advance called the base timing, and then add progressively more timing as the engine speed increases. This setup is full of compromises — it gives us optimum performance under only a few operating conditions and just enough timing advance to get by under all other circumstances.

If you take a look under the hood of nearly any modern automobile, you will find that more and more auto manufacturers are moving toward engines using DIS, or distributorless ignition systems. DIS setups typically use a separate ignition coil for each pair of cylinders or sometimes for each individual cylinder.

When an ignition coil discharges its energy in a spark form, it must begin to recharge itself and get ready for the next trigger event. The amount of time it takes for the coil to fully charge is called the coil saturation time.

As the engine RPM increases, the amount of time between cylinders firing decreases. This means that the amount of time a coil has to store up energy gets smaller and smaller, resulting in diminishing quality of spark output.

For example, a V-8 engine using a distributor and one coil must fire four times per revolution. At 6,000 rpms, the engine goes through 100 revolutions per second! That means the coil has to fully charge and discharge its spark about 400 times per second! As the engine speeds climb even higher, the situation becomes even worse.

With the advent of computer-controlled ignition timing, automakers found that they could divide the amount of work needed from the coils between the cylinders. This meant that if we used our V-8 engine with four coils, then each coil would be responsible for two cylinders, instead of one coil for all eight. Each coil will fire only once per revolution, thus giving four times the amount of coil saturation time! The engine running at 6,000 rpm will now only have to fire each coil 100 times per second! If we decided to add four more coils, then we could cut that time down even further!

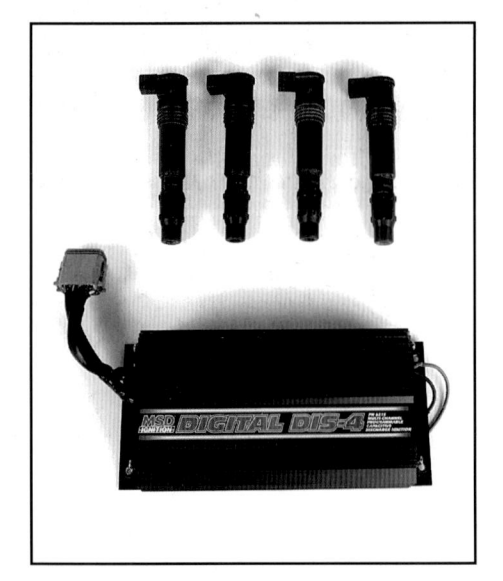

A modern ignition system consists of an ignition amplifier and individual coils for each cylinder. Using a separate coil for each cylinder means the coils have more time to recharge before firing each spark plug, providing for a more efficient ignition event.

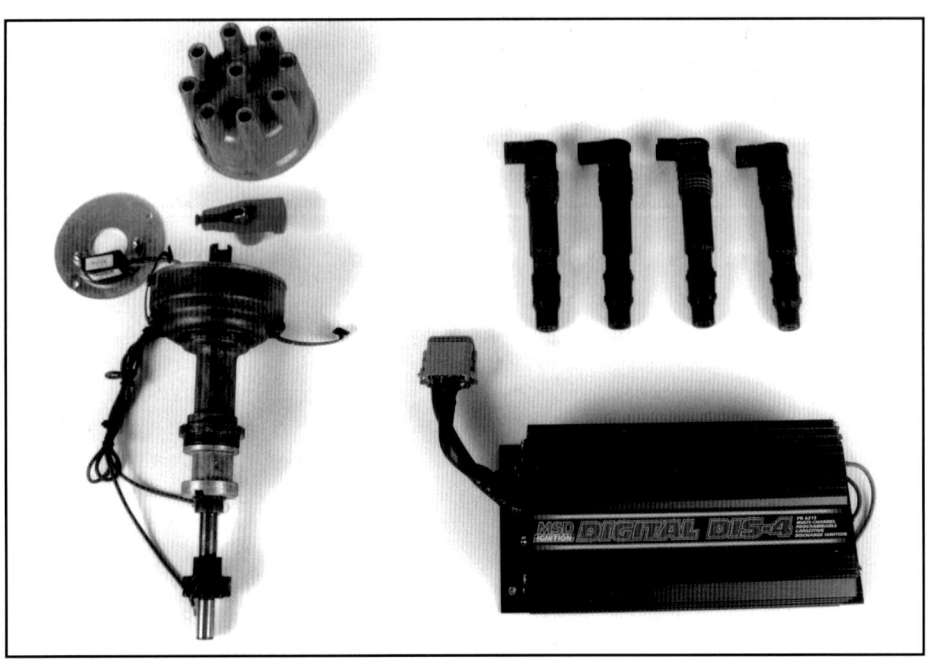

Distributorless ignition systems operate more efficiently by dividing the workload over multiple coils instead of using a distributor to spit the power output of a single coil between all the cylinders. Some distributorless systems use one coil for every cylinder, and some use one coil for every two cylinders.

Building and Tuning High-Performance Fuel Injection

Chapter 2

The Basics of Electronics

While most aftermarket EFI systems are fairly user friendly, it is a good idea to brush up on your "basic electronics 101" in case anything goes wrong and you need to diagnose small problems. Most fuel-injection problems can easily be solved with even just a rudimentary understanding of electricity.

When working with aftermarket fuel injection systems, it is helpful to have a basic knowledge of electricity and its principals. However, it isn't required that you have a degree in electrical engineering to be able to install and use one.

In order to understand and use electronic fuel injection systems effectively, it is necessary to have at least a basic understanding of some of the general principles of electricity and electronic devices. This will allow you to easily set up your system and will greatly aid you in troubleshooting the little gremlins that will inevitably show up somewhere in your projects. It is not necessary for you to be an engineer or have a degree in computer programming or electronics to be able to successfully navigate your way through a modern EFI system. Most are very user friendly and can be easily manipulated to get the desired results. However, it certainly helps if you know how to use the basic testing equipment and diagnostic methods to ensure your electronic components are working properly.

This chapter will briefly cover the general principles of electricity and electronic devices, but if you wish to really dig in and grasp some of the more technical subjects, a trip to the local bookstore will provide access to any number of books covering topics from the basic principles all the way through to the most complex circuits and their functions. The subject of electricity is so broad itself that covering everything involved is well beyond the scope of this book. For now, we'll just

Building and Tuning High-Performance Fuel Injection

address the aspects that will directly relate to building and troubleshooting an EFI project.

Voltage

The volt is probably the most recognizable term in any discussion about electronics, though it is often misunderstood and misused. Basically, the voltage of any electrical circuit is a measurement of the electromotive force, or EMF, within that circuit. It is this force, or electrical pressure, that we are talking about. The potential amount of work that can be done in any situation depends on the amount of available force you have to get the job done with. The more work there is to accomplish during a given amount of time, the more force is required to do it. In electricity, voltage is our force. The more voltage we have, the more muscle we can flex when trying to get our mission accomplished. Technically, a volt is defined as the electromotive force that causes a current of one ampere through a resistance of one ohm.

In real life it might be easier to imagine a garden hose spraying water. The water pressure in the hose is similar to our volt. If the size of our hose stays the same and we require a higher volume of water from the hose, then we must increase the pressure. In much the same way if we increase the voltage in a circuit of constant resistance, the size of our hose in this case, we will see a corresponding increase in the current flow through the circuit. Voltage is to water pressure, what amperage is to water flow, and the resistance in ohms is comparable to the size of our garden hose. So as you can see, if you want an increase in amperage (or water flow), you either have to decrease resistance (increase hose size), or add voltage (increase water pressure). Also, amperage can and will be decreased by a drop in voltage or an increase in resistance.

Voltage, amperage, and resistance are interrelated, as we will see shortly, through a law of physics called Ohm's law.

Amperes

Amperage, or amps, as it is most commonly called, is the measurement of the flow of electrons through a circuit; the flow of water though our garden hose, if you will. When we induce voltage into a circuit of some resistance, we cause electricity to move through the circuit. How much electricity, or how many electrons flow through the circuit, is our amperage.

One amp is measured as the amount of electrical flow that happens in a circuit with one ohm of resistance when a pressure of one volt is applied to it.

For example,

1 volt = 1 ohm x 1 amp, or V = O x A

Sometimes, the term amperage is referred to as inductance. The letter "I" is used to represent inductance or current. Likewise, at times resistance is used to refer to ohms, and is represented by the letter "R". Using these terms, our formula would look like this: V = R x I

I find it easy to remember this formula by associating the letters with other things. So, when I need to recall how to calculate a circuit's parameters using this particular formula, I just speak the phrase "Vermont equals Rhode Island" (V = R x I). However, I do realize that I am not the world's most entertaining author of unique acronyms, so I would encourage you to come up with whatever phrase you find that helps you remember the formula best!

If you look back again to our garden hose, you will see that if we can fill a one gallon bucket in one minute with a one inch diameter hose at a given pressure, then in order to fill the bucket faster, we need more flow of water from the hose. To achieve this, we can either keep the pressure the same and use a bigger diameter hose, or keep the hose

Batteries can be used to store and create their own voltage. Technically, a volt is defined as the force that causes a current of one ampere through a resistance of one ohm.

The ignition coils are used to store energy and send current, or amperage, to the spark plugs. One amp is the amount of electrical flow that happens in a circuit with a resistance of one ohm when a pressure of one volt is applied to it.

The Basics of Electronics

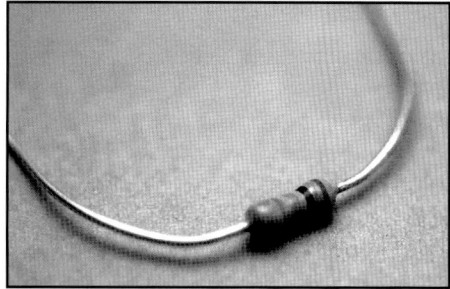

A resistor like this one is capable of adding more resistance to a circuit. The technical term for the resistance of an electrical circuit is the ohm. An ohm is defined as the amount of resistance a circuit has when a force of one volt passes through it and produces a current flow of one amp.

Many modern ECUs like this one from F.A.S.T. have built-in aluminum fins called heat sinks, which allow them to dissipate the heat generated from the internal circuitry.

Voltage is similar to the water pressure inside a garden hose. Imagine a garden hose spraying water. If we increase the pressure, more water will flow through the hose. Similarly, if we increase the voltage in a circuit, we will see a corresponding increase in the current flow through the circuit.

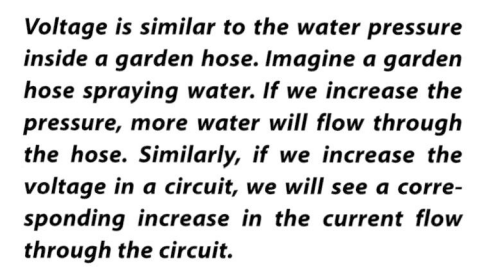

diameter the same and increase the pressure to push more water out. Think of amps as the gallons-per-minute rating of our hose circuit.

Resistance

The technical term for the resistance of an electrical circuit is the ohm. It is defined as the amount of resistance a circuit has when a force of one volt through it produces a flow of one amp of current. In other words, if we wish to keep referring to our lowly garden hose, ohms would be the size of our hose. A smaller hose has more resistance to water flow than a larger one, so if the water pressure in the hose always remains the same, then a larger hose will have less resistance and therefore will pass more water. In the same manner, a circuit of constant voltage will pass more current as the resistance goes down and less current as the resistance (or ohms) goes up.

Ohm's law relates all the functions of volts, amps, and ohms to each other. In an electrical circuit there is a mathematical balance between the three. They must all coexist within certain boundaries and a change in any one of these three values will always have an equal effect on at least one of the remaining two. Basically, Ohm's law states that when resistance in a circuit changes, but the source voltage remains the same, then current flow will also change in an inverse proportion. This means if we increase the circuit's resistance, then we will decrease the current flow by the proportional amount. Conversely, if we lower the resistance in the circuit, then we will raise the current flow by proportional amount.

Voltage plays a role here too, in that if we keep the resistance in a circuit the same and increase the voltage on the circuit, then the current flow will also increase. Anyone who has ever melted a wire while installing a car stereo or theft alarm can relate to this. If we have a small wire and too much voltage, then the amount of current that tries to pass over the wire will usually result in copper and plastic goo that has a wafting odor of burned popcorn!

Current passing though a circuit produces heat energy that needs to be expended. This usually occurs naturally though convection to the atmosphere, but sometimes an ECU will use a heat sink to draw heat away from it and into the atmosphere or sometimes even a fan to blow cool air on its components.

This heat that is generated is why a short to ground usually causes some kind of damage to the components in the circuit. A short circuit happens when a part of a circuit becomes damaged and results in a path of electron flow that leads directly to a ground source. Electricity always follows the path of least resistance, so if you provide a means to bypass any resistance in the circuit and go directly to ground, the electricity will gladly take it. Do you remember what happens if we lower the resistance of a circuit? That's right, the current goes up — a lot in this case. When a short to ground occurs, the current flow gets so high that it usually produces enough heat to destroy the circuit it is traveling on. At best, it will cause the circuit to cease operation. At worst, it can potentially cause a fire if left undiscovered.

Now that we have discussed a few of the basic terms and principles of electricity, lets take a look at how these factors and the changing of them affects our fuel-injection strategy.

Catch a Wave

When we are measuring voltage we sometimes find that the voltage in a particular circuit will vary in a pattern. When voltage changes in these constant patterns, we refer to them as waveforms. There are two basic styles of waveforms that we are concerned with in automotive applications: the sine wave, and the square wave. A special piece of equipment called an oscilloscope is required to actually see these wave formations. They happen over a period of time, and a standard voltmeter isn't designed to measure circuits over any amount of time. We'll talk more about these later in the chapter on tools and equipment. However, it should suffice to know that the ECU in our fuel injection system is constantly monitoring these waveforms and making decisions based on the information derived from them.

Sine Waves

Basically, a sine wave is pretty simple. It is a pattern of voltage that slowly builds to a peak over a given amount of time and then slowly decreases to a valley or trough.

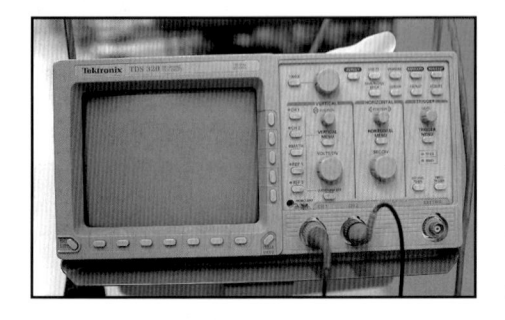

This special piece of equipment called an oscilloscope is required to actually see wave formations since they happen over a period of time. A standard voltmeter isn't designed to measure circuits over any amount of time.

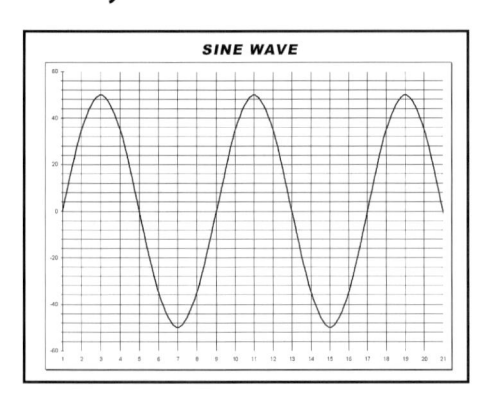

A sine wave like the one drawn here consists of a pattern of voltage that slowly builds to a peak over a given amount of time and then slowly decreases to a valley or trough.

For instance, when a piece of metal passes though a magnetic field, it creates a spike of voltage. As the metal passes out of the field again, the voltage drops. This is essentially the way a pickup coil inside a distributor works. The ECU monitors the average voltage across the field and each time it sees the spike at the top of the sine wave, it recognizes that a tooth from the distributor shaft has passed the pick-up coil or VRT. VRT stands for variable reluctance transducer, which is a fancy name for a device with a magnetic field that produces a sine wave when a piece of metal passes it by.

It is possible for a shaft to spin in proportion to engine speed, with a tooth on the shaft to represent each cylinder. Each time a tooth passes the VRT or pickup coil, the ECU knows that it is time to fire another cylinder. In this way, the ECU can also calculate the speed of the engine by counting the number of peaks in the sine wave per minute.

Square Waves

Unlike a sine wave, the square wave is a fairly complex pulse of on-off signals created to measure or control various functions. Because the signal is measured in an on-again, off-again fashion, the ECU looks at the high or low voltage for a signal, and nothing in the middle. The circuit is either on or off and the ECU normally only sees high voltage when the circuit is considered on and low or no voltage when the circuit is off.

Here is a shot of an actual VRT. VRT stands for variable reluctance transducer, which is a fancy name for a magnetic device that produces a sine wave whenever metal passes by it.

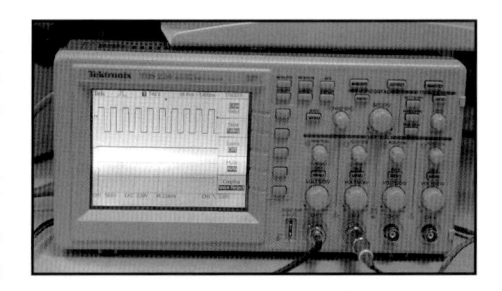

Unlike a sine wave, the square wave is a fairly complex pulse of on-off signals created to measure or control various functions. The circuit is either on or off, and the ECU normally only sees high voltage when the circuit is considered on and low or no voltage when the circuit is off.

Some sensors measure square waves like crankshaft or camshaft speed sensors, and some actuators, such as injectors or ignition coils, are controlled by square waves.

Essentially there are four parts of the square wave we are concerned with: amplitude, frequency, pulse width, and duty cycle. We will be discussing each one and its significance to our EFI system at many places throughout this book, so they each deserve a little discussion now, rather than backtracking later on.

Amplitude

The amplitude of a square wave is the amount of voltage change from low to high that occurs when the circuit is turned on or off. For instance, many crankshaft speed sensors use amplitude of five volts. The ECU monitors when it sees zero volts and when it sees five volts to know when the parameters of the circuit have changed. Usually a technician won't be testing the amplitude of a circuit, but rather they will be testing to be sure that there is some change in amplitude to know whether the circuit is operating at all.

Frequency

The frequency of a square wave is simply a measurement of how many complete on-off transitions happen over a given amount of time. The typical standard of measurement for frequency is the hertz. The term hertz

The Basics of Electronics

represents cycles per second. A frequency of 40 hertz, or Hz, would mean that the on-off transition happened 40 times in one second. You may have also heard the term megahertz or kilohertz. These are simply exponential measurements of the hertz. The term kilo equals one thousand and the term mega stands for one million. It is difficult to grasp that computers are so fast that they can process information in megahertz. Imagine being able to do a million math calculations in one second! Whew — if you could do that, then you probably could've read this entire book about ten million times in the length of time it took you to read this sentence!

Pulse Width

The pulse width is the amount of time that our square wave is in the high stage, or how long the circuit is turned on. In reality the pulse width of a circuit can be any amount of time — seconds, days, or years — but in our fuel-injection applications, we normally measure pulse widths in thousandths of a second, or milliseconds. An injector pulse width refers to the amount of time the injector is held open and is directly related to how much fuel the injector sprays out during that cycle. Since the fuel pressure remains constant, the length of time the injector is open will dictate the volume of fuel it will pass. The fuel pressure at the injector is held constant under all conditions by the fuel pressure regulator, so when the ECU monitors how much air has entered the engine, it can calculate how long to open the injector in order to supply the correct amount of fuel to maintain the desired air-fuel ratio.

Duty Cycle

Unlike the pulse width, which is only a measurement of the amount of time the circuit is on, the duty cycle is a measurement in percent of the amount of time that the circuit is on versus how long it is off. A high duty cycle would be when over a period of time, a circuit is on more often than when it is off. A duty cycle that is too high will often cause damage to components. This is because a circuit that is passing current will need to dissipate heat, and if the circuit has a duty cycle that doesn't allow sufficient time at rest, the heat will not be able to leave the circuit and will eventually cause damage.

In tuning a custom EFI system, it is important to keep an eye on the duty cycle of the injectors so they do not overheat and fail at an inopportune moment.

It is possible to calculate the maximum allowable pulse-width that an injector can be given in order to stay within an acceptable range of duty cycle for any given engine speed.

It works like this:

First, divide engine speed (RPM) by 60 to get revolutions per second.

6,000 rpm / 60 seconds per minute = 100 revolutions per second

Then, divide 1 second by the revolutions per second = seconds for one revolution

1 second / 100 revolutions per second = 0.01 seconds per revolution

Now multiply the seconds for one revolution by 2 to get amount of time for one complete engine cycle (In a four-stroke engine, it takes two revolutions to complete a four-stroke cycle).

0.01 seconds per revolution x 2 = 0.02 seconds per complete 4-stroke cycle

This is the amount of time it will take to complete one complete four-stroke cycle, which is also the maximum amount of time we have before the next cycle begins and we need to worry about filling the cylinder with air and fuel again. The amount of pulse width compared to the amount of time available to complete the engine cycle will give a percentage equal to the duty cycle. If the amount of pulse width required of the injector in order to supply enough fuel to achieve the desired air-fuel ratio produces an unacceptably high duty cycle, then you will need injectors that can supply a greater amount of fuel for any given pulse width. This is usually referred to as the injector's flow rate, and can be measured in pounds per hour, cubic centimeters per minute, or grams per second.

From the example above, you can see that at 6,000 rpm it takes 20 thousandths of a second, or 20 milliseconds, to complete each four-stroke cycle. That means if we have an injector pulse width of 15 milliseconds at 6,000 rpm, then our injector duty cycle would be 75 percent.

15 milliseconds / 20 milliseconds = .75, or 75%

As the engine speed goes up, the amount of time it takes to complete the four-stroke cycle decreases, so if the pulse width remains the same, then the duty cycle will increase.

Most engine tuners feel that about 85 percent duty cycle is the maximum acceptable limit of normal injectors. If you find that in order to obtain your desired air-fuel ratio, you have to order pulse widths that produce duty cycles higher than 85 percent, then you may want to consider using larger injectors.

ECU OUTPUT CONTROL

When our ECU sends out control commands to the actuators in order to perform any function, it uses one of two basic methods of control: analog control, or pulse width modulation.

When the ECU uses analog control, it is simply turning an actuator on or off. Things like shift lights, torque-converter lock-up clutches, and A/C, radiator fan, nitrous-oxide, and fuel-pump relays are controlled by the ECU using simple analog control. The ECU simply tells them when to turn on and when to turn off essentially the same way a light switch works.

Pulse-width modulated (PMW) control takes a bit more effort than simply turning on or off an actuator. The ECU not only has to tell something when to turn on, but for how long and how often. The ECU has to determine what factors necessitate the functioning of a given device, determine how much of that function needs to happen to get

Chapter 2

A fuel-pump relay like the one shown here is a good example of a circuit that is switched on and off by the ECU in an analog fashion. It is either all the way on, or all the way off.

the desired results, and finally give the required command to the device in question. All this takes quite a bit of sophistication and requires the ECU to act quickly. Luckily, it can.

For instance, at an engine speed of 7,000 rpm, most ECUs can obtain information from between 10 and 30 sensors, process the info, make a decision about what to do, and actually carry out its command about 40 times before the engine travels through just one degree of rotation! At that engine speed, it takes about .0000238 second to travel through one degree of engine rotation. That is a true testament to the speed to precision of OEM and aftermarket ECUs.

As an example of a pulse-width modulated circuit, the ECU gathers information from the engine sensors about how much air has flowed into the engine. It then must decide how long the fuel injectors should remain open in order to achieve the target air/fuel ratio. Because the engine's airflow changes dramatically based on several factors, we cannot always open the injectors the same amount of time, otherwise we would have no means to control the air/fuel ratio. For this reason, we must modulate the amount of time the injector is open on each firing cycle, or we must modulate its pulse width, hence the name pulse-width modulation.

Some other actuators that require pulse width modulation are: idle air control (IAC) valves, exhaust gas recirculation (EGR) valves, additional injector outputs, and cold-start valves.

In the next chapter we'll talk about

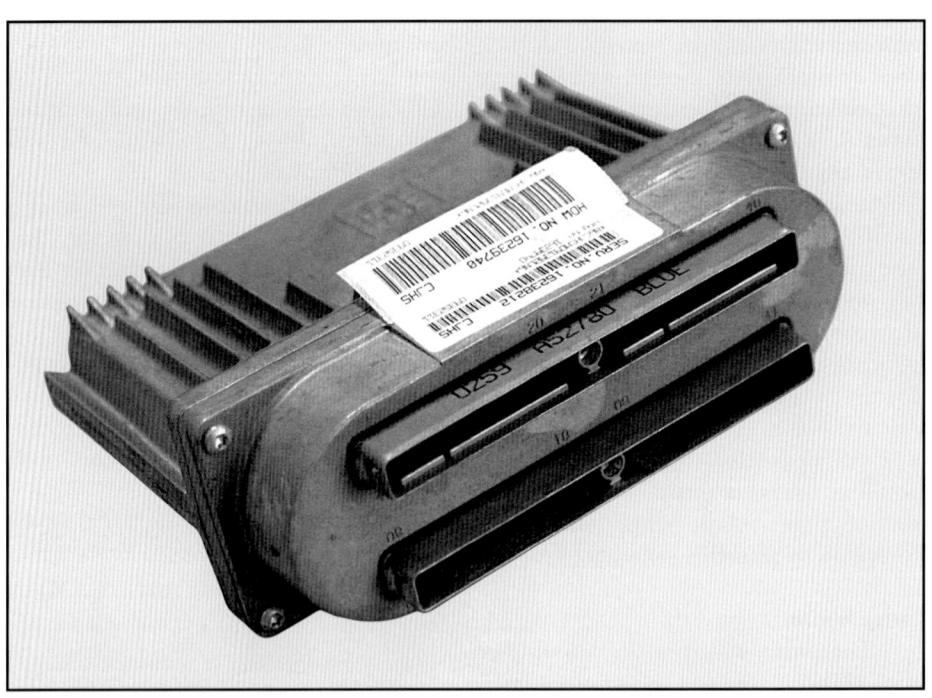

At 7,000 rpm, an ECU like this one can obtain information from about 20 sensors, make a decision about what to do about that information, and output commands about 40 times before the engine travels through just one degree of rotation! At 7,000 rpm, it only takes about .0000238 of a second for the crankshaft to rotate that one degree.

An idle air control (IAC) valve is switched on and off by the ECU in a pulse-width modulated (PWM) fashion. The ECU can open the valve anywhere from zero to one hundred percent using PWM control.

the tools and procedures you'll use to troubleshoot some of the electrical functions we've learned about in this chapter.

Chapter 3

Tools and Equipment

During the course of building your fuel-injection system, there are many specialized tools to help you along the way with everything from wire harness construction to troubleshooting a faulty sensor. Some equipment is very simple to use, while other pieces like the ones shown here are a bit more complex and take some special knowledge to use effectively.

In the course of building your custom EFI systems there will be many times that you will need to have access to some tools and diagnostic equipment. While in the building stages, you will need tools that help aid in the construction of the wire harness, and then once you have the system running, there will inevitably be some problems that you will need some diagnostic equipment to find. Finally, in order to make your engine run well, you will need to data gathering equipment to ensure you are going in the right direction. In this chapter we will take a look at some of the tools and equipment you will need to know how to use, and we discuss some basic procedures for using them.

While it will not be necessary for you to be an expert diagnostic technician, a "super tuner" with the laptop, or even be a veteran dynamometer operator, you will find that if you at least have a basic understanding of how these things work, it will make the overall project go much more smoothly.

DVOM

One of the most-often used tools in any EFI builder's toolbox will be the DVOM, or digital volt and ohm meter. This is a multipurpose tool that will come in handy about a million times before you wear it out!

The typical DVOM has two test leads or probes coming out of it that can be connected to an electrical circuit for the purpose of testing the circuit for any number of the electrical properties that we talked about in the last chapter.

Most are capable of testing the resistance of a circuit, spark plug wire, or sensor. It can also be used to test voltage at just about any source. Most can read from just a few thousandths of a volt to up over 400 volts and commonly can read either AC or DC circuits. Also they can sense resistance values from down in the hundredths or

Building and Tuning High-Performance Fuel Injection

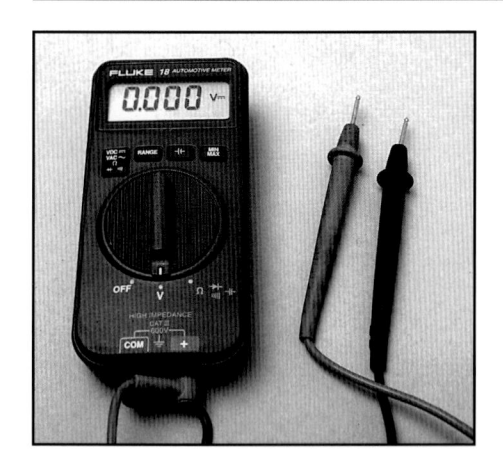

Chapter 3

One of the most often used tools in any EFI-builder's toolbox will be the DVOM, or digital volt and ohm meter. This is a multipurpose tool that will come in handy about a million times before you wear it out!

even thousandths of an ohm to circuits that are basically infinite — usually when there is a short circuit, the DVOM will show a very high number in mega-ohms or millions of ohms!

This is a useful tool when testing the different sensor circuits for continuity in your EFI system. Many times a poor running engine has nothing to do with a poor calibration, but more to do with the fact that a sensor has malfunctioned or the wire harness has failed to deliver the signal from a particular sensor to the ECU. By using the two leads of the DVOM at each end of the wire from the sensor in question to the ECU, one can check the circuit's resistance to ensure there is a proper route for the signal to travel on.

Another good use is to test the operation of many of the sensors in the EFI system. Since most of these sensors rely on the basic principles of electronics like voltage and resistance, the DVOM is the perfect tool for investigation. For example, the ECU monitors the resistance value of the water temperature sensor to determine the right amount of correction factors to add or subtract from the base calibration maps when the engine temperature is outside the normal operating conditions. So, when the operation of this sensor is in question, we can use the DVOM to check the resistance values of the sensor at a certain temperature and compare that information to published data from the sensor's manufacturer.

The throttle position sensor is yet another example of a common test for which the DVOM is required. This sensor is a linear potentiometer, which is a device that changes its resistance in proportion to the amount of travel it moves through. As the throttle opens, this sensor's resistance decreases and the voltage that travels across it increases, so it is a simple test to rotate the sensor and watch the values on the DVOM to make sure operates correctly.

There are many more uses for a good DVOM, and no serious EFI technician should be without one. The user's manual will normally have lots of useful information on how to use the meter efficiently and get the best results. These meters can be found reasonably priced and are readily available at most electronic stores and even hobby shops or hardware stores. There are still some older analog meters available, but I wouldn't recommend buying one, as they are not suited well for the small voltages and current flows of a modern EFI system.

TEST LIGHT

A test light is a very simple yet fast and accurate way to test for voltage on a circuit. Basically it is a device that has a probe on one end that can be used to quickly connect the light to a circuit. The other end of the test light usually has some length of wire and a means of quickly attaching to the end of the circuit to be tested, usually a ground source. If there is power available where the probe end of the light is touched, then it will travel up the probe and cause the bulb to light up, assuming you've made a good ground on the other end.

I find it very quick and easy to use a test light for checking the condition of automotive fuses. These fuses are almost always in an uncomfortable location to access and are difficult to visually inspect without removing them from the fuse panel.

I simply connect the alligator clip end of my test light to a ground source, and then touch the probe end to each side of the top of the fuse where the metal is exposed. If it lights the bulb on both sides of the fuse, then it is good. If

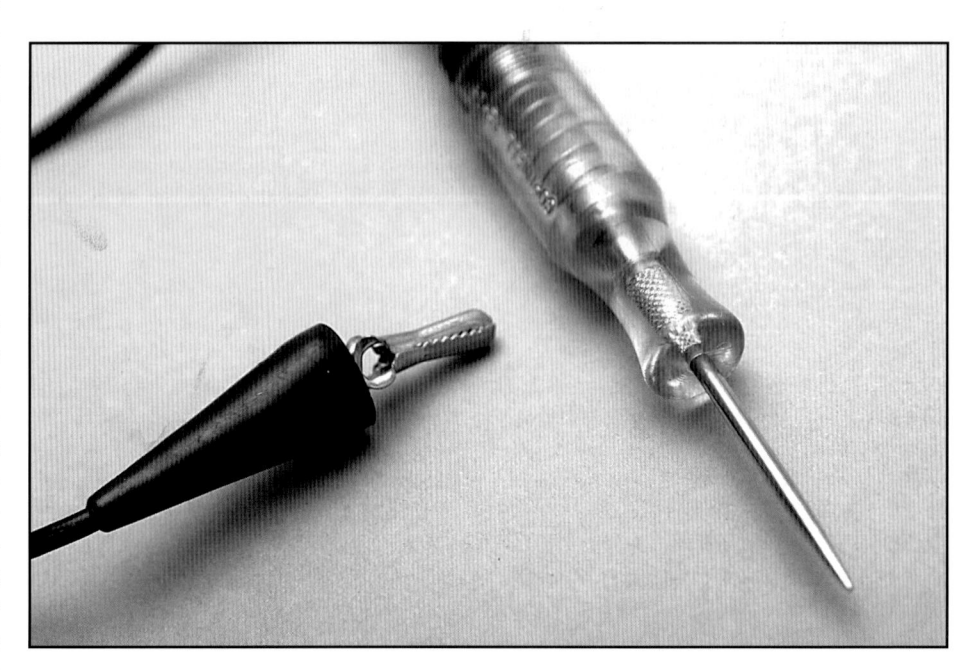

A test light is a very simple yet fast and accurate way to test for voltage on a circuit. Basically, it is a device that has a probe on one end and a small clamp on the other end. You can clamp one end to a ground and probe the circuit with the other. The bulb will light if voltage is present on the circuit.

---

24 **Building and Tuning High-Performance Fuel Injection**

Tools and Equipment

not, then I simply remove the fuse and install a new one!

Another place I find it helpful to have a test light is when I suspect a wire has been damaged somewhere down the line, but I cannot be certain where. I usually will connect my light to ground and begin to probe the wire in question, progressively moving along the length of it until I find a spot where there is no longer voltage. This saves me from removing the entire length of wire from the car and instead only replacing the pieces that I have to.

Again, test lights are very inexpensive tools that can be found at any electronics store, hobby shop, or hardware outlet. I always keep a spare light bulb for my test light, because they do burn out on occasion, and it's important to check its operation before condemning a circuit as being faulty!

Powered Test Light

This tool is very similar to a normal test light, except for the fact that it has two leads and requires both power and ground to operate. Once the light has been properly supplied with power and ground, it has a logic circuit connected to the probe end that can decipher whether a circuit has power or ground on it. Normally, when the probe touches a ground circuit, a colored LED (light-emitting diode), usually green, will illuminate. When a power circuit is touched, another LED of a different color, usually red, will light up.

These lights are usually surge protected, which means they will not allow large spikes of voltage or current to pass through them to the circuit being tested. For this reason, this is the only type of test light that should be used when testing any circuit that is directly connected to the ECU. It is very easy to damage the delicate circuitry of the modern ECU, and care must be taken to avoid a catastrophe in your garage!

Often times I find this tool to be extremely helpful in troubleshooting an engine that is not running, or one that is running poorly. I like to use it to determine whether an injector is firing. I can use it on the signal side of the wires going to the injectors to verify that the ECU is outputting a signal to them to actuate, and then on the other wire you can watch the LED lights flash back and forth from red to green as the circuit opens and closes to fire the injector. A normal test light will not normally pick up the slight fluctuation because it happens so quickly that not enough current passes through the injector to fully light the bulb.

Vacuum Pump

A handheld vacuum pump is probably not the first thing that comes to mind when one thinks about tools in the EFI tuner's toolbox. Yet I find it to be a very handy piece of test equipment when testing pressure sensitive devices like a MAP sensor or a fuel pressure regulator.

You can use it in conjunction with a DVOM to apply vacuum to a MAP sensor and watch the voltage and resistance change on the signal wire of the MAP sensor. It is also useful to use in conjunction with a fuel pressure gauge to make sure the fuel pressure regulator is dropping the fuel pressure in proportion to engine vacuum signals.

These can be very inexpensive, or can be rather pricey, depending on what features you want. Most can be found at an automotive parts retail store and should be kept in a dry storage place, as moisture can affect the operation of the diaphragm inside the pump.

Fuel Pressure Gauge

A fuel pressure gauge is an absolute must-have item for testing a fuel-injected engine. This is a simple pressure device that connects to the fuel delivery line in order to measure the amount of fuel pressure the injectors are receiving from the regulator and pump.

The amount of fuel pressure there is available at the injector has a dramatic effect on the amount of fuel the injector will spray out during a given period of time. Since most aftermarket computers do not actively measure fuel pressure and make compensations based on it, the calibration of the engine relies heavily on a good constant fuel pressure. If the pressure changes for any reason, the ECU will not know it. As a result of this situation, many "electrical" problems are solved by fixing problems in the fuel system.

Not all EFI systems have the same types of fittings to connect to a univer-

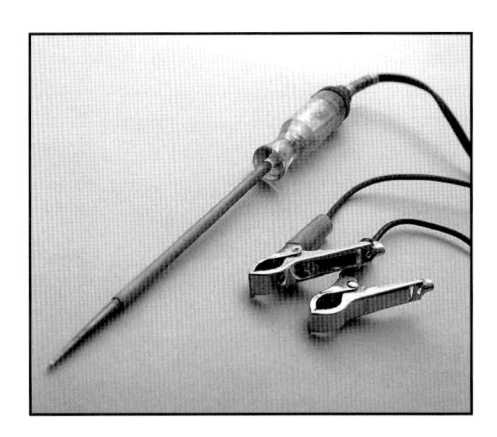

A powered test light is very similar to a normal test light except that it has two leads and requires power and ground to operate. Once the light has been properly supplied with power and ground, it has a logic circuit connected to the probe end that can decipher whether you are touching it to a power or ground.

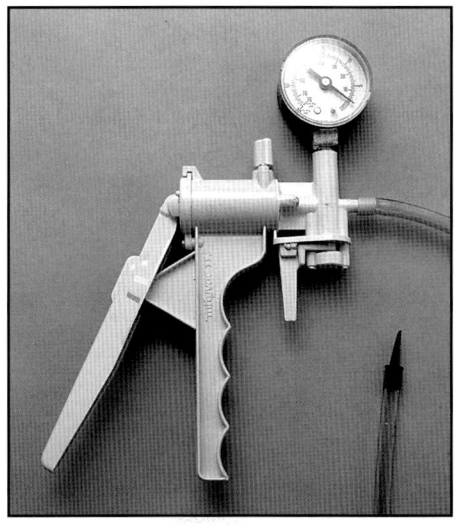

A handheld vacuum pump is probably not the first thing that comes to mind when one thinks about the tools found in the EFI tuner's toolbox. However, I find it to be a very handy piece of equipment when testing pressure-sensitive devices like MAP sensors or fuel pressure regulators.

Chapter 3

A fuel pressure gauge is an absolute must-have item for testing a fuel-injected engine. This is a simple pressure device that connects to the fuel delivery line in order to measure the amount of fuel pressure the injectors are receiving from the regulator and pump.

Some aftermarket ECUs, like this one from MoTeC, have the ability to actively measure and record fuel pressure. This allows the ECU to compensate for the changes in fuel pressure so they don't affect the air/fuel ratio.

stantly monitored, and some people go as far as installing a pressure sensitive switch in the fuel delivery system to cut the ignition and inhibit engine operation in the event of a fuel-system failure. This greatly reduces the chances of engine damage occurring due to leaning out the engine when there is a problem with fuel delivery.

OSCILLOSCOPE

The oscilloscope is a fairly complex instrument used mostly by electronics technicians that is not usually readily available to the hobbyist or general EFI technician. However, it merits a mention here because of its importance in measuring the circuits commonly used in the performance EFI system.

Basically, it operates similar to the DVOM, except that is it designed to measure voltage and time and display them together. Using this strategy allows you to monitor a system's change in voltage over time.

As an example, you might want to connect the scope to an injector to verify its pulse width, amplitude, or duty cycle.

Alternatively, when an ignition is given the command to fire, it must have a certain amount of time to charge with energy to release to the spark plug. This is called the dwell time. An oscilloscope is the perfect tool to use when you'd like to watch this happen and find the right amount of time to turn on the charge circuit for the coil. Most EFI systems do this for you automatically, but a few require that you supply them with this data from the ignition coils you wish to use in your system.

These instruments are quite expensive and the knowledge of their use is normally quite complex and beyond the necessity of the user's reading this book. I just felt that if you were at least aware of the uses of the oscilloscope, that if/when you to need a circuit tested on one, you would know what to look for in a diagnostic shop or technician.

DYNAMOMETERS

The dynamometer, or dyno, is such a complex instrument that we could

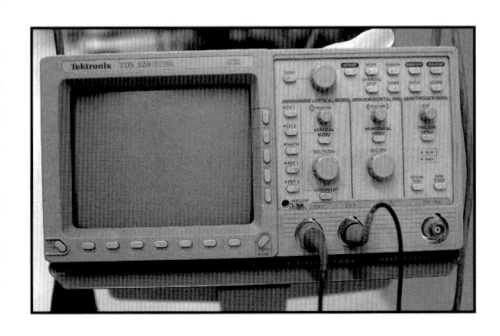

The oscilloscope is a fairly complex instrument used mostly by electronics technicians. They aren't usually readily available to the hobbyist or general EFI technician.

dedicate an entire book to it. However, in this book we will discuss what it is, the different types there are, and how to use them to tune your system properly.

A dyno is a tool that allows an engine or vehicle to be placed under simulated real-life operating conditions in a contained environment, so that the operation of the engine can be closely monitored without the variables and dangers associated with actual operation. There are two basic types: the engine dyno, and the chassis dyno.

The Engine Dyno

The engine dyno is basically an engine stand where engine can be run with a load or strain with all the engine's accessories connected and operational. The dyno collects performance data, and the operator can then decide what changes to make. Most engine dyno facilities have the ability to hold an engine at any given speed and load point constantly so that a tuner can calibrate the base fuel and ignition maps in real time, based on the data from the dyno console and from the other measuring devices on the dyno, such as temperatures, pressures, and air/fuel ratios.

The Chassis Dyno

The chassis dyno is probably the most accessible and easy-to-use dyno for the average hot-rodder. The chassis dyno is basically the same tool as an engine dyno; only it has a set of rollers that can be driven by the wheels of the vehicle. With a chassis dyno, not just the engine, but the entire vehicle can be

sal fuel pressure gauge, so be sure to buy one that has a variety of fittings if you plan on working on more than one type of fuel-injected engine.

Some people prefer to have a permanent fuel pressure gauge installed in the system so that pressure can be con-

Tools and Equipment

Tuning on the Dyno

The engine dyno is an engine stand where all the engine's accessories can be connected and run while the dyno puts a load or strain on the engine. The dyno collects performance data, and the operator can then decide what changes to make to the engine. Needless to say, an engine dyno is a very valuable tool for tuning an engine and EFI system.

evaluated. Plus you can test an engine that is already installed in a vehicle, which is nice. The shops that own these dynos usually have a public rental fee that allows you to bring your vehicle and have them secure it and operate it while you make the necessary changes to the calibration. Some shops even offer a service for them to do the actual tuning and calibration for you.

The most common chassis dynamometers are the inertia type. These dynos use a heavy roller of a known resistance to calculate horsepower based on the amount of time it takes your car to accelerate it. The advantage of this type of dyno is that the results are very repeatable because the roller never changes, and so the power is calculated by how fast you can spin it. If you make changes that increase your engine's power, it will show up in the quicker acceleration time of the roller and vice versa.

The problem with this setup though, is that we don't always drive our automobiles at full throttle, and we must be able to operate the engine over a wide range of loads and speeds to calibrate all of the available units in the maps. Since the inertia dyno can only

Sometimes when you are tuning an engine that is already in a vehicle on a chassis dyno, a lot of strange things can happen that you should be aware of.

First of all, it is important to keep an eye on all the things that are happening. It can be very difficult to keep track of engine temperature, manifold pressure, air/fuel ratios, and engine torque and horsepower readings all at the same time. It will take some practice to get comfortable with all of this while the wheels are spinning.

Try to pay attention to things like traction of the tires on the rollers. Many cars that produce big power can easily overpower the amount of tire adhesion to the roller, and this will dramatically affect the amount of power the dyno records. If you aren't applying all the power to the roller, it can't tell how much power you are making. On a dyno chart, this can normally be seen as an abnormal spike in engine speed and a corresponding drop in power and torque readings.

It is also important to remember that if you are recording air/fuel ratios with anything but the most high-speed exhaust analyzers, it is very common to get false readings when the engine accelerates too quickly. This happens because the engine speed changes so rapidly that the exhaust meter cannot update its sampling rate quickly enough. By the time it processes a sample and displays it, the engine can be well beyond that operating range and be dangerously lean, or grossly over fueled. This makes it nearly impossible to record data and make accurate changes to the calibration.

Always use the best tires you can on the dyno, and be aware that having too little tire pressure can cause the tire to deform on the roller and actually decrease surface contact! Soft compound racing slicks usually have the same effect and are not ideal for use on a chassis dyno. Your best bet is to use a good radial street compound tire and strap the vehicle down tightly against the rollers.

The chassis dyno is basically the same tool as an engine dyno, only it has a set of rollers that are driven by the wheels of the vehicle. Thus, the entire vehicle, not just the engine, can be evaluated. Chassis dynos come in handy for tuning engines and EFI systems that are already installed in a vehicle.

Building and Tuning High-Performance Fuel Injection 27

Chapter 3

Dynos can load the engine at any operating point, which makes it possible for you to tune all of the sites in the base fuel and ignition maps. They can also measure power in real time, so you can make changes on the fly.

calculate power from acceleration, it is impossible to tune for power and correct air/fuel ratios at steady operation.

Whenever possible, I try to use a chassis dyno equipped with a load source, called a brake, and a load cell that physically measures the torque and power being applied to it, rather than having to calculate these numbers.

There are several different kinds of brake dynos, but the most common are the water brake absorbers, which use an impeller in a case that drives against the resistance of water, and the eddy-current brake absorber, which uses two opposing magnetic fields to generate friction and can be regulated by the amount of current passed through them.

These dynos can load the engine at any operating point just like an engine dyno, so we can tune all of the sites in our base fuel map and ignition map. They can also measure power in real time so that you can make changes on the fly. The best part, is that most of these dynos will allow you to make inertial type acceleration runs to test the power in the same way an inertial dyno does. That way, the numbers can easily compare when you go to a different dyno facility.

AIR/FUEL RATIO MONITOR

In my opinion, the stand-alone air/fuel ratio monitor is by far the single most important tool for calibrating the EFI system.

A Word About Lambda

When tuning an engine's air/fuel ratio, we often use the term "lambda". The word lambda comes from the Greek language and means ideal.

When we talk about lambda in reference to automotive uses, we mean that an engine is operating at the ideal ratio of air to fuel for a perfect combustion event. This point, also referred to as stoichiometric, is the point where there is no excess of air or fuel left over after the combustion takes place.

While it is commonly stated that and air/fuel ratio of 14.7:1 is lambda, this is only partially true. In this sense, lambda is often misunderstood.

Depending on the available energy in the type of fuel you are using, the correct air/fuel ratio to achieve lambda can change, but a value of lambda 1.00 is always the same. Numbers of less than 1.00 mean that the air/fuel ratio is richer, or that there is an excess of fuel. Numbers of lambda more than 1.00 mean that there is an excess of oxygen, or a lean mixture.

So, even though a gasoline engine gives a lambda value of 1.00 at an air/fuel ratio of 14.7:1, it doesn't mean that this is always the correct ratio of air to fuel for every case. Different fuel types require different air/fuel ratios to obtain a lambda of 1.00. For instance, an engine using methanol for fuel would require an air/fuel ratio of 6.40:1 to obtain a lambda of 1.00.

Below is a chart to show that while lambda values remain constant, the type of fuel used will affect the air/fuel ratios necessary to obtain the same value of lambda.

Engines will want to run at or near lambda 1.00 or higher for best efficiency, and around Lambda 0.80 to 0.90 for full power and high load. This extra fuel helps to keep the cylinder temperatures within reasonable limits. The best exhaust emissions can be found right around lambda 1.00.

Lambda to Air/Fuel Ratio Chart

Lambda	Gasoline	Diesel	Methanol
0.75	11.0:1	10.9:1	4.8:1
0.80	11.8:1	11.6:1	5.1:1
0.85	12.5:1	12.3:1	5.4:1
0.90	13.2:1	13.7:1	5.8:1
0.95	14.0:1	13.8:1	6.1:1
1.00	14.7:1	14.5:1	6.4:1
1.05	15.4:1	15.2:1	6.7:1
1.10	16.2:1	16.0:1	7.0:1
1.15	16.9:1	16.7:1	7.4:1
1.20	17.6:1	17.4:1	7.7:1
1.25	18.4:1	18.1:1	8.0:1

Tools and Equipment

A good stand-alone air/fuel monitor, like this one from MoTeC called the PLM (professional lambda meter), is an invaluable tool for tuning a fuel-injected engine. The meter reads and displays data about the exhaust mixture so that the user can understand what is happening inside the engine.

As modern engines like this supercharged, electronically fuel-injected Cadillac Northstar become increasingly complex, the need for precise measurement of air/fuel ratios becomes even greater. Tuning these engines without an exhaust analyzer is a sure bet for failure.

The correct way to tune the engine to the proper air/fuel ratios under all operating conditions is to have the values in the base fuel table closely match the target air/fuel ratios in the calibration software. This car uses full-time air/fuel correction and logs all the information to data files for later review.

This is a device that uses a high-speed oxygen senor that is placed in the engine's exhaust stream to sample the amount of oxygen in the exhaust.

The sensor's voltage output is directly proportional to the ratio of air/fuel that is present in the exhaust stream, but not all sensors are extremely accurate, so once the monitor receives the signal, it corrects it for accuracy and then it displays this value.

Most high quality stand-alone monitors such as the ones from Autronic or MoTeC are very expensive and extremely accurate. These monitors are fast enough to monitor air/fuel ratios in real time, even on very quick acceleration runs. Most even have a data output function that can be used to send information to a dyno or a data logger, which is a nice function on a high-powered vehicle that accelerates very fast. The tuner must be watching a great deal of parameters all at the same time, and it helps to be able to save the data from a run and analyze it afterwards to determine the changes necessary.

There seems to be a lot of hype in the industry about the use of wideband oxygen sensors for tuning or for closed-loop operation of a racing engine.

Let me start by saying that I don't dispute the use of a high-quality wideband oxygen sensor in a closed-loop configuration on an engine operating under light loads at or near stoichiometric air/fuel ratios. However, if you study a chart of the voltage output curve for most oxygen sensors, you will find that even though they will output voltages to represent very rich or lean air/fuel ratios, their accuracy is greatly diminished anywhere away from the stoichiometric mixtures.

I do not believe there are any wideband oxygen sensors that are available to the hobbyist that by themselves have the accuracy required to operate an engine under all conditions.

Many aftermarket EFI manufactures use this marketing ploy to make people believe that their systems will run themselves and some even say they can tune themselves by the use of wideband oxygen sensors. This is simply not an acceptable fix for a poorly calibrated base fuel map. However, many think that by inserting target air/fuel ratios that this wideband option will take the place of expensive rental time at the local dyno. This is just nonsense. There is no replacement for good tuning using information from a good stand-alone air/fuel monitor with output correction. Period.

The correct way to do things is to tune the engine to the proper air/fuel ratios under all operating conditions, and then have these values closely match the target air/fuel ratios in the calibration software. This way the sensor can be accurate enough to make gentle corrections as necessary. The software shouldn't have the power to make more than about 3-5% correction to the base map, otherwise the air/fuel ratios begin to oscillate around the desired numbers due to the fact that the sensor response time is much slower than the ECU can react. The system begins to overcompensate for small changes and it swings back and forth trying to get the numbers right. By giving the closed-loop function a smaller control range, the changes necessary to hit the target air/fuel ratio are much more subtle and normally don't produce large changes in the mixture, which prevents this oscillation.

Building and Tuning High-Performance Fuel Injection

Chapter 4

ECU Inputs

There are many different sensors and actuators that make up the components of a fuel-injection system. In this chapter we will take a look at some of the more common ones used in most aftermarket EFI systems.

The term MAP represents manifold absolute pressure — the amount of vacuum or boost inside the manifold at any given time. The MAP sensor uses absolute pressure because this type of reading will always be constant and will not be affected by changing atmospheric conditions like a normal pressure gauge would.

In this chapter we will cover some of the basic working components of the EFI system and the theory behind how they work independently and as part of the entire system. We will begin with a look at the inputs the ECU uses to collect information, and then in the next chapter we will look at the outputs, which it uses to carry out its commands.

MAP Sensor

The MAP (manifold absolute pressure) sensor is most commonly used as the primary input for determining the engine's load. The term load in this instance describes how hard the engine is working at any given engine speed. In other words, the amount of air that flows through the engine per cycle does not necessarily increase simply because of an increase in engine speed. The overall amount of air moving through the engine is greater for a given amount of time, but the amount per cycle doesn't vary greatly unless there is a change in engine load.

As an example, picture a car sitting at idle in neutral. In order to get the engine to climb up to say, 5,000 rpm, the operator need only push down very lightly on the accelerator pedal. Now picture the same car in overdrive going 20 miles per hour and going up a steep hill. In order to get the engine speed up to 5,000 rpm the accelerator pedal will need to be pushed to the floor and the engine will be working much harder because the load on the engine is greater for the same engine speed.

The MAP, manifold absolute pressure, is the amount of vacuum or boost inside the manifold at any given time. The sensor uses absolute pressure because this type of reading will always be constant and will not be affected by changing atmospheric conditions like normal gauge pressure would.

30   **Building and Tuning High-Performance Fuel Injection**

ECU Inputs

The MAP sensor consists of a flexible diaphragm that conducts electricity. The resistance of the diaphragm changes when it flexes or bends. When pressure is applied to the MAP sensor, it causes the diaphragm to flex. The resistance acting on the electricity passing through the sensor changes in proportion to the actual pressure acting on it, and the computer is able to read the changes in the signal that returns to the ECU.

If we have a tire pressure gauge and we connect it to a tire that reads 32 psi, we can say that the tire filled to a gauge pressure of 32 psi. So by adding our gauge pressure to the known atmospheric pressure (14.7 psi), we have an absolute pressure of 32 psi + 14.7 psi = 46.7 psi absolute. A tire is like a manifold in that it can hold a certain amount of pressure — assuming there aren't too many leaks.

Before we go any farther it will be useful to briefly touch on what absolute pressure is and what the units of measurements are that represent it. Normal atmospheric pressure is rated in units of pounds per square inch, or psi. The pressure at sea level is 14.7 psi. As the altitude changes, so does the density of the air. An increase in altitude produces a decrease in air density and a corresponding decrease in the measured pressure. It is also worth mentioning that as the altitude increases, the temperature of the air decreases in direct proportion. The air's altitude, pressure, density, and temperature are all related, and a change in any one of these factors affects all the others.

If we have a tire pressure gauge and we connect it to a tire that reads 32 psi, we can say that the tire is filled to a pressure of 32 psi. This number is referred to as the gauge pressure. The absolute pressure that actually exists inside the tire would be the atmospheric pressure plus the gauge pressure. So, if we measure the tire's absolute pressure at sea level the tire would have an absolute pressure of 14.7 + 32 = 46.7 psi absolute.

It is important that we only use absolute pressure when dealing with calibrating our ECU. That way, when the vehicle is operated in different geographic areas, at different altitudes and air densities, the calibration for any given manifold absolute pressure will remain the same.

Again, it is important to remember here that the density of any quantity of air is directly related to its absolute pressure. The higher the pressure, the denser the air will be for that given volume. This is easily recognizable in engines that are supercharged or turbocharged. The more boost you have to pressurize the engine with, the more total airflow it uses, and thus the more power it makes.

It will help here to also understand that nearly all automotive computers measure absolute pressure in metric units of bars, or kPa, meaning kilopascals. The reason for doing this is because when the absolute pressure inside the engine is less that 0 psi, it is operating in a vacuum. When discussing amounts of vacuum, we typically use terms like inches of mercury, or InHg, and when we talk about positive pressure or boost in an engine, we use pounds per square inch, or psi. It can be very tricky and time consuming to constantly convert these units to make them something easy to understand.

Instead, we use metric units of pascals. A pressure of 14.7 psi is considered to be one atmosphere, or 100 kPa. One kPa represents 1,000 pascals. Also a pressure of 14.5 psi is equal to one bar, so the two terms are very closely related in actual measurements, and are often used in place of each other. A bar of boost, which indicates a manifold pressure of roughly 14.5 psi gauge pressure or 25.2 psi absolute (at sea level). These measurements are also the same as having 200 kPa of manifold pressure.

When referring to automotive ECUs, we typically only use measurements of kPa. Thus, an engine operating in vacuum would have a manifold absolute pressure of something less than 100 kPa, and when the engine is at wide open throttle in a state where it has no vacuum or boost, it would have a MAP value of about 100 kPa. When the engine sees positive pressure, or boost, the MAP signal would be higher than 100 kPa. This means that a gauge pressure in the manifold of 14.5 psi of boost

Building and Tuning High-Performance Fuel Injection

Chapter 4

Tools for the Dyno

Whenever you get ready to tune an engine either on an engine dyno or in a car, be sure to assemble a small toolbox with troubleshooting tools such as test lights and a DVOM.

You will find that inevitably during your tuning projects there will come a time when those pesky little electrical gremlins pop up. Some dyno shops have tools available for customers to use, but most do not.

You can quickly use a test light or a DVOM to test for poor connections in the wiring or faulty relays.

You might also want to bring along some screwdrivers and a few wrenches just in case those darn hose clamps spring a leak on the radiator hose or intercooler tube!

Always be sure you have the proper size lug-wrench to ensure the wheels are tight before starting too! The last thing you want to happen while on the chassis dyno is for a tire or wheel to have a problem.

At some point during your tuning, you may also find it necessary to change the engine oil and filter. Be sure you have enough extra oil, and a fresh filter to use. Also bring an approved oil container to catch all the used oil you will remove from the engine, and bring plenty of rags to clean up any spills. The quickest way to offend a dyno owner or operator is to make a mess in their shop! Always be courteous and aware of your surroundings.

Manifold absolute pressure directly relates to the amount of air that exists inside an intake manifold. A higher MAP value indicates greater airflow, and thus greater engine load, while a smaller MAP number indicates less load and airflow in the engine.

would be equal to 200 kPa, and a gauge pressure of 29 psi would net a MAP value of 300 kPa and so on.

All this may sound complicated, but it helps to just remember that less than 100 kPa is vacuum, and more than 100 kPa is boost, and every 100 kPa is equal to about 14.5 psi of positive gauge pressure.

Now we can begin to discuss the actual method the MAP sensor uses to relay information to the ECU. The actual MAP sensor signal is an electrical value sent from the sensor to the ECU. The ECU determines the amount of pressure inside the engine from that signal.

The MAP sensor consists of a flexible diaphragm that conducts electricity. The resistance of the diaphragm changes when it flexes or bends. So, one side of this diaphragm is exposed to a closed circuit leading to the manifold pressure signal coming from the engine. When the pressure is applied to the MAP sensor, it causes the diaphragm to flex an amount that is proportional to the actual pressure acting on it.

The ECU sends a small amount of voltage, usually 5 volts, to the sensor and then measures the amount of voltage that returns to it through the resistance of the MAP sensor. The more pressure that is applied to the sensor, the more its resistance value changes. This now affects the amount of voltage that is sent back to the ECU. The sensor's resistance is carefully calibrated to be exactly the same value for any given amount of absolute pressure so that the ECU can mathematically calculate the pressure against it for any voltage value.

Once the ECU receives the electrical signal from the MAP sensor, it uses that value, along with values from several other sensors, such as the engine speed, water temperature, and air temperature sensors, to determine the actual density and mass of air inside the engine. It does this using a property of mechanical physics called $PV=NrT$.

This equation explains how the computer knows how much air is in the engine and is the very essence of our EFI system.

P: represents the absolute pressure in the engine

V: represents the volume we are measuring

N: represents the mass of air (which is what we are trying to find)

R: represents a real gas constant for air, which is used in all air calculations (287.05 for dry air)

T: represents the absolute temperature of the volume being measured

If we can produce all but one of these variables, we can then apply them to this formula to find the missing one. In our case, we have pressure from the MAP sensor (P), we have volume (V), which is the size of our manifold, and we have temperature from our intake air temperature sensor (T), which we will discuss shortly. The R is a constant num-

ECU Inputs

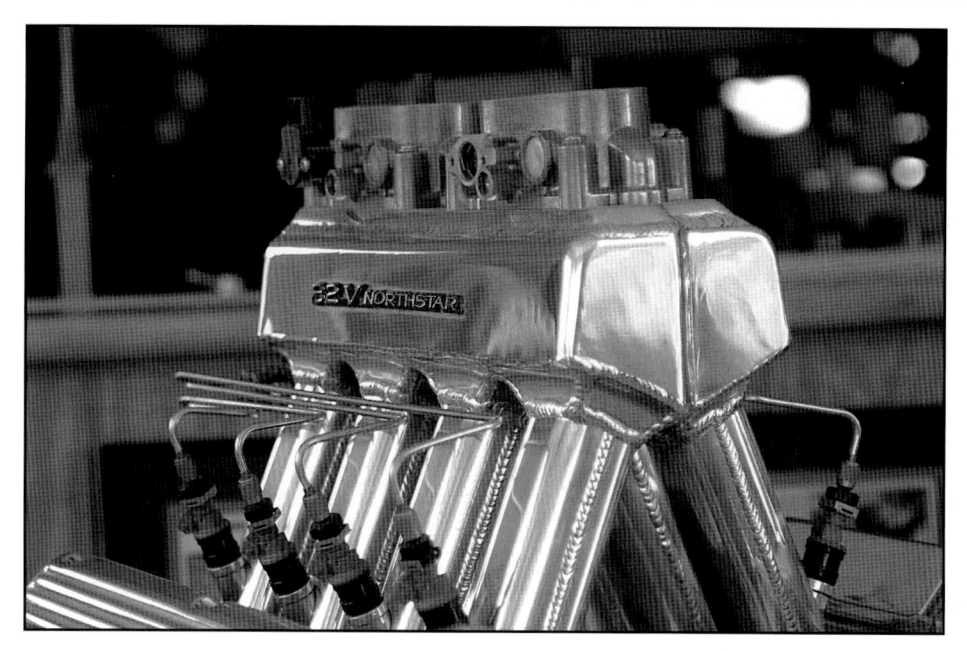

Using the PV=NrT formula, and ECU can calculate how much air there is inside the manifold. Although you won't actually need to know how to use this formula, it is fun to at least understand how it all works! Things happen fast inside a manifold like this one, so if you use the formula to solve for one of the variables, the answer you get will only be true until the throttle plate opens or some of the intake charge gets sucked into one of the cylinders.

One of the projects the author has completed was the swap of a '97 Ford Explorer engine using MAF-based fuel control into this '46 Sportsman Woody convertible. Modern fuel-injection systems allow older cars to be driven much more comfortably and reliably.

ber, called the real gas constant, which is always the same for air. So the only thing we don't know is the mass (N).

Once we figure out the mass, we will have a quantity, which can be easily related to other quantities like the amount of fuel. Then we can obtain an air/fuel ratio. It is this method that the ECU uses to determine how long to turn on our injectors to obtain the correct mixture of air and fuel for the engine to operate properly.

Take heart my friends in knowing that you will never need to actually do any of these calculations in the process of building and tuning your own EFI system, as this is all being done behind the scenes in the software for us by the lovely engineers who manufacture these systems. I just felt it necessary for you to understand the basic concepts behind how the system works in order to really appreciate the value of each component!

MAF Sensor

I would like to briefly mention another type of sensor commonly used by automotive manufacturers called the MAF sensor. The abbreviation MAF stands for mass airflow sensor. This sensor is plumbed into the intake air stream of the engine and is used to directly measure the mass of air entering the engine, thus eliminating one step in the process of calculating the correct amount of fuel to inject into the engine. Since the MAF gives us the mass, we do not need to solve any equations to figure it out.

The sensor works by having a fine mesh screen that all the air entering the engine must pass through. Woven into the screen is a wire that the ECU sends electrical current through. This wire becomes hot because of this current, and the air passing by the sensor absorbs some of this heat. The more air that passes over the wire, the more current that ECU will have to pass to maintain the wire temperature. So, the ECU measures how much current it takes to keep the wire at a specified temperature, and from that, it is able to calculate the exact amount of air entering the engine. This sensor is calibrated in much the same way as the MAP sensor so that it is very accurate.

The only real drawback to this system is that the sensor must sit directly in the way of all of the air entering the engine, and therefore the sensor itself becomes somewhat of a restriction to airflow, because the amount of air the engine can inhale is limited to the maximum flow capacity of the MAF sensor itself. Also, engines using radical camshaft timing may suffer from a poor

Chapter 4

Typically, OEM-manufactured sports cars like the ones seen here use MAF-based fuel calibrations. Most aftermarket engine management systems convert these to MAP-based systems because of the ease of adjustability and flexibility when making changes for new hardware.

The sensor is normally connected to the throttle shaft and rotates along its axis as it is moved by the throttle linkage. The farther the throttle is opened, the more the sensor's resistance value changes, and the signal to the ECU is changed proportionally.

The throttle position sensor (TPS) is a device that tells the ECU how far open or closed the throttle is and how quickly it changes from one position to another. In this picture, the TPS is found on the side of the throttle body, where it can measure the movement of the throttle blade.

idle as the reversion in the intake manifold can cause air to move backwards through the sensor and be measured twice.

It is important to note that this method is commonly used only by OEM manufacturers and is typically not found in high-performance applications or in aftermarket EFI systems. But of course, there are always exceptions.

Throttle Position Sensor

The throttle position sensor is a device that tells the ECU how far open or closed the throttle is, and how quickly it changes from one position to another.

This type of device is called a linear potentiometer. A linear potentiometer is a unit that can be fed a certain amount of voltage and the amount of voltage that can pass through the senor and return to the computer is proportional to its linear travel. What this means is that the more the position of the senor changes along its limit of travel, the more its resistance to voltage changes.

The sensor is normally connected to the throttle shaft and rotates along its axis as it is moved by the throttle linkage. The ECU sends a small amount of voltage to the sensor, (usually 5 volts) and measures the amount that is sent back after it passes through the resistance of the sensor. The farther the throttle is opened, the more the sensor's resistance value changes, and the signal to the ECU is changed proportionally. The ECU normally learns in its memory what the minimum and maximum voltage values are and can then understand the exact amount of throttle opening in a percentage from zero to 100 percent.

When the throttle is opened rapidly, a large rush of air enters the engine in a very short period of time. Because air is lighter than fuel, it tends to move much faster, and when the throttle is snapped open, the engine could see a momentary condition where there is an excess of air, or a lean condition.

To solve this problem, the ECU measures the percentage of throttle change over a period of time. If the ECU determines that the throttle has been opened very rapidly, it can decide to add some extra fuel from the injectors for a short period of time to compensate for the momentary lean condition that occurs.

Also, if the throttle is closed very rapidly, the ECU can detect this and may decide to shut down the injectors momentarily to avoid a situation where there is an excess of fuel, or a rich condition.

When and how much extra fuel can be added or subtracted during transient throttle conditions is normally a user-programmable function of aftermarket ECUs. That way, the user can tailor the calibration to meet the requirements of their particular engine. We will talk about how to do that in a later chapter.

34   *Building and Tuning High-Performance Fuel Injection*

ECU Inputs

The engine coolant temperature supplies vital information that the ECU needs to determine the correct air/fuel mixture for any given engine temperature. This sensor acts like a choke would in a carburetor. When it is cold outside, the coolant temperature sensor tells the ECU to add extra fuel until the engine warms up.

Coolant Temperature Sensor

The engine coolant temperature is another vital part of information the ECU needs to determine the correct fuel and air mixture for any given operating condition.

When the engine is very cold, the air and fuel that enters it does not tend to atomize very well. Sometimes the fuel will actually not atomize at all, and thus will not readily mix with the air. The heavier fuel tends to form droplets and fall out of the airstream. It builds puddles along the intake manifold floor or on the port floors of the intake runners in the cylinder head. The fuel can also cling to the walls of the port, and either of these two situations can lead too poor combustion because of uneven air and fuel distribution to the cylinders.

During cold engine operation, the ECU can choose to add extra fuel into the mixture to ensure that enough atomized fuel actually makes it into the combustion chamber.

At other times, such as when the engine is very hot, the fuel going into the combustion chamber can be used to actually absorb some of the excess heat and take it out the exhaust to be dispersed into the atmosphere. The computer senses when the engine is overheating and can add extra fuel to accomplish this.

In order for the ECU to make these decisions, it must draw information from the coolant temperature sensor. The coolant temp senor is actually a device called a thermistor. A thermistor is an electrical conductor that changes its resistance based on its temperature. There are two basic types of thermistors, the NTC and the PTC.

NTC is the most commonly used and it stands for negative temperature coefficient. This means that the electrical resistance value of the sensor changes at an inverse proportion to its temperature. For example, if the temperature of the sensor is cold, its resistance will be very high. However as the temperature of the sensor goes up, its electrical resistance goes down in directly proportional amounts.

It is for this reason that most automotive ECUs use the NTC type of coolant temperature sensors. The ECU feeds a small amount of voltage (usually 5 volts) to the sensor and monitors the amount of voltage it sees in return. As the engine's water temperature gets hotter, the voltage that passes through the coolant temperature sensor gets higher because the sensor's resistance value is dropping.

The ECU can also use the coolant temperature sensor's information for other things regarding the safety of the engine, such as limiting the amount of boost the engine will be allowed to make when the engine is cold, or having a lower rev limit for the engine when it is outside the normal operating parameters.

Again, most aftermarket ECUs allow the end user some degree of input on when to use and how much affect these limits can control the engine.

Intake Air Temperature Sensor

The ECU is busy collecting data from the engine sensors in order to calculate the mass of the air present in the manifold. Adding into the mix is the information that it receives in the form of an electrical signal from the intake air temperature sensor.

We have already mentioned earlier that when we want to solve our PV=NrT equation for the mass of air in

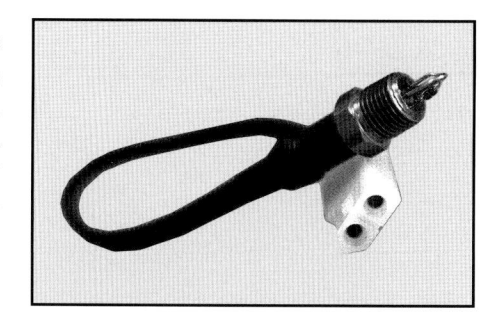

The intake air temperature sensor is a type of thermistor and is normally always of the NTC type. As the temperature of the engine's air intake goes up, the resistance of the sensor goes down.

the manifold, we would need to know the temperature of the air. This is because as the temperature of the air changes, its density changes in direct proportion to it. Basically, as the air gets hotter or colder, the density of the air changes — assuming the volume remains the same.

Think about it like this: We have a balloon and we blow it up and tie a knot in it so that no air can get in, and no air can get out. Then we begin to heat the balloon up and we notice that it begins to get larger in size. No more air has entered the balloon, so how do we explain this? It is because the air is expanding when it is heated, so the same amount of air that we started with now occupies a larger volume, but if we wanted to keep the volume constant, we would have to release some of the air as it got hotter to keep the shape/size of the balloon.

As you know we cannot, within the realm of practicality, increase or decrease the volume of our intake manifold. So, it follows that when the air entering the manifold gets hotter, that the actual mass of the air will be less because of the loss in air density. The reverse is obviously true for a drop in temperature of the intake air — the colder the air (for a given volume), the more dense it is.

The colder, denser air contains more oxygen for a given volume to contribute to the combustion process. This fact explains why your car always seems to be a bit more powerful on a cool evening than on a hot day in the desert.

Building and Tuning High-Performance Fuel Injection

Chapter 4

The intake air temperature sensor is a critical component of the engine management system. In order for it to work properly, it must be placed directly in the incoming airstream. This allows the ECU to react quickly to changes in air density.

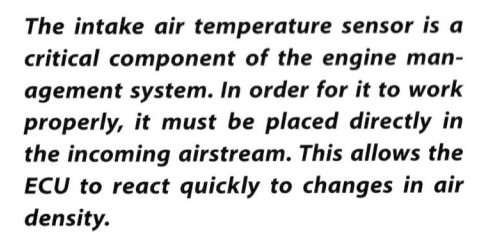

The intake air temperature sensor is also a type of thermistor and is normally of the NTC type. This sensor differs slightly from the coolant temperature sensor in that it is designed to have a much higher sensitivity to very small changes in temperature, and is also not designed to endure continuous exposure to liquid. Even very small changes in air temperature can affect its density, so the sensor must have a very fine sensitivity to temperature change. Also, the change in voltage output to the ECU must be equally precise in order for the ECU to make accurate calculations.

ENGINE SPEED

Obviously, one of the most critical pieces of information about how the engine is running is engine speed. Without this, we cannot process any information about how much air is in the engine, how long to switch the injectors on, when to fire them, how much ignition timing we need, and a host of other parameters.

The ECU gets information about engine speed in the form of electrical impulses either in sine wave or square wave digital form, which it uses to perform a counting procedure to calculate engine speed. Which type of wave form the ECU sees is dependant on the type of sensor used.

One of the most critical pieces of information about how the engine is running is engine speed. Without knowing the engine speed, we cannot process any information about how much air is in the engine, how long to switch the injectors on, when to fire them, or how much ignition timing we need.

There are two basic types:

The first is the VRT, or variable reluctance transducer. This is what has been commonly referred to as a pick-up coil.

Basically it has in iron or magnetic core wrapped tightly with a multitude of coiled wire along its entire length. When a piece of ferrous metal passes close by it, the metal interrupts its magnetic field and induces a voltage spike in the wires coiled around magnetic core. The voltage spike is seen from the ECU as a sine wave. The ECU counts the number of pulses it sees over a period of time, and then divides that number by the number of cylinders to determine the engine's RPM.

The second type is the Hall-effect sensor. This sensor uses a transistorized circuit, which is fed a small amount of voltage from the ECU. The circuit contains a magnetic field that holds the contacts of the transistor circuit closed and allows the voltage from the ECU to pass through it and return to the computer.

When a piece of metal passes through the circuit and the magnetic field, it momentarily interrupts the magnetic field and allows the transistor circuit to open up. This stops the flow of electricity through the circuit and redirects it to a ground source. At this

The VRT, or variable reluctance transducer, is what has been commonly referred to as a pick-up coil. It has an iron or magnetic core wrapped tightly with a coiled wire along its entire length. When a piece of metal passes close by, it interrupts the magnetic field and induces a voltage spike in the wires coiled around it. The ECU is able to interpret this signal.

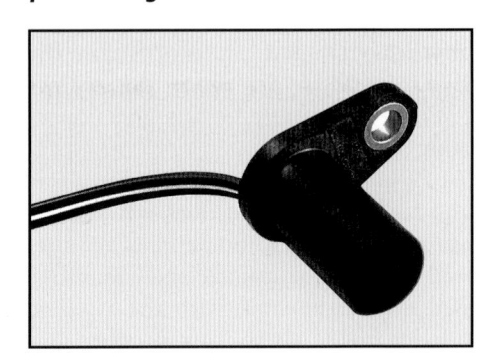

The Hall-effect sensor uses a transistorized circuit that is fed a small amount of voltage from the ECU. The circuit contains a magnetic field, which holds the contacts of the transistor circuit closed and allows the voltage from the ECU to pass through it and return to the computer.

point, the ECU no longer receives the voltage signal and views this change as a square wave signal. The ECU then counts the high and low signals, and in much the same way as the VRT, divides the number of pulses by the number of cylinders to obtain the engine speed.

CAMSHAFT POSITION SENSOR

In applications that use a direct-fire ignition system, or a sequential fuel-injection strategy, which fires each

Building and Tuning High-Performance Fuel Injection

ECU Inputs

Most aftermarket engine management systems do not use knock sensors for calibration. Fine-tuning a knock sensor to detect the exact harmonic frequency of a particular engine experiencing detonation requires very sophisticated diagnostic equipment.

injector in the firing sequence of the engine, the ECU must have a way of knowing where the engine is in the firing order sequence at all times. The easiest way of doing this is to use a sensor connected to the camshaft that operates the same way the engine speed sensor does — it sends a signal to the ECU each time the number-1 cylinder reaches top dead center. This way the ECU knows when it is time to begin the firing sequence again and can repeat the order of injector outputs correctly.

KNOCK SENSOR

Some aftermarket ECUs allow the use of a piezoelectric acoustical sensor called a knock sensor. This sensor is tuned to output a voltage signal to the ECU whenever it senses a certain frequency of noise generated as the engine experiences pre-ignition or detonation.

Often this frequency is inaudible by the human ear, so the sensor can relay information to the ECU, and the computer can take action to correct the situation by retarding the ignition timing to prevent further occurrence of knock before the operator ever hears it.

Not all aftermarket ECUs carry this function, and those that do normally have limited tuning ability. Typically, the end user can select the threshold of knock that the sensor can operate above, and how much control over the ignition timing the function has.

Knock sensors are difficult to tune for the correct frequency of a high-performance engine, because high-performance engines tend to generate higher noise levels than stock engines. For this reason, most aftermarket ECU manufacturers choose to omit this feature, as it is easy to fool the sensor into thinking the engine is experiencing pre-ignition when it is not. Still, having the capability to monitor the engine's tendency to knock is beneficial, and the knock sensor can serve as a helpful tuning tool.

Another way of detecting engine knock that several manufacturers have been exploring is called ion sensing. When the ignition system fires and the mixture in the combustion chamber is burned, a certain amount of energy is released in the form of electronic impulses called ions.

The amount of ions released during and after the combustion event can be monitored through the amount of electrical feedback it causes in the ignition components such as the spark plugs, ignition coils, and spark-plug wires.

By closely watching this process, manufacturers have developed a means of detecting when improper combustion has taken place, either in the form of low mixture-burn efficiency, or on the other end of the scale, when the extreme situation of pre-ignition, or detonation, has taken place. With this information, the ECU can be programmed very accurately to detect and prevent the damaging situations where detonation occurs.

While several manufacturers have experimented and actually implemented this method of knock detection and correction, its use in the aftermarket is likely still some time off.

OXYGEN SENSOR

The oxygen sensor is the last in line to give its information to the ECU. This

---

Detecting Engine Knock

There are several engine knock detection and control units available on the market to aid in tuning your engine. Some can detect engine ping or knock and display a message to the user, while others can actually take control of the ignition system and retard the amount of timing the engine uses to try and prevent any damage. Many units, such as the ones sold by J&S KnockGaurd, are fairly inexpensive (compared to the price of engine components), and are easy to use.

Knock sensors work by using a small piezoelectric microphone that attaches to the engine block and listens for a specific noise frequency that is only created when the engine experiences pre-ignition or detonation. When the frequency is detected, the microphone outputs a voltage signal to the ECU or display unit to tell it that knock is occurring. The ECU, or the user, can then decide to take preventive measures, such as retarding the ignition timing, or adding extra fuel to prevent further knocking.

Be aware though, that most engines, especially those with mechanical valve train, will produce an excessive amount of noise at high engine speeds. This extra noise can often either drown out the noise from knocking, or completely overwhelm the microphone and cause the unit to think that knock is occurring more than it is.

While knock detectors are great tools for tuning, you shouldn't allow them to replace good common sense and the thorough inspection of spark-plugs!

Building and Tuning High-Performance Fuel Injection

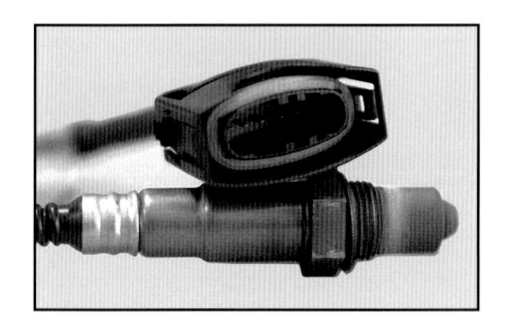

The oxygen sensor, or lambda sensor, is placed in the exhaust stream of the engine and can detect whether or not the engine is operating in a rich, lean, or stoichiometric state. They are also sometimes referred to as O2 sensors

is because its information is used as feedback, so that the ECU can evaluate the effectiveness of its output commands on the combustion event.

The oxygen sensor, or lambda sensor as it is sometimes called, is placed in the exhaust stream of the engine. It can detect whether or not the engine is operating in a rich, lean, or stoichiometric state. The ECU can then use this information to make subtle corrections to the next series of output commands on the following engine cycle.

The sensor has a tip made of zirconium dioxide that produces an electrical signal when it senses a difference in the level of oxygen in the exhaust compared with the level of oxygen in the outside atmosphere. In this way, an oxygen sensor is like a car battery in that they both use a chemical reaction to create a flow of electrons, i.e., electricity.

When the mixture is rich, meaning there is too much fuel, there is a great difference in the amount of oxygen present compared to that of the outside atmosphere, so the voltage signal is higher. When the mixture is leaner, the difference between the amount of oxygen in the air outside and the exhaust mixture is smaller, and subsequently, the voltage output of the oxygen sensor is less. Typically, the voltage range of the sensor is about 1 volt. When the engine is very lean, the oxygen sensor output voltage is near .1 volts. As the engine's air/fuel mixture becomes very rich, the sensor's output to the ECU is near .9 volts.

When the engine operates at the stoichiometric value of 14.7:1 air/fuel ratio, it is considered to be at a lambda value of 1, or have perfect combustion. At this point, the engine is not considered to be rich or lean and the oxygen sensor voltage is near .5 volts (in the middle of the scale).

The engine only operates at 14.7:1 while idling or cruising under light loads, because the heat generated from full-power operation under heavy loads requires more fuel to keep the cylinder temperatures under control. Trying to operate the engine at very lean mixtures under heavy loads is a sure way to produce melted engine parts. The extra fuel used from the rich mixture serves to absorb some of the heat in the combustion chamber and carry it out the exhaust pipe to disperse into the atmosphere.

Typically, the engine produces the most clean exhaust emissions when it is operating at or near the stoichiometric point.

There are two basic types of oxygen sensors: a narrow band, and a wideband. While both of these are capable of detecting the oxygen content within the exhaust, the main difference is that the accuracy of the narrow band is greatest at or near air/fuel ratios of 14.7:1, and loses its accuracy very rapidly at mixtures richer or leaner than this point. This is because the sensor was originally to be used only when it could be useful to accurately control the fuel mixtures around stoichiometric. With a narrow-band oxygen sensor, any small deviation from this point could be seen very quickly and easily corrected.

The wideband sensor's output is calibrated to be much more linear, so that its accuracy is the same from very rich to very lean conditions. This sensor allowed manufacturers to use feedback information from the sensor to control the engine's fuel mixtures for nearly any operating condition.

EXHAUST GAS TEMPERATURE SENSOR

An exhaust gas temperature (EGT) sensor can be used by some aftermarket fuel injection systems as another way of gathering feedback information about

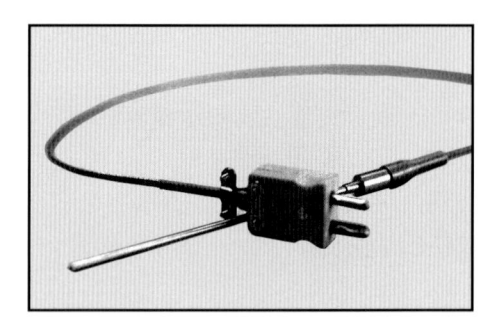

An exhaust gas temperature (EGT) sensor like this one is sometimes referred to as a K-type thermocouple. This instrument is used to evaluate the efficiency of the combustion inside an engine.

the combustion efficiency of the engine.

When the engine's air/fuel mixture is too lean, the exhaust temperature will normally reflect this by becoming elevated. Conversely, when an engine is running rich, the temperature of the exhaust will be lower.

It is important to note though, that the ignition timing has a dramatic effect on exhaust gas temperatures and can cause the EGT reading to be very misleading. As an example, an ignition event that happens very early in the cycle will give the heat created from combustion more time to be dissipated into the piston, piston rings, cylinder walls, combustion chamber, and water jackets before going out the exhaust tube. This tends to create a much lower exhaust temperature. Conversely, when the ignition even happens later in the cycle, there is little time for the engine to absorb the heat from combustion, so the resulting exhaust gas temperature is much higher. Both of these situations can affect the EGT regardless of the air/fuel mixture in the cylinder.

For this reason, it is always preferable to trust the air/fuel monitor over the EGT sensors for actual calibration. The EGT sensors do provide useful information about the condition of the engine and its relative margin of safety, so they should also be considered to perform the best calibration possible based on the amount of information available. Be careful when using EGT for tuning though, since it isn't necessarily a clear indicator of the air/fuel mixture, and damage can occur.

Chapter 5

ECU Outputs

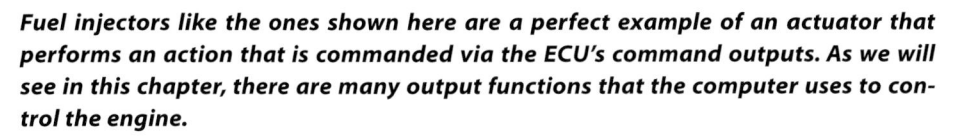

Fuel injectors like the ones shown here are a perfect example of an actuator that performs an action that is commanded via the ECU's command outputs. As we will see in this chapter, there are many output functions that the computer uses to control the engine.

The coil, or coils, that make up the secondary ignition system receive their signal to fire from the ECU. Once the computer decides it's time to fire a specific cylinder, it sends an output signal to that particular coil. These coils are from Electromotive.

Once the ECU has collected a sample of the data provided to it from the engine sensors, it has essentially enough information to create a snapshot of the engine's running state at that instant.

From this snapshot, the computer can look up values stored in each of the tables that make up the calibration called maps. These maps are basically a matrix of grids that interact with each other and provide the ECU with information on how to decide what commands it will output to the various controls like injectors, ignition system, and auxiliary devices like A/C compressor clutches, shift lights, etc.

Once the ECU has decided to output a command, it must send a signal to each of the actual devices that act on those commands. In this chapter, we will briefly discuss what those outputs are, and try to gain a general understanding of how each of them works.

Ignition Outputs

When our ECU has decided to fire the spark plugs at a certain amount of time before top dead center, called ignition advance, it must send a signal to the ignition coil, or to an igniter, which is used in most cases to amplify the signal from the ECU that goes to the coil. This

Building and Tuning High-Performance Fuel Injection 39

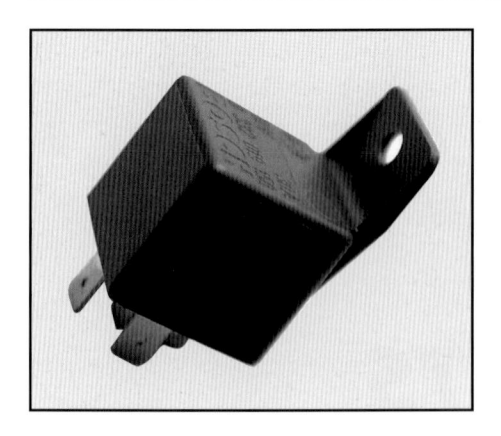

Chapter 5

The ECU turns on a fan relay when it detects that the engine coolant is high enough to warrant more airflow across the radiator. The relay allows direct battery voltage to be applied to the fan without drawing it through the ECU itself.

is done in order to prevent drawing large amounts of current through the ECU itself. By doing this, the manufacturers have found it easier to prevent excessive heat build-up within the circuitry of the ECU.

Some ECUs have the ability to give the end user control over how long the output signal is transmitted to the coil, or igniter (which comes before the coil).

The amount of time the signal is sent is called the dwell time. Simply put, it is the length of time that the ignition coil needs to fully charge. When the coil isn't fully charged (if there isn't enough dwell time provided by the system because of increasing RPM), it will not be able to get a healthy spark from the spark plug.

Dwell time is usually ordered in amounts less than 10 milliseconds, or 10 thousandths of one second. Any more than this, and at high engine speeds there would not be enough time between engine cycles to fully charge the coils.

Fan Relays

When the ECU sees that the information given to it from the coolant temperature sensor is telling it that the water temp is beginning to get too hot, the ECU can send a signal out to a relay in order to switch on the radiator cooling fans. A relay is used to connect the power source that runs the fans directly to the car's electrical system to avoid pulling too much amperage through the ECU.

Often times, the vehicle may have other data sensors, such as a vehicle speed sensor, which gives information to the ECU about the car's speed. The ECU can then decide not to turn on the fans when the vehicle is at speed because of the large amount of air already flowing across the radiator. That way, there will be less wasted energy. In an aftermarket ECU, most of the fan control functions are user programmable, so the user can decide when to turn the fans on or off according to what they believe is best.

Air Conditioning Relays

Some aftermarket ECUs are capable of controlling the output to the A/C relays in your car when they are told to do so by the switch on the dashboard. When you turn on the A/C request switch on the dash, a signal goes to the ECU, and the computer can decide whether or not to output a signal to the relay that controls the clutch on the A/C compressor.

When you turn on the A/C, a signal goes to the ECU, and the computer can decide to output a signal to the relay that controls the clutch on the A/C compressor. So the ECU cycles the compressor on and off by way of the A/C relay, which is located in the fuse box.

There are three basic methods for firing the injectors on the engine: the batch-fire method, the multi-point method, and the sequential method.

Building and Tuning High-Performance Fuel Injection

ECU Outputs

A multi-point system is one that fires all of the injectors simultaneously, once every revolution. A multi-point system only requires a signal from the engine sensors to tell it the engine speed, so it knows when to fire the injectors. Throttle-body injection (TBI) systems like the one shown are an example of a multi-point system.

A batch-fire system, sometimes called a bank-to-bank system, is one that fires half of the engine's injectors on each engine revolution. This way each injector must only fire once every other revolution. It may be difficult to tell a batch-fire system from a sequential system by looking at them since they both use individual injectors.

Again, a relay is used to prevent large amounts of current from flowing through the computer itself. If the engine speed is very high, the ECU may decide to shut off the A/C compressor clutch signal to avoid over spinning the compressor and wearing it out. Also, by cutting it out under heavy loads, the power it takes to turn the compressor can be conserved for more important tasks, like acceleration!

Once again, this function is almost always programmable by the end user to allow the tuner to decide when to turn the compressor clutch on or off. Factors affecting compressor-clutch engagement can include engine speed, engine load, or engine coolant temperature — it is completely up to the user to decide.

INJECTORS

Possibly one of the most critical steps when setting up your EFI project is understanding and selecting the proper injectors. First though, lets discuss the types of systems that are available and the strategy they use to fire the injectors. There are three basic methods for firing the injectors on the engine: the batch-fire method, the multi-point method, and the sequential method.

A system that uses a sequential injector firing sequence requires a signal from the camshaft position sensor to tell it when the engine is at top dead center for the number-1 cylinder. That way, it can begin its sequence there and follow through the engine's firing order until the last injector has fired, and then begin again at the first cylinder.

These systems work well with engines that use very large injectors. Sometimes these injectors can be so large that when fired together, they can nearly empty the amount of fuel inside the fuel rail. Since it takes a bit of time for the fuel system to keep and up refill the fuel rail, this can cause fluctuations in the fuel pressure present at the injectors. This in turn leads to improper control of the engine's air/fuel mixture, because the amount of fuel an injector can flow for any given amount of time open depends heavily on the actual fuel pressure at the injector.

A multi-point system is one that fires all of the injectors simultaneously, and only requires a signal from the engine sensors to tell it the engine speed, and then it can fires the injectors once every revolution.

Typically, this type of system will be found on an engine using a throttle body injection system. These systems operate much like a carbureted engine, in that the fuel is injected at the opening of the intake manifold and must be evenly distributed throughout the engine by the manifold itself. While these systems can be highly effective, they still suffer from some of the same drawbacks as a carbureted system because of the wet fuel flowing around inside the manifold.

A batch-fire system, sometimes called a bank-to-bank system, is one that fires half of the engine's injectors on each engine revolution. This way each injector must only fire once every other revolution.

Batch-fire systems are commonly found on OEM engines that have one injector per cylinder. While this system is highly effective because it injects the fuel directly behind the intake valve and eliminates the problems with the wet-flow manifold system, it is still not is ideal as a sequential system. This system fires half of the injectors at once to somewhat lessen the problem of fuel-pressure fluctuations, but the real problem is that only one of the cylinders being injected with fuel will have an

Building and Tuning High-Performance Fuel Injection

Chapter 5

> ## Wiring Tips
>
> While researching this book project, I had the opportunity to come into contact with many highly skilled individuals who were more than glad to share their knowledge with all of us. One of those people was Dino Dobbins.
>
> Dino's illustrious career started after graduating from Palomar College in Palomar, California. There, Dino studied courses in electronics technology. Dino soon found work handling all of the wiring requirements for Nissan Performance Technology, Inc. Nissan Performance Technology built the now-infamous GTP racing cars that dominated several racing series in the late 1980s and early 1990s. From there, Dino went on to work for such companies as Toyota Racing Development, and Caldwell Development, Inc., who campaigned many successful ventures into the famous 24 Hours of LeMans!
>
> Dino was happy to share some tips on building quality and reliability into your wiring project. First, Dino recommends using no smaller than 20-gauge wire for any of your fuel-injection wire-harness needs. Anything smaller cannot carry the current necessary to drive the injector and ignition circuits. Smaller wires also have a much higher tendency to break during heavy use.
>
> Dino also suggests that any crimped connections should be done using high-quality crimping tools, and that you should always give the connection a good strong tug to ensure it will not come out. The chances of the wire coming out on its own are quite small if you cannot pull it out by hand!
>
> Dino suggests that a soldered joint is normally a better connection than a crimped joint, but notes that improper soldered joints can become brittle and break after long-term use. He also suggests that all soldered joints should always be double heat shrunk using a high-quality heat-shrink material.
>
> The moral of his story is that if you always strive to make good wire connections, you will have a good chance at a trouble-free wire harness!

MATCHING INJECTORS TO THE ENGINE

In order to match the type of injector you have to the type of system you wish to use, and vice versa, you will need to understand the basic differences in the types of injectors and how to know what kind you have.

There are two common types of injectors: saturated, and peak-and-hold. The main difference between the two is how the ECU uses electrical current to tell them to open.

A saturated injector is one that is always full of voltage and has a fairly high resistance. The resistance value of this type of injector will normally be in the 7-14 ohm range. Because the resistance is high in these injectors, very little current is used to open them.

A peak-and-hold injector is one that must be fed a signal of high current in order to quickly open to its maximum flow point, and then uses a slightly lower amount of current to hold it open. This is a feature normally only found on higher-flowing injectors, because of the higher magnetic load required to open the larger injector coil. The extra current helps to open intake valve. The rest of the cylinders will have fuel injected behind the intake valve while it is still closed. This fuel must then stop and wait for the valve to open before it can move into the cylinder. This stopping and starting can cause some minor fuel-mixture control problems at low engine speeds when using very large injectors.

All of these systems work quite well, and numerous OEM have used them for various applications. Obviously, the OEM prefer the multi-point and bank-to-bank systems because of their relatively inexpensive cost to manufacture, and the fact that they can be made quite efficient. Normally, the OEM will opt for a sequential-firing injector scheme only when extreme standards of exhaust emissions must be met, or unusually high performance levels are required.

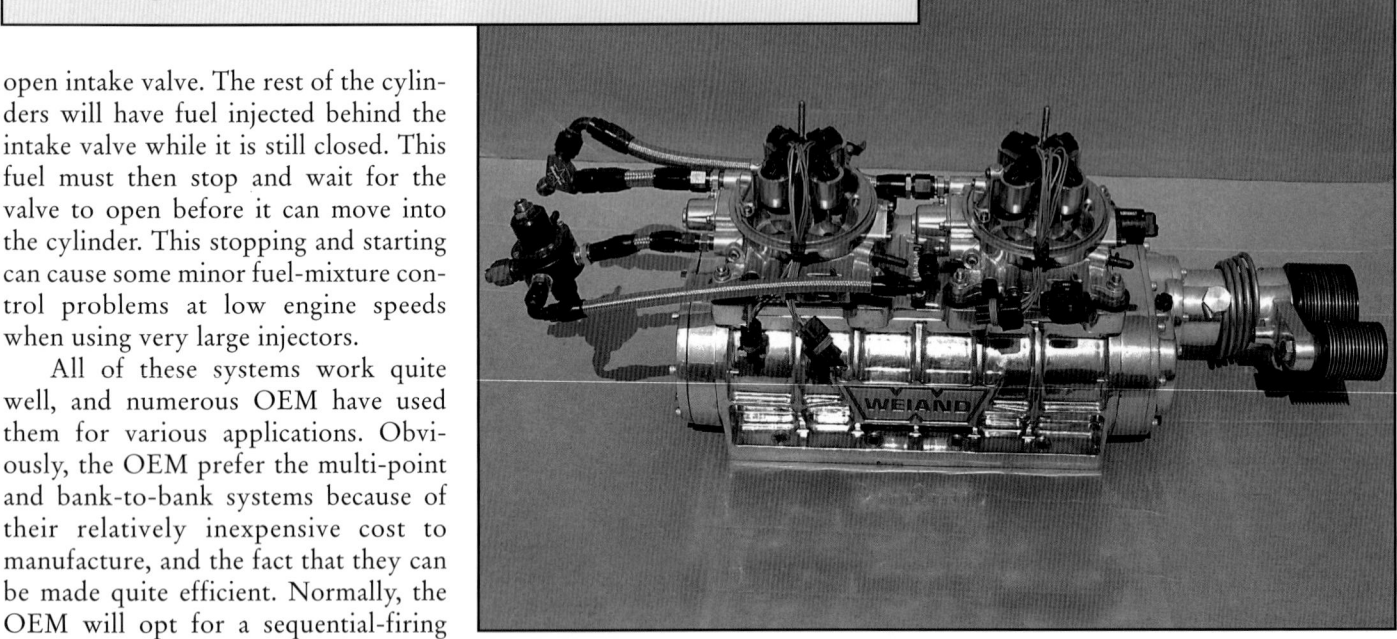

The pressure at which the fuel is supplied to the injector will affect the actual flow rate. A higher pressure will cause more fuel to pass the injector nozzle for any given amount of time that the injector is open. A lower pressure will flow less fuel.

ECU Outputs

get the job done. These injectors normally have a resistance value of anywhere from .2 to 4 ohms.

It is important to know what the resistance value of your injector will be in your project when ordering your new ECU. This will prevent any problems with incompatibility issues between your injectors and the ECU injector drivers. Mixing and matching the high-current drivers and injectors improperly could cause damage to the injector drive circuitry inside your ECU or to the injectors themselves. Always be sure to check with your manufacturers if you are uncertain if your ECU and injectors are compatible.

Knowing the flow capacity of your injectors will ensure you are using the proper size of injector to supply enough fuel for your engine to run properly. There are two common units of measurements for fuel injectors: pounds per hour, and cubic centimeters per minute.

Which rating your injector manufacturer uses is entirely up to them and is rather unimportant. If you have an injector that is rated in lbs/hr and would like to know what its rating is in cc's/min, there is an easy calculation to help you convert it. It goes like this:

lbs/hr x 10.2 = cc's/min

For Example:

55 lbs/hr x 10.2 = 561 cc's/min

Conversely, if you have an injector rated in cc's/min and would like to know its flow rate in lbs/hr the calculation works in reverse, like this:

(cc's / min) / 10.2 = lbs/hr

For Example:

(440 cc's / min) / 10.2 = 43 lbs/hr

It is also important to know that all injectors are rated at their static pressure, which is usually 43.5 psi. This figure is usually provided by the manufacturer.

The pressure that the fuel is supplied to the injector at will affect the actual flow rate. A higher pressure will cause more fuel to pass the injector nozzle for any given amount of time the injector is open. A lower pressure will flow less fuel.

Since we know that the amount of fuel pressure available to the injector will affect its flow capacity, we need a way to determine what your injector flow rate will be at various fuel pressures. To do so, just use the flowing formula:

New Flow Rate = √ (New Pressure / Old Pressure) x Old Flow Rate

For Example:

We have an injector that flows 32 lbs/hr at a pressure of 43.5 psi.

Brake Specific Fuel Consumption

Brake specific fuel consumption, or BSFC, is a common measurement of an engine's efficiency regarding how well it uses the energy available in the fuel it consumes. Normally it is measured in lbs/hp/hr, or pounds of fuel used for each horsepower, per hour.

An engine will consume a certain amount of fuel (pounds per hour) to produce a given amount of power. Depending on their efficiency, it is possible for two engines to produce the same amount of power while using vastly different quantities of fuel. By the same token, the two engines could just as easily make two very different amounts of horsepower while using the same amount of fuel!

For example, lets say we have an engine that produces 400 horsepower and has a .5 BSFC.

hp x BSFC = pounds of fuel used per hour

400 x .5 = 200 lbs of fuel per hour

Now let's say the same engine could produce the same 400 horsepower with a .4 BSFC.

hp x BSFC = pounds of fuel used per hour

400 x .4 = 160 lbs of fuel per hour

This second engine is more efficient, because it used less fuel to make the same amount of horsepower!

BSFC can be influenced by many factors, and it is important to look at these numbers when testing and tuning an engine to help determine if the fuel system is up to the task of keeping the fire burning in the combustion chamber.

When sizing your injectors for a particular engine, it is also helpful to use the BSFC numbers, along with the engine's horsepower potential, to calculate how much fuel will be required of them. We will discuss how to properly size your injectors later in the book.

Here are some basic guidelines for BSFC numbers if you don't have access to a dyno to actually measure them:

- Naturally aspirated engines using carburetors: .48-.55 BSFC.
- Naturally aspirated engines using EFI: .45-.50 BSFC.
- Forced induction engines using carburetors: .62-.66 BSFC.
- Forced induction engines using EFI: .60-.65 BSFC.

Of course, these are general guidelines and are displayed quite conservatively. If you have access to a dyno to tune your engine, then it is much easier to actually measure these figures. Remember though, that many factors influence an engine's BSFC, and it is possible, and quite common, to obtain numbers different than those used for this writing. I have heard of people tuning some very high horsepower four-cylinder engines and recording BSFC numbers in the low .4s and even high .3s!

Building and Tuning High-Performance Fuel Injection

Chapter 5

Not all engines will use one injector for every cylinder. Some V-8 engines like this one use a 4-barrel throttle body that has four very large injectors attached to the top of it. Keep this in mind if you are calculating your injector size, as you'll obviously have less than one injector per cylinder.

First, have a realistic estimation of how much power the engine will make. Then, use a realistic BSFC number. A brake specific fuel consumption number is an indicator of how much fuel the engine will use to make a given amount of power. For a typical naturally aspirated engine, a BSFC of .45-.50 is a good place to start. Turbocharged, supercharged, or air-cooled engines will be slightly higher, around .60-.65 BSFC.

At this point you can multiply the amount of power you will make by your BSFC number to get an overall fuel quantity. Then divide that quantity by the number of injectors you are planning to use to find the amount of fuel each injector will need to supply.

For example, if we have a 500 hp engine with a BSFC of .50 and eight injectors:

hp x BSFC = pounds of fuel used per hour
500 x .50 = 250 lbs/hr

pounds of fuel used per hour / Number of Injectors = Injector Flow Requirement

250 / 8 = 31.25 lbs/hr

So, we would need an injector that flows about 32 lbs/hr for each of the eight cylinders.

It is important also to note that this will indicate what the injector flows at its maximum duty cycle. Injectors will not last very long if they are forced to operate at or near their maximum duty cycle.

The industry standard is not to push the injectors past about 80 percent duty in order to keep them operating safely. You can add this extra value into your fuel-requirement calculations by dividing the final injector requirement by .8 to be safe.

(31.25 lbs/hr) / .8 = 39 lbs/hr

At this point, we have covered just about all the basic components of our EFI system and we are ready to being discussing how to actually use and tune our system in the next chapter!

How much would our injector flow at 60 psi?

New Flow Rate = √ (60 / 43.5) x 32

New Flow Rate = 37.58 lbs/hr

While this formula serves to show that raising the pressure to the injector yields a higher flow rate, it is important to note that there is a point of diminishing returns, meaning that as the pressure continues to rise, the flow rate does not rise proportionately. You will eventually reach a point where raising the fuel pressure will no longer net a gain in fuel flow because of the physical size limitation of the injector. Also remember that the higher the fuel pressure is, the harder it is for the injector's magnetic field to actually pull the injector open. At times when the fuel pressure overcomes the injector's magnetic strength, it will "lock" the injector closed and cause to be unable to flow any fuel at all until the pressure subsides! This could be a bad situation if the engine is producing lots of power and heat at that very moment! It is best to find an injector with a flow rate that is sufficient at its normal fuel pressure rating to supply enough for the engine. This will prevent any problems with high fuel pressure clamping the injector nozzle shut.

Choosing an Injector

Once you have selected the electrical type of injector you will use, it may help to use a few quick formulas to estimate the required size of injector you will want to use.

Based on the amount of power your engine will produce, and how efficiently it makes that power in terms of fuel consumption (brake specific fuel consumption, or BSFC), you can determine how much fuel flow each injector will need to flow, given one injector for each cylinder.

CHAPTER 6

TUNING MAPS AND BASIC ENGINE CALIBRATION

Okay, now that we have covered all of the basic components that make up the fuel injection system, and the simple physical properties of nature that we use to operate the engine, we are ready to begin the process of calibrating the software to run the engine properly. This is a time-consuming and tedious process, so don't get in too much of a hurry to get it all done, especially if it is your first time tuning an engine.

Consult a professional when looking for advice. There are all too many people willing to give out free advice about how everything in the world works, but remember that few hot-rodders have successfully tuned their own fuel-injected engines, and there is a lot more to it than meets the eye. This book will serve as a great reference when questions come up, but nothing can take the place of the experience you'll gain from jumping in there and getting your hands dirty!

Be sure to take great caution when making changes to the program calibration, as it is very easy to get lost and make mistakes. When tuning an engine using EFI, it is quite simple to make a change that could be detrimental to your engine. Always consult the manufacturer's user manual or technical support group before attempting any changes you are unsure about.

Tuning an engine using software to manage the EFI system will require you

In this chapter we'll take a look at some of the practices and equipment for properly tuning an engine. Many tuners in the performance aftermarket prefer to use a chassis dynamometer such as the one shown here to calibrate an engine.

to input numbers or values into a variety of maps. These maps each control a certain engine function or operation. Often they work in conjunction with each other and in order to tune the engine properly, so more than one map must be used to get the desired result. Before we begin discussing the actual tuning of any maps, let's take a brief overview of what the more common maps are and what they do.

BASE FUEL MAP

The single most common map that will be tuned in any engine is the base fuel map. This map consists of a grid matrix of values that the computer uses

---

Building and Tuning High-Performance Fuel Injection — 45

Chapter 6

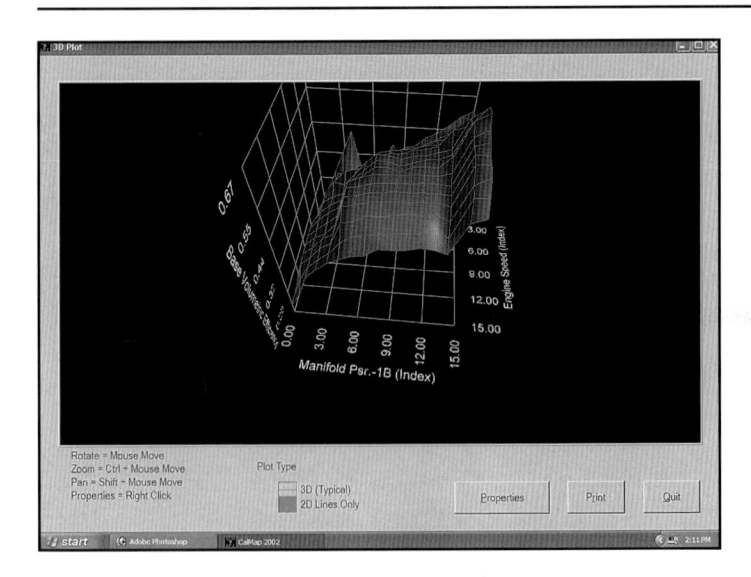

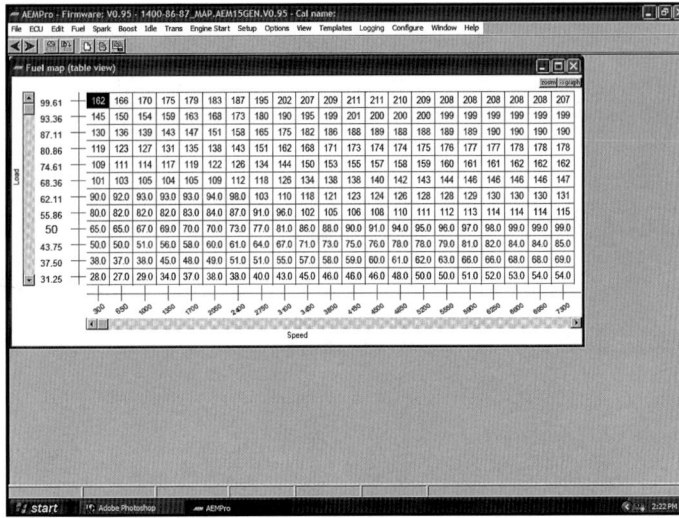

The single most common map that will be tuned in any engine is the base fuel map. This map consists of a grid matrix of values that the computer uses to look up the correct amount of fuel to add to the engine under any given operating condition.

This map represents how much air the engine is using at that exact moment. Normally it does this by having a two-axis grid. One axis represents the engine speed, and another represents engine load. It is usually called either the VE (volumetric efficiency) map or the base fuel map.

to look up the correct amount of fuel to add to the engine under any given operating circumstance.

All of the engine's basic fueling requirements are taken from this table. Any adjustments for temperature, altitude, or for special circumstances, like for use during cold starting, are made against this map, so it is important to always tune it first to avoid chasing one's tail later on. Typically, this map shows the engine's volumetric efficiency, or how much air the engine is using at that exact moment.

The base fuel map shows the engine's VE on a two-axis grid. One axis represents the engine speed, and another represents engine load. In this case, the most often used unit for load is MAP or manifold absolute pressure. The computer uses information from the MAP sensor to determine how well the engine is filling with air, and compares that value to the engine speed to

Volumetric Efficiency

There is an age-old adage that goes something like "an engine is nothing more than an air pump." The saying has been around forever and is usually understood to mean that because an engine ingests air and mixes it with fuel for combustion, only to discharge it again out the exhaust pipes, it is merely pumping air in and out.

The term "volumetric efficiency" (VE) is used in measuring and engine's performance as a guideline for establishing its ability to completely fill and discharge its cylinders with air and fuel. Obviously, the higher an engine's volumetric efficiency, the more power it will be able to produce.

It begins filling with air each time the cylinder moves down on the intake stroke. When the cylinder volume is completely full, it is considered to be 100% volumetrically efficient. This is where we get the term engine displacement. A five-liter engine would displace five liters of air and fuel on each complete engine cycle if it were operating at 100% volumetric efficiency.

Of course, there are many factors that affect how well the engine will fill itself, such as intake and exhaust components, camshaft profile, and most importantly, engine speed. As the engine speed climbs, the amount of time the cylinder has to fill decreases and because of this the engine doesn't always fill completely. As an example, our five-liter engine operating at 80% VE would actually only displace four liters of air and fuel.

From this example, it is clear that in order to improve the power output of any engine (with a given displacement), we must improve the ability to flow air in and out. In certain circumstances, it is possible to have a VE that is greater than the engine displacement. One example would be a supercharged five-liter engine that has twice the pressure in the manifold as the outside atmosphere. In this case, the engine airflow would be approximately double that of the normal five-liter and would, of course, produce nearly twice the power output!

Tuning Maps and Basic Engine Caibration

The throttle position sensor, usually located on the side of the throttle body, can also be used to determine engine load. The more throttle angle the ECU sees, the more air it assumes is entering the engine. The throttle shaft connects through the throttle body to the actual sensor.

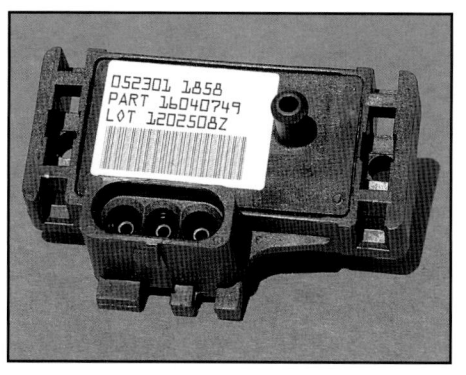

Typically, throttle angle by itself is not used in an engine where boost is present. This is mostly due to the fact that the manifold pressure can change wildly under full throttle conditions as boost increases, and there is no way for the throttle position sensor to register this change. In this case, using a MAP sensor is the better choice.

When an engine has very radical camshafts or individual throttle bodies, it can sometimes have a very weak or even erratic MAP signal. This makes it difficult to tune the engine efficiently. In this case, using the throttle position signal is the better choice.

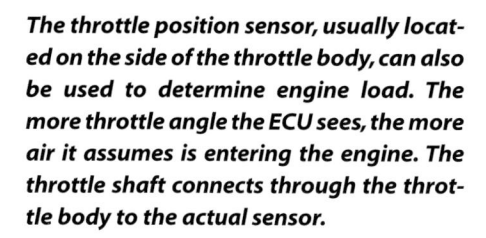

see how many times it is filling in a given period of time.

The throttle position sensor can also indicate engine load. The more throttle angle the ECU sees, the more air it assumes is entering the engine. The ECU compares the angle of throttle opening to the engine speed to get an estimate of the engine's volumetric efficiency.

Typically, throttle angle by itself is not used in an engine where boost is present. This is mostly due to the fact that the manifold pressure can change wildly under full-throttle conditions and there is no way for the throttle position sensor alone to register this change. In this case, the MAP sensor is the better choice.

When an engine has very radical camshafts or individual throttle bodies, it can sometimes have a very weak or even erratic MAP signal because the overlap period of the camshaft causes pressure to fluctuate in the intake manifold. This makes it difficult to tune the engine efficiently using only the MAP sensor signal. In this case the throttle position signal is the better choice for mapping, because it ignores these tiny fluctuation in manifold pressure and can more accurately control the air/fuel mixture at low engine speeds.

Some ECUs have the capability to use both methods at the same time. This allows unique engine applications, such as a radically cammed engine using individual throttle bodies and turbochargers! This way the ECU can ignore the small changes in manifold pressure at low engine speeds where they are unimportant, yet fully recognize the larger variations in manifold pressure when the engine becomes pressurized from forced induction. Keep this feature in mind when shopping for an ECU to fit the needs of your particular project.

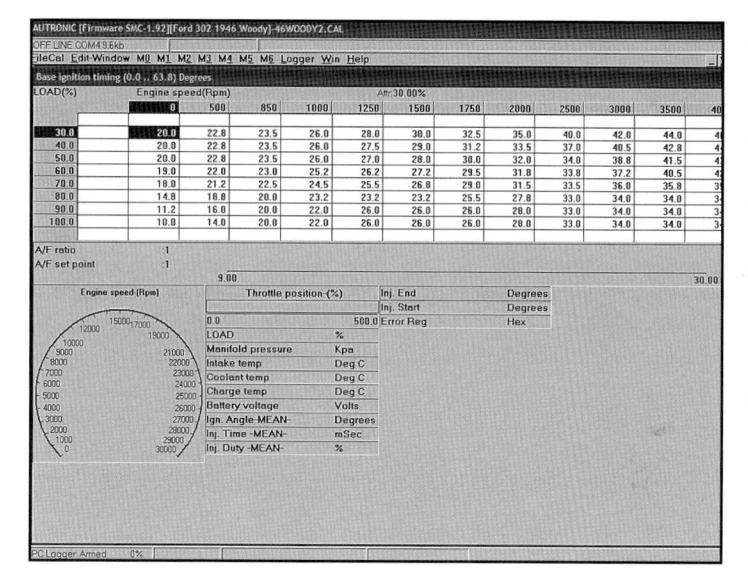

Once you have determined the load scale for the base fuel map, you will generally want to use the same scale for the base ignition map. This will keep all your tuning methods the same and avoid confusion when changing between maps during tuning. The load scale is the side of the table or map that represents how hard the engine is working (how much air it is flowing).

The base ignition map is essentially the same as the base fuel map in that it represents the engine's volumetric efficiency. All of the engine's basic ignition requirements are taken from this table.

BASE IGNITION MAP

The base ignition map is essentially the same as the fuel table in that it represents the engine's volumetric efficiency at any point in its operating range. The words "table" and "map" are interchangeable, and both represent the matrix-style grid of numbers for the fuel, timing, airflow, etc. All of the engine's basic ignition requirements are

Chapter 6

Controlling Big Injectors

When tuning a small-displacement engine with very large injectors, you may have trouble establishing a good, solid idle. This occurs because some ECUs do not have the injector driver strength needed to open and close these injectors for the short period of time necessary to control the fuel consistently. Other than using a better quality fuel injection computer than what you already have, (assuming you've already purchased one), there are a few tricks to help you along.

First, always make sure that your ECU is getting at least full battery voltage, if not some extra from the alternator. The ECU will have a much harder time staying consistent if the supply voltage is not up to par.

Second, use a little more ignition advance at idle than normal to help the engine produce slightly more torque and keep itself running a little better.

Lastly, try lowering the base fuel pressure just slightly to take the pressure off of the magnet coil inside of the injector. The less pressure it has to open the valve against, the easier time the injector driver will have when trying to open it. You don't want to go down too low though, or poor fuel atomization can occur and make the poor idle situation even worse!

I have found that some of the better ECUs like those from MoTeC, Autronic, and EFI Technology have very little problems controlling very large injectors on even the smallest engines. If you are looking at purchasing a fuel-injection system for your project and idle quality is a concern, these might be good systems to look into. It is often beneficial to look at all the pros and cons of owning a particular brand of fuel-injection system, other than just the initial cost alone.

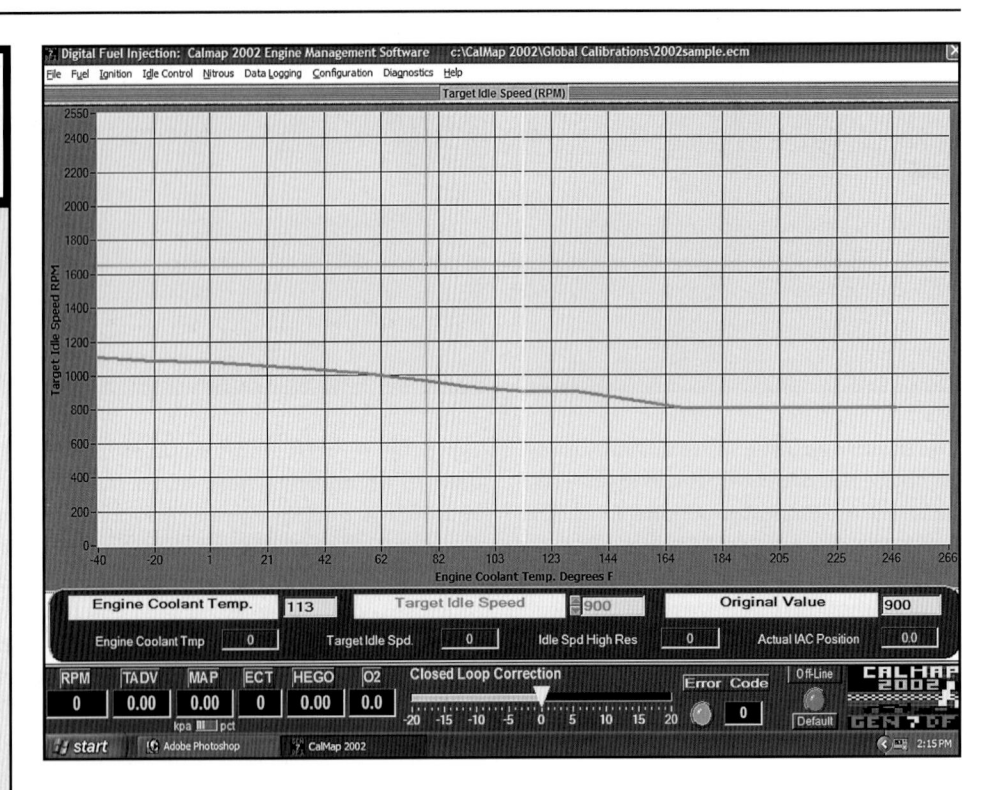

The target idle map is used to control the ignition timing while the engine is at idle. Usually this map uses a small grid of engine speed versus temperature, battery voltage, or some other reference point to accurately control the ignition event during idle conditions.

The target idle map is also used to control the idle speed via the idle air control valve, or IAC. Once the engine speed is determined, this map uses the values in the table to determine the correct amount of ignition timing and IAC opening to get to the desired idle speed.

taken from the base ignition map. Any adjustments for temperature, altitude, or during cold cranking are made against this map, so it is important to always calibrate this map first.

As stated earlier, the same grid and load scale functions used in the base fuel table apply here, so that tuning is easier to understand. This way you can compare fuel and timing values for a given point on the map easily without any conversions.

This map allows the user to adjust the ignition advance as necessary anywhere in the engine's load or speed ranges. Careful tuning here will result in a very efficient and smooth-running engine. Use caution here, because even small changes in the amount of ignition advance you supply to the engine can have dramatic effects on the margin of safety. It is easy to cause damage to the engine by adding too much advance, so go slowly, and conservatively creep up on the optimum amount to avoid trouble.

IDLE SPARK MAP

This map is used to control the ignition timing while the engine is at idle. Usually this map uses a small grid of engine speed versus temperature, battery voltage, or some other reference point to accurately control the ignition event during idle conditions. The user can fine-tune the engine's performance by slowly testing different values in this table with trial and error.

Often this map is also used to

48 *Building and Tuning High-Performance Fuel Injection*

Tuning Maps and Basic Calibration

control the idle speed via the idle air control valve, or IAC. This is a small valve located near the throttle opening that can be used to allow extra air to bypass the throttle to affect the engine speed without moving the actual throttle. Once the engine speed is determined, this map uses the values in the table to determine the correct amount of ignition timing and IAC opening to get to the desired idle speed. When the engine speed changes and moves away from the desired value, this map jumps into action and controls the IAC and ignition timing values to correct the situation.

COOLANT TEMP CORRECTION

This map can be used to make corrections to both the base fuel and base ignition tables. The map uses a small grid of engine speed compared to the coolant temperature to make corrections and get the desired engine performance.

When the engine is cold, extra fuel and timing can be added to aid in fast warm-up. This extra fuel is used to create more heat and aid in warming the engine up sooner, and also to stabilize the air/fuel mixtures when some of the cold fuel doesn't atomize well and doesn't make it into the combustion chamber.

The map can also be used for a safety backup by adding extra fuel and reducing the amount of ignition timing the engine sees during periods of high engine temperature or even overheating. This will cause the engine to produce less heat within the combustion chamber and relieve some of the load from the cooling system.

AIR TEMP CORRECTION

When the ECU runs through its calculation to figure out the mass of air entering the engine, it must use the absolute temperature of the air as one of its parameters.

Once the engine has been tuned, this map can be used to make gentle corrections for changes in air temperature to ensure the correct operation of the engine under all circumstances. This map can also be used to correct the base ignition timing values under very cold or very hot inlet air temperature conditions for best performance.

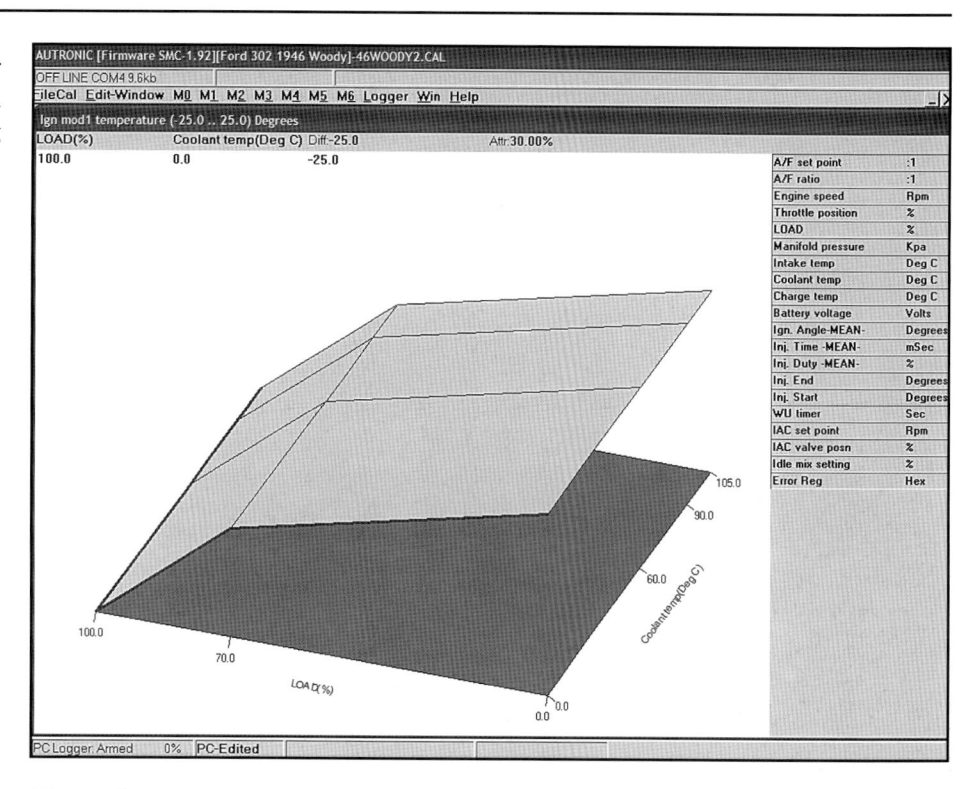

The coolant temperature correction map is used by the ECU to make changes to the fuel and ignition curves based on engine temperature. This software from Autronic, like many others, allows the user to program how much correction is made.

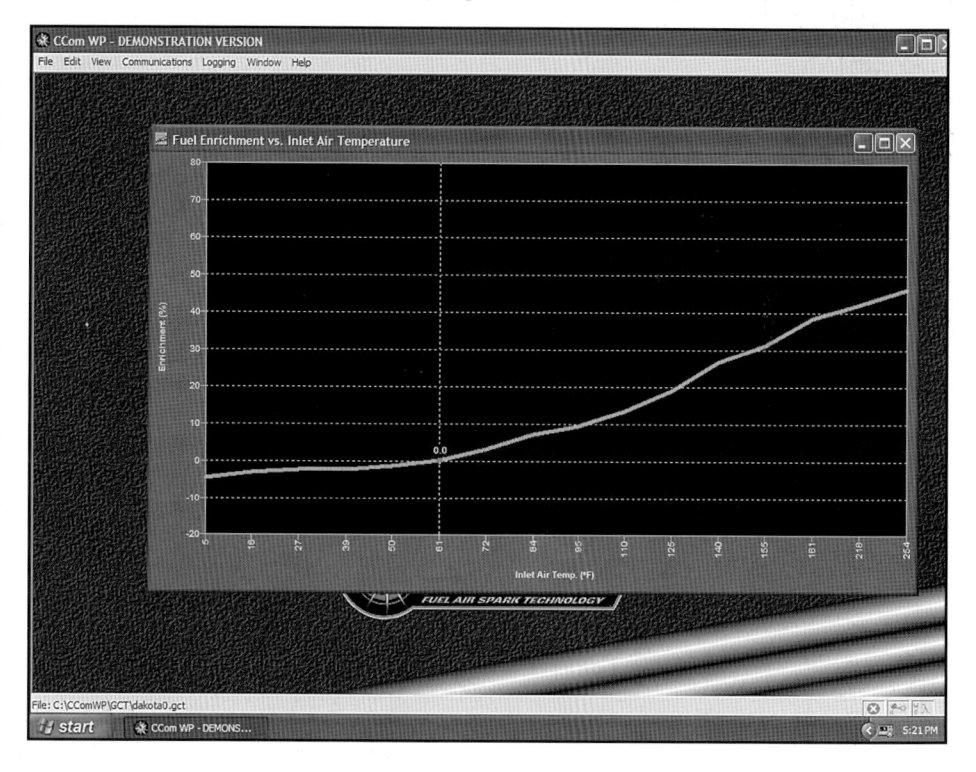

The ECU must make corrections to the base fuel and ignition tables based on the temperature of the air entering the engine. To do this it uses the air temp correction maps, like the one shown here.

Building and Tuning High-Performance Fuel Injection 49

Chapter 6

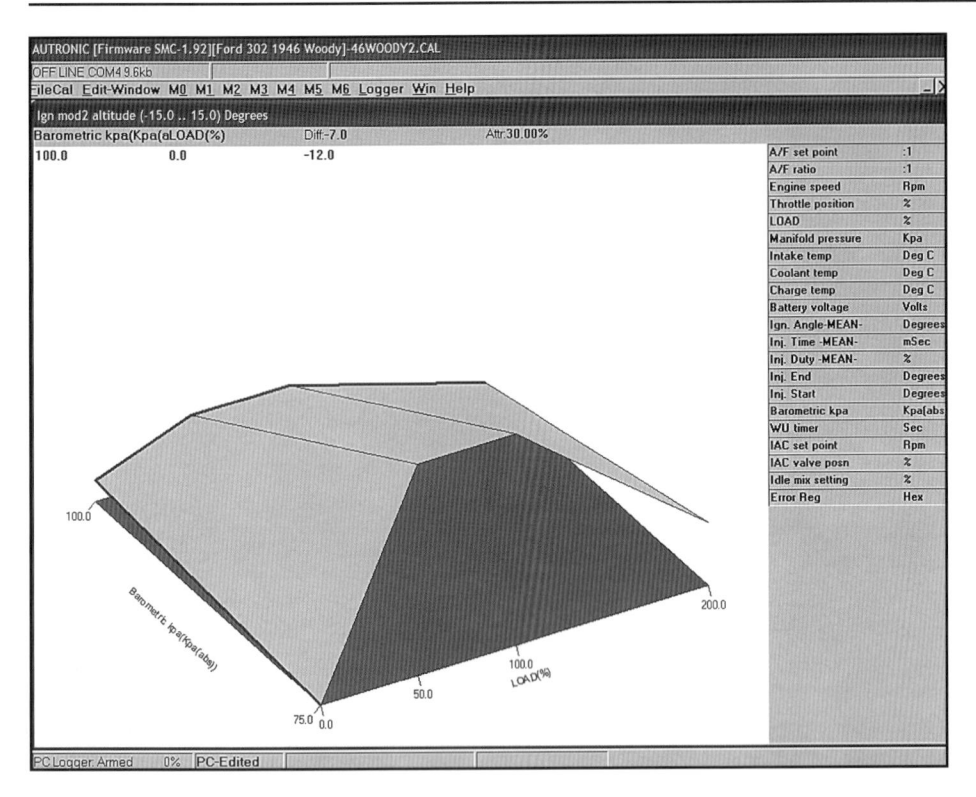

The altitude compensation map allows the user to compare values at different operating altitudes and make the necessary changes to the base maps. This comes in handy when a vehicle will see dramatic changes in altitude, such as climbing Pike's Peak in Colorado.

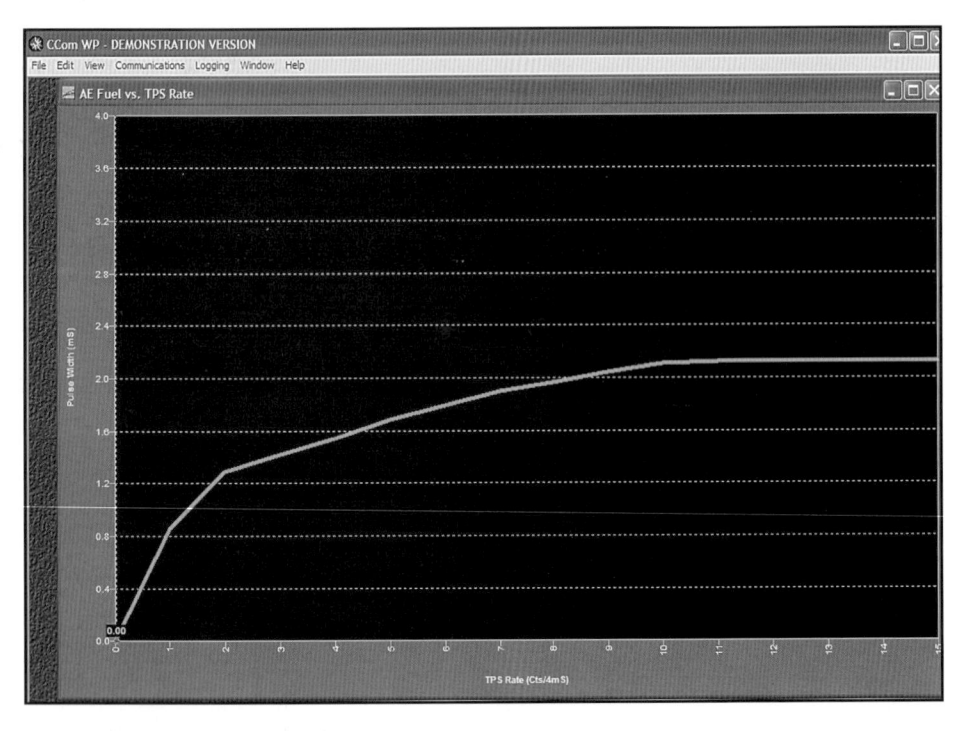

When the ECU sees the signal from the throttle position sensor change very rapidly, it must add extra fuel to the injection cycle. It does this by temporarily lengthening the injector pulse width. To set this up, there is a table, like this one from F.A.S.T., for calculating the necessary amount of extra fuel versus how much the TPS signal has changed.

Altitude Correction

When the engine is tuned correctly, it will run properly under almost any atmospheric condition. Again, this is due to the fact that we normally reference absolute pressure inside the manifold, and not gauge pressure. This way, when the atmospheric conditions change because of altitude, the absolute pressure in the manifold changes accordingly. However, there are times when slight corrections could be necessary. Very large changes in altitude could be one reason.

This map allows the user to compare values at different operating altitudes and make the necessary corrections to the base maps. With proper tuning, an engine will operate just as smoothly at all altitudes whether in Death Valley, California, below sea level, or in Denver, Colorado, almost a mile high. Patience is the key when tuning these maps. Trial and error is the only way to find the exact setting for these situations.

Acceleration Enrichment

This map allows the user to add an extra shot of fuel during transient throttle changes. When the throttle is opened this maps uses a value from the grid based on engine speed and the amount the throttle has been opened to determine the correct amount of extra fuel. Most of the time this function is totally user programmable, meaning you can add as much or as little extra fuel as you require for any given condition.

Deceleration Enleanment

The engine consumes a lot of air and fuel when it runs at high speed with the throttle wide open. When this condition suddenly changes due to a sharp closing of the throttle, it is easy provide too much fuel to the engine causing fouled spark plugs, backfires, and poor fuel economy.

This map allows the user to cut back the amount of fuel that the base fuel map calls for in order to prevent backfires and improve fuel mileage and even throttle response by keeping the

Building and Tuning High-Performance Fuel Injection

Tuning Maps and Basic Engine Calibration

spark plugs clean and healthy.

These are just a few of the wide variety of maps available to tune your engine for the maximum performance efficiency.

The various manufacturers offer slight differences in their software about what corrections can be made to their particular systems, so it is important to consult the user's manual for details on your particular unit. Almost all of the systems actually use all of these and other methods of real-time correction to the base fuel maps. Some are available to the user, while some systems make these changes automatically and have them take place behind the scenes. In any case, make the best use of all the tools that your system offers.

Basic Engine Calibration

Once you have read this book, and after you have read and understand the owner's manual for your system, you are ready to begin installing and tuning your own EFI system.

In the old days, tuning an engine was simply a matter of digging out your screwdriver and box-end wrench to change the jets in the carburetor and adjust the ignition timing by rotating the distributor housing. This was a crude but effective way of tailoring the amount of fuel and air entering the engine, and of making sure the engine received enough ignition advance to properly burn that mixture.

These days, the demands on performance and fuel economy require a bit more sophisticated approach, involving the use of some fairly technical equipment. For now though, we are going to concentrate on the actual calibration part of tuning that takes place on your laptop computer.

Before you begin your calibration process, be sure to check over all the basics like ensuring the engine has no water, oil, or fuel leaks, as these can cause problems later. Also check to make sure you have no vacuum leaks in the engine, as this will greatly affect the tuning process by throwing off all the MAP sensor values. Lastly, check that the fuel system is operating correctly and verify that the fuel pressure is set to where you

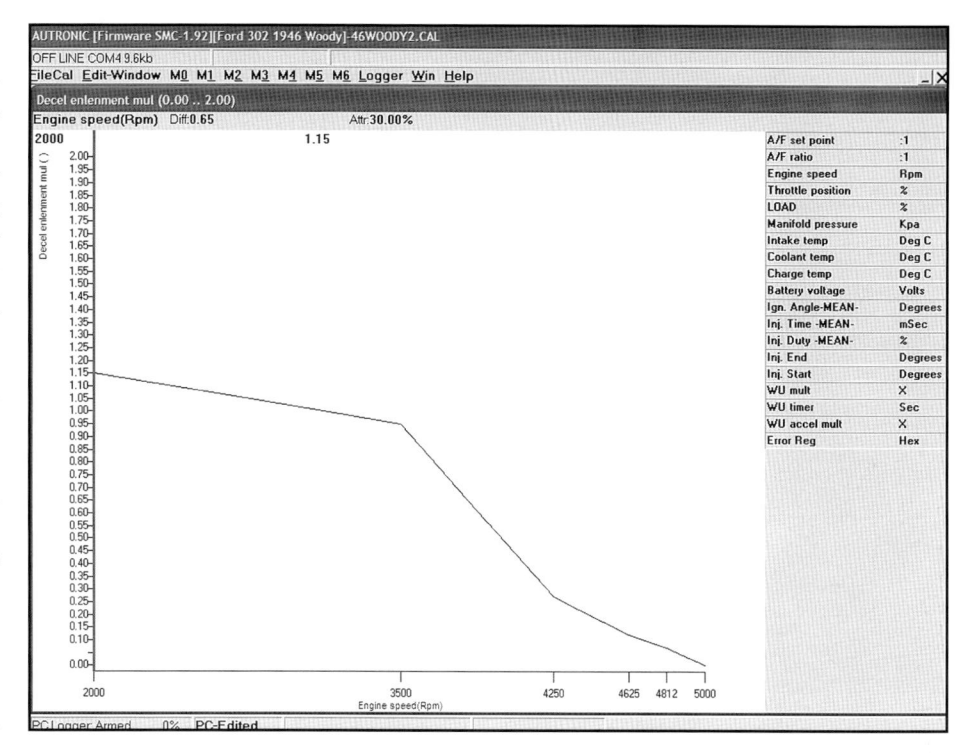

When an engine running at high speed suddenly has the throttle closed, it is common practice to shut down the injectors momentarily in order to preserve fuel economy and throttle response. There are maps, like the one here from Autronic, that allow the user to customize this feature.

In the old days, tuning an engine was simply a matter of digging out your screwdriver and box-end wrench to change the jets in the carburetor and adjust the ignition timing by rotating the distributor housing. This Demon carburetor works very well, but still requires the use of basic hand tools to make adjustments.

Building and Tuning High-Performance Fuel Injection 51

Chapter 6

Most aftermarket fuel-injection systems will have an adjustable fuel pressure regulator like the one shown here. Always set the base fuel pressure accurately before you begin tuning to avoid trouble later on.

Racing and high-performance engines like this monster will need to idle richer because typically they have lots of overlap ground into their camshafts. This overlap allows high-RPM power to build easily, but also causes a large amount of intake manifold reversion at low engine speeds.

desire it to be. The industry standard is to set the fuel pressure around 43.5 psi. In this case, 45 psi will work fine. Once you set the fuel pressure in the beginning, try to avoid changes later on, as they will affect all of the tuning you have done up until that point.

Now that you are up and running with the engine and your laptop has successfully communicated with the ECU it is time to begin tuning. Remember to always concentrate on tuning the base fuel and ignition tables first and then work on your correction tables. Working on any corrections before having the base tables fully tuned will result in improperly tuned sites on your base table and make it difficult to make the engine run to its full potential.

You will want to begin tuning mainly with the base fuel table and alternate tuning between this and the base ignition table for the most thorough tune.

Idle Fuel Requirements

Often you will find that performance engines will want to idle with fuel mixtures a fair bit richer than the typical 14.7:1 air/fuel ratio most people talk about. More docile street-going engines, and especially engines designed for high fuel economy, will idle very lean, often as lean as 16 or 17:1. Because the engine isn't generating a lot of heat and energy at this point, the cooling system can easily keep up with the demand. So for best emissions and economy, it is usually best to keep the idle as lean as possible without experiencing a condition so lean that it causes a misfire in the cylinder. A lean misfire happens when the fuel molecules in the cylinder are spread so far apart that the flame in the cylinder cannot reach all of them. Adding a small amount of extra fuel will easily correct this situation.

The reason that racing and high-performance engines will need a richer idle is because typically they have lots of overlap ground into their camshafts. These camshafts allow high-RPM power to build easily, but they also cause a large amount of intake manifold reversion at low engine speeds.

Because of this reversion the intake charge tends to get contaminated and therefore not all of the fuel stays atomized and makes it into the combustion chamber with the air. Adding more fuel under these circumstances will allow the engine to idle more smoothly. Most racing engines will like to idle in the 13.0-14.2:1 air/fuel ratio range.

Part-Throttle Requirements

Most engines, regardless of their level of performance, will want to run fairly close to stoichiometric, or even much leaner, under lightly loaded or part-throttle conditions. At this point the engine speed can be relatively high, while the engine's volumetric efficiency is still rather low. The engine is not producing much power at this point, and is therefore not generating too much heat inside the combustion chamber, so it can afford to run quite lean.

Some engines will run happily at stoichiometric, while others will run just fine at air-fuel ratios as lean as 16 or 17:1. Keep an eye on the knock sensor values and pay attention to the engine performance. If you are using a dyno to

52   Building and Tuning High-Performance Fuel Injection

Tuning Maps and Basic Engine Caibration

Most engines, regardless of their level of performance, will want to run fairly close to stoichiometric (14.7:1) or even much leaner under light-load or part-throttle conditions. This helps with both exhaust emissions and fuel economy.

tune, you may see a decrease in power, or on the street you may find a slight misfire induced by the lean condition. At this point, you will want to richen the mixture slightly and leave it there.

Full-Throttle Requirements

When you are at full power and you've got the pedal buried in the floor, it is the most exciting time during tuning! However, it can be quite scary and it is also the most treacherous time to be poking wildly at those little keys on the laptop. Things are happening very quickly now and it is easy to lose track of what is happening.

Most importantly, try not to get fixated on any one single engine condition, like say, air/fuel ratio for instance. While this is extremely important, remember that there are lots of other things that could harm the engine in very short order, such as overheating, lack of oil pressure, or loss of fuel pressure to name just a few.

A good tuner will learn how to watch all of these functions, while also monitoring the dynamometer readings or road conditions, listening for engine noises or problems and make changes on the laptop all at once!

You may want to enlist the help of a professional or seasoned tuner for this part of the tuning exercise on your first attempt.

Here are some general guidelines:
Typically every engine will be producing its largest amount of power and heat at wide-open throttle. Some of the fuel going into the combustion chamber will be used to absorb heat and help

Tuning a very powerful engine at full throttle can be very exciting, and very dangerous at the same time! Be very mindful of your ignition timing and air/fuel ratios when performing your high-power tuning.

Building and Tuning High-Performance Fuel Injection 53

Chapter 6

What is Detonation ?

Detonation is a destructive force that often happens inside the combustion chamber of an engine. This force is often misunderstood and goes completely undetected until it is too late.

When a cylinder is full of a mixture of air and fuel, it is the spark plug's job to ignite the mixture. When the mixture begins to burn, it wants to expand very rapidly. Since the expansion is contained inside the engine, it causes the pressure within the cylinder to rise. It is this pressure that pushes down on the piston and creates useful power inside the engine.

Under normal circumstances, the pressure in the cylinder rises at a controlled rate and builds up against the piston over a period of time. Because of the materials we use in the construction of our engines, there are physical limits to the amount of pressure the components within the engine can withstand. When detonation occurs, the pressure in the cylinder spikes almost instantaneously and can easily exceed the structural limitations of the engine.

In a high-powered racing engine, the cylinder pressure builds to somewhere between 1,200 and 2,000 psi over a period of a few milliseconds. During detonation, the pressure in the engine rises instantaneously to as much as 5,000 to 6,000 psi! No wonder the parts fail under these conditions.

What actually happens during detonation is that the air/fuel mixture becomes ignited somewhere in the cylinder before the spark plug has a chance to do its job. Anytime a flame begins to burn in a closed cylinder like this it begins to radiate away in a circular wave that increases in size over time. The flame front started elsewhere in the cylinder collides at some point with the normal flame front started by the spark plug. When the two flame fronts collide, they have the effect of two thunderhead clouds meeting in a storm: A tremendous amount of energy is released and its direction and speed is totally uncontrollable.

The things that cause detonation, or pre-ignition, to occur are numerous, but they all lead back to the same thing — too much heat inside the cylinder. This can be a result of the ignition sequence being started too early and releasing too much heat in the cylinder, or from carbon buildup on the piston that retains heat and glows like an ember of charcoal. Whatever the reason, great care should be taken to avoid detonation at any cost.

keep things under control so that the chamber stays in one piece! For this reason, almost no engine will operate very long at full power with air/fuel ratios nearing stoichiometric.

This is in direct contrast to what most newbies I've talked to believe. Everyone always talks about the buzzwords like stoichiometric, but I have found that there are few who truly understand what this means. Stoichiometric is simply the point of perfect combustion, meaning that all parts in the mixture were burned completely.

That is why 14.7:1 air/fuel ratios provide very clean emission readings. But this is simply not enough fuel to safely operate the engine under full-power conditions and remain reliable. The heat generated inside the cylinder can easily melt and destroy engine parts if not for the help gets from the extra fuel absorbing some of the heat.

Most engines that are naturally aspirated will like air/fuel ratios in the area of 13.5:1, with the optimum being somewhere slightly richer or leaner depending on the specific engine combination.

High-compression engines will want just a bit more fuel to help them stay cool within reasonable limits and still make good power. Air/fuel mixtures as rich as 12.5:1 may be needed to control the temperature inside the cylinder in these cases.

When an engine is turbocharged or supercharged, the game changes significantly. The air entering the engine is already much hotter and this tends to elevate the combustion chamber along with it. Using a lot more fuel here will not only serve to help cool the chamber, but it will also go a long way in preventing the dreaded detonation.

Typically, supercharged engines are less efficient than turbocharged engines

Remember that an engine that makes any real power, such as this blown small-block Ford, will experience a lot of damage if you attempt to tune the full-load fuel curves to a near stoichiometric air/fuel ratio. The added fuel from running richer than stoichiometric helps keep the combustion chambers cool.

54 — Building and Tuning High-Performance Fuel Injection

Tuning Maps and Basic Engine Calibration

in terms of air temperature, but the turbocharged engine will also make more power because of this, which results in more heat.

Finding the perfect air/fuel ratio for your engine can be difficult and very time consuming. I typically try and use a dynamometer for this operation, but my recommendation is that for under 15 psi of boost, most water-cooled engines will be happy from 12.2-12.5:1, and most air-cooled engines will want to be slightly more rich.

Engines with very high boost levels will require special attention and may want to be far richer than these numbers. It is not uncommon to see an engine running 30 psi of boost with an air-fuel ratio of 10.5:1! Test carefully and be aware of engine conditions all the time, and remember to check your sparkplugs for signs of trouble.

Understanding Ignition Timing

In the course of tuning the engine, you will also need to determine the optimal ignition timing setting for the operating conditions. This is most effectively done on an engine dyno, as results are very easy to see and compare back-to back.

The normal procedure would be to operate the dyno and observe the instantaneous power and torque readings, while changing the ignition timing values for any given speed and load point. Remember to observe the engine's tendency to knock or exhibit detonation and make adjustments accordingly.

As this method of tuning is not always readily available to the average tuner, the next best thing to do would be to use a chassis dyno and tune it in roughly the same fashion, using more of a trial-and-error approach.

The amount of ignition timing the engine will require varies greatly depending on several factors, including engine speed, engine load, atmospheric conditions, and fuel quality. Also, some engine designs will tend to burn the fuel mixtures more efficiently than others, thus requiring less advance to properly burn the entire mixture.

The idea here is to ignite the mixture

The easiest way to tune the ignition map is with the engine being held at a constant speed and load on a dyno. If you don't have access to an engine dyno, try renting some time on a local chassis dyno.

at the proper amount of time before the piston reaches the top of the cylinder (or when the piston is a certain distance from reaching top dead center). This is necessary in order to allow enough time to create the pressure that forces the piston back down in the bore without doing it too soon and causing the piston to have to fight its way to the top.

Having too little advance (firing too late) will result in poor power and throttle response because of the lack of pressure available to push the piston back down the cylinder once it reaches top dead center. In extreme cases, at very high engine speeds, the piston can actually run away from the expanding flame front.

On average, the flame in a cylinder propagates at about 900 ft/sec. Knowing this, it would be theoretically possible to calculate the perfect amount of ignition timing for any given engine speed based solely on the size of the bore. However, this rarely works because of all the other variables involved.

Here are some basic guidelines for setting the ignition tables for a given type of engine. These are only general suggestions and the idea here is to get you thinking about the factors that affect your engine's operation and ignition requirements, and also about what is happening in the cylinder at any given time.

Bore Diameter

Larger bores need more advance to get the flame all the way across them; smaller bores typically need less.

Chapter 6

Typically engines using forced induction, like this turbocharged '02 Subaru WRX will require less ignition advance than a similar naturally aspirated engine. This is the case because the higher density of air and fuel in the turbocharged engine will burn faster.

Combustion Chamber Size

In much the same way, a larger combustion chamber needs a bit more advance to give the flame enough time to build pressure, while smaller chambers tend to be more efficient and require less timing.

Compression Ratios

Engines with lower compression ratios tend to build less pressure on their own and therefore need the help of some extra advance to get things going. Engines with higher compression ratios will benefit from pulling the timing back a little bit, allowing them to build pressure on their own, and also reducing the amount of heat in the combustion chamber.

Fuel Octane

The octane rating of a fuel is simply a measurement of the fuel's burn rate, or its resistance to knock. Fuels with higher octane ratings tend to burn more slowly and are good for use in high-temperature combustion chambers. The higher the octane number of a fuel, the more ignition timing it will tolerate.

Combustion Chamber Design

More efficient chamber shapes like heart shaped, pent-roof, and multi-valve designs tend to burn the mixture very efficiently. For this reason, they normally require a lot less ignition advance than more traditional bathtub or hemi-shaped chambers.

Forced Induction

Engines using forced induction have a much higher energy content present in the combustion event, and the flame front can travel from molecule to molecule much easier because of their close proximity to each other. As a result, they typically require less advance to ignite the mixture. The lower amount of advance also serves to lower combustion-chamber temperatures.

CORRECTION MAPS

Once you have successfully tuned your engine completely using the base maps for fuel and ignition, you will have a pretty decent-running car. At this point you may want to take a break, let the car cool down, and start thinking about making subtle corrections using the other correction maps.

My advice is to get up early in the morning after the engine has rested all night and get it started and begin tuning immediately. This allows you to tune the correction maps in real time as they are working. Once the engine is up to normal operating temperature, you will have to wait until it cools down completely to get the same opportunity again.

The object is to get the engine to run the same way under all operating conditions. Cold weather, hot weather, high altitude, and sea level all require a slightly different tune, and it is these maps that allow you to touch up the base maps just the right amount. Use them carefully, and remember that they should only be small corrections. If you find yourself needing very large corrections, you may want to take another look at the base maps first!

There are many correction tables that must be tuned to have a perfectly running engine. Always tune correction tables last, as they affect the base fuel and ignition values. Changing these maps before fully tuning the base tables will result in very erratic values in your base settings.

Introduction to Part 2

In part two of this book we will take a look at some of the most popular brands of aftermarket fuel-injection systems. We will address manufacturers who build kits for you to purchase and fit to your own projects. Some of these will have plug-and-play systems that will fit directly on your engine using existing sensors and wire harness. Others will require custom installation of everything from the wire harness to the fabrication of mounts for unique sensors. Some of these systems will have premade maps for you to install that will work well with your engine, while others will require extensive tuning in order to get the most out of your project.

I have gathered information on each manufacturer in this manual from personal experience, detailed research, talking with other knowledgeable people in the industry, and from speaking directly to most of the manufacturers. Whenever possible I will try and pass on information about each company's history and their philosophy towards engine management.

Once you finish reading this book you will be able to return to it often as a valuable resource for information on each system, and as a means for determining which system best fits your application in terms of features, budget, and ease of installation.

I will try and cover the features of each system so that you can compare them against one another. At the beginning of each chapter I will have a short summary that you can use to get a general feel for the overall value of that particular manufacturer based on its performance in each of three categories: Cost, Features, and Ease of Installation and Tuning. It is important to remember that this summary info is based on a comparison of each system to the other systems in this book, and is simply the author's opinion. My experience in dealing with each manufacturer or their product has led me to these conclusions. Feel free to make your own decisions based on your own experiences. I have simply made an attempt to classify each system in a manner that will help you make an educated choice about which one is right for you.

Also remember, just because I sing the praises of one system, that doesn't necessarily mean that a particular system will work for everyone. For example, a system such as EFI Technology is of extremely high quality, but it is also fairly expensive and the wire harness can only be obtained through the company's specialized manufacturing facility on a custom basis. Also, the software interface for these units is a very complex tool that has so many features that it may be above the skill level for a novice fuel-injection tuner. On the other end of the scale, you might find the complete kits offered by Edelbrock, which has limited features, yet the installation and tuning is very simple for even a first-time user. In reality, I do not believe there is any one perfect system for every application in terms of cost, features, and usability.

I have made every attempt to make the list of features and methods of tuning as accurate as possible. However, since the market changes so rapidly and manufacturers are continuously developing new products, I recommend that you check with the manufacturer before you make your final choice to ensure the features you require will be intact.

I hope that as you read through this section of the book you will find it informative and exciting. Good Luck!

CHAPTER 7

ACCEL / DFI

ACCEL's latest offering is the Gen7 engine management system. The preceding system, Gen6, did not offer real-time tuning (on the fly) or closed-loop fuel corrections. The Gen7 offers these features, as well as many more. ACCEL's ECUs all come as a complete unit with the software and data cable needed to utilize your laptop and tune your engine. Some manufacturers have an additional charge for these items, so be sure to check before completing your order.

The ACCEL brand of engine management systems has been in the game for a while now, and in fact was one of the early systems to gain popularity in the United States. ACCEL/DFI is a part of the massive company called Mr. Gasket. This relationship has allowed them the opportunity to create a very large variety of kits that are very easy to install on a diverse array of engine types. They also have tons of premade maps to help get you up and running.

There are two basic versions that are popular. The first, which has been around for probably ten years or better now, is their Generation 6. This was the system that came onto the hot-rod scene and brought fuel injection into the realm of possibility for enthusiasts and racers alike.

The second and latest version is called Generation 7. The new Gen7 hardware and software has dramatically improved the appearance and performance of the ACCEL systems.

Some of the best tuning features of the new Gen7 software are its start-up calibration help menus. With this software, the user can answer simple questions about their engine concerning displacement, injector size, camshaft specs, etc., and the software will automatically generate a base fuel and ignition curve to aid in getting the engine up and running smoothly.

ACCEL Gen 7

COST: $1,500 to $2,500

FEATURES: This system has lots of capability for extras like nitrous solenoids or torque converter control. You can grow into some of its features.

EASE OF INSTALLATION AND TUNING: The software has an easy learning curve, and its simple premade harness makes for direct plug-in to the sensors.

This feature, along with the software's ability to graph the fuel and ignition tables into a nice 3D image, allows the user to quickly find errors in the tables and eliminate common tuning pitfalls that some less experienced users might encounter.

These days, the ACCEL Gen6 units are becoming less and less common, and for that reason, we will spend most of our time on the newer Gen7 units.

The following is a list of the standard components that come in an ACCEL Gen7 kit:

- ECU
- Wire Harness (typically custom-fit to application)

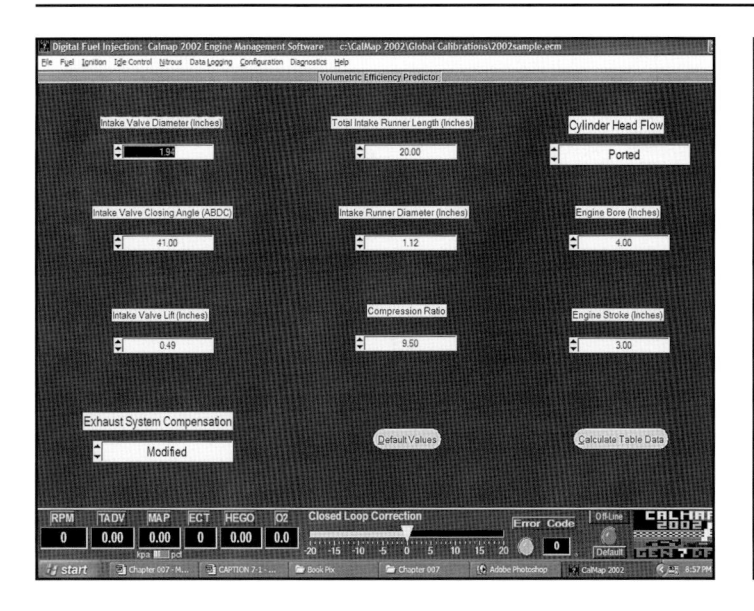

ACCEL/DFI

One of the best tuning features of the new Gen7 software is the start-up calibration help menu. With this software, the user can answer simple questions about their engine concerning displacement, injector size, camshaft specs, etc., and the software will automatically generate a base fuel and ignition curve to aid in getting the engine up and running smoothly.

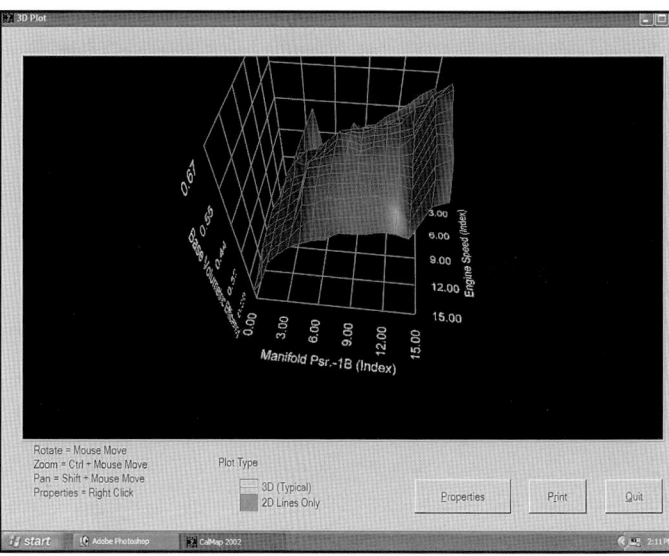

The software's ability to graph the fuel and ignition tables into a nice 3D image allows the user to quickly find errors in the tables and eliminate common tuning pitfalls that some less-experienced users might encounter.

- Ignition Adapter (per installation)
- Fuel Pump and Main Power Relays
- Coolant Temp Sensor
- Intake Air Temp Sensor
- Manifold Surface Temp Sensor
- Oxygen Sensor
- Data Cable & Calibration Software

Most of the basic kits from ACCEL are custom-fit for a specific application, so when you call the dealer to order a kit for your project, be sure to tell them exactly what it is you would like to accomplish so that they can make sure you get the right parts to do the job. You don't want to get a box full of parts for a Honda if you are building a small-block Chevy for your project!

If you are planning on having the ECU control lots of other functions, ACCEL also has a variety of options that are available. Be sure to mention these options when you are placing your order.

Here is a list of the optional equipment offered by ACCEL:

- Idle Air Control Valves
- Wideband Oxygen Sensing
- Ignition Modules (for specific ignition types)
- Radiator Fan Control
- Torque Converter Control
- 3 Stages of Nitrous Relay Controls
- Knock Sensing
- Check Engine Light Function
- Air Conditioner Relay Control

The ACCEL Gen7 can be ordered with a variety of fuel-injection modes in fully sequential, batch fire, and staged injection. The Standard Gen7 ECUs can be ordered to fire standard GM HEI and Ford TFI ignitions, in addition to their ability to recognize standardized trigger patterns from both Hall-effect

The ACCEL Super Ram kit shown here comes with everything needed to install their fuel-injection system on a small-block or big-block Chevy engine. These kits make it very easy for a first-time user to get up and running quickly.

This system is a custom kit for a supercharged small-block Chevrolet engine. You can order a kit from ACCEL to suit a wide variety of different engine types. Be sure to inform your dealer about your project so that they can get you the right combination of parts.

Building and Tuning High-Performance Fuel Injection

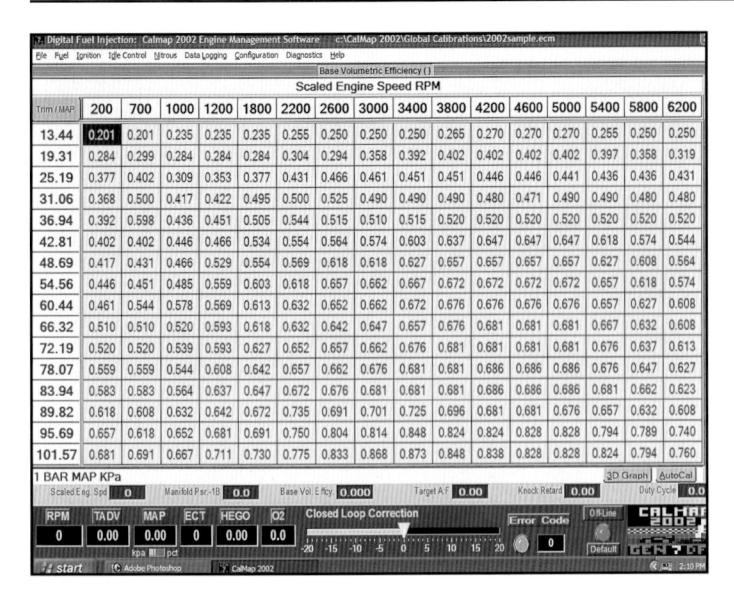

Chapter 7

Tuning with the Gen7 software is made easier by using the table and graphical features of the base fuel and ignition maps. Input all of the numbers in the table and then check the graph for visual errors before troubleshooting a poor running condition. The base fuel and ignition maps share their RPM and load ranges. There can be a total grid size of 16 RPM by 16 load points, giving the user 256 possible points to tune the engine. The user can also determine what the breakpoints between engine speeds are.

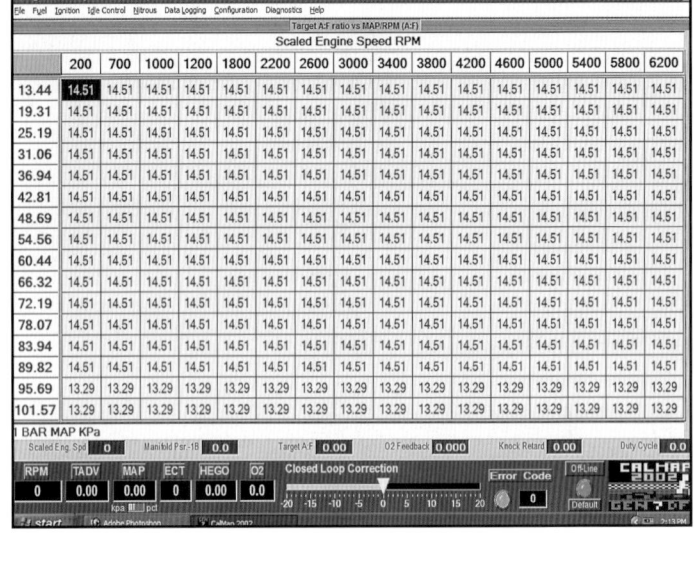

When using the tuning software, the user also has the option to use the target air/fuel ratio map to input their desired air/fuel ratios. At this point, the ECU will relay information to the software from the oxygen sensor to help it find the target numbers.

and inductive pickups found in most distributor and crank trigger setups in 4-, 6-, and 8-cylinder configurations.

Tuning with the ACCEL Gen7 software is quite easy when using either the graphical or numerical displays of the fuel and ignition tables. Your laptop should be at least Windows 98 or higher, and at least 400 MHz is recommended in order to take advantage of Gen7's powerful graphing functions.

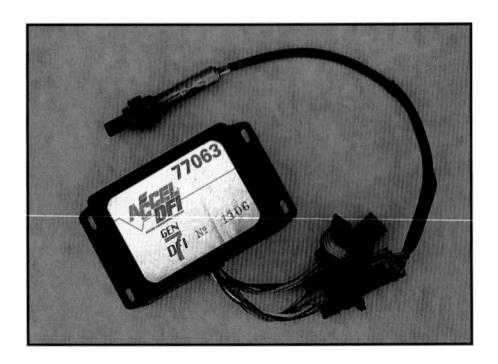

Setting up the base maps is very user friendly due the software's ability to conform to the user's defined inputs. You can custom tailor the RPM ranges that you wish to tune in increments of 10 rpm. This function allows you to tune the map so that areas of small change in volumetric efficiency (VE) can be covered fairly generally, and then the map can be adjusted to have much more resolution where the engine's VE changes dramatically over a small range of engine speed.

The base fuel and ignition maps share their RPM and load ranges and there can be a total grid size of 16 rpm by 16 load points on the grid, giving the user 256 possible points to tune the engine. The user can also specify whether to have load represented as a function of MAP sensor value, or for engines having more radical camshafts, the throttle position sensor values can be used. However, unlike some other systems, the two values cannot be blended or used together.

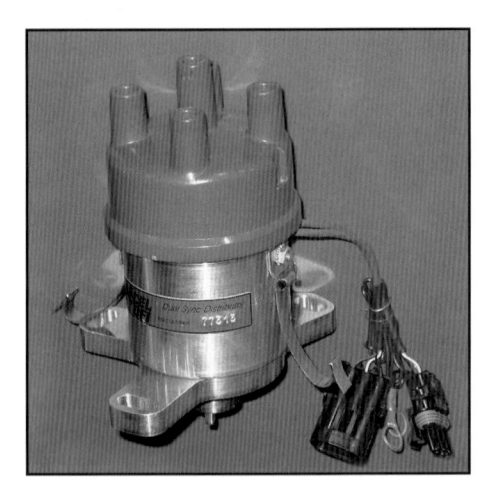

One of the many options of the ACCEL Gen7 engine management systems is this wideband oxygen sensor controller. This unit takes information from the oxygen sensor and makes corrections to the voltage signal based on its temperature and sends the corrected output to the ECU.

In order to address specific issues with installing an ACCEL Gen7 ECU into a Honda B-series engine, ACCEL offers this dual-sync distributor. It is designed to be a plug-in replacement for the stock unit. This unit installs easily and gives the ECU all of the signals it requires.

When using the tuning software, the user also has the option to use the target air-fuel ratio map to input their desired air/fuel ratios. At this point, the ECU will relay information to the software from the oxygen sensor about how close the actual air/fuel ratio is to the target air/fuel ratio. Then the user can make the required change to the base fuel maps to ensure that the actual air/fuel

60 Building and Tuning High-Performance Fuel Injection

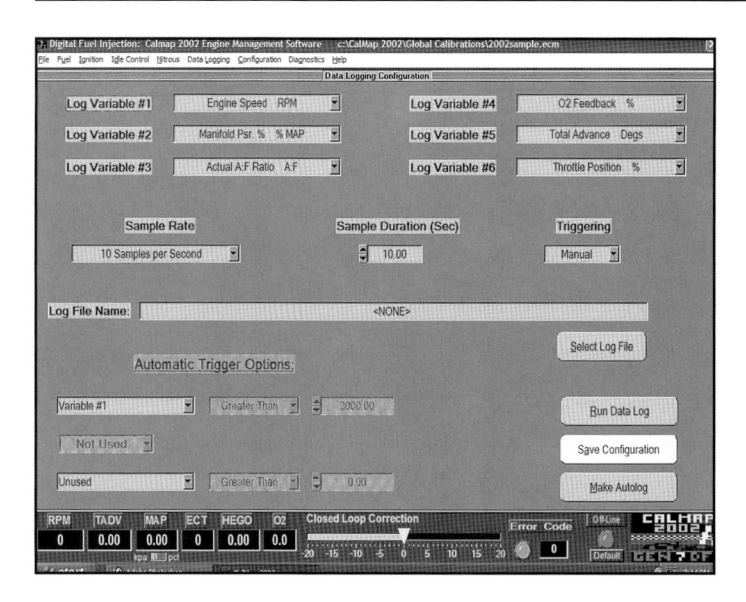

ACCEL/DFI

Another very helpful feature of the ACCEL Gen7 software is that it gives the user the ability to data-log information on their laptop. This allows the tuner to make changes to the maps during the tuning process, make an actual run, and then download and save the information from the engine sensors to review later on. Another very helpful feature of the ACCEL Gen7 software is that it gives the user the ability to data-log information on their laptop. This allows the tuner to make changes to the maps during the tuning process, make an actual run, and then download and save the information from the engine sensors to review later on.

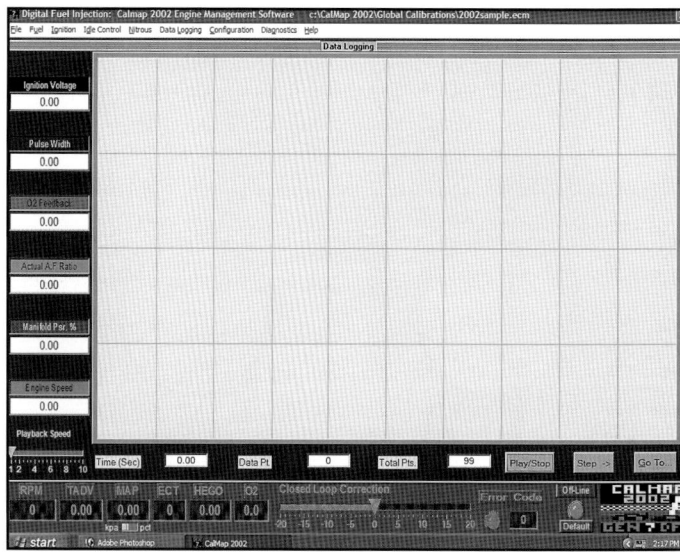

Being able to look over the data from a run after it has been completed will allow you to take your time and go over things that you may have missed in the bustle of high-speed tuning. This screen displays all the data that was logged during the run.

ratio closely matches the target values.

This is a very handy tuning tool, especially when used with the wide band oxygen sensor option. The ACCEL Gen7 system also offers its users the ability to adjust each cylinder's fuel independently. This helps compensate for differences in the manifold and intake systems, which can affect the ability of any one cylinder to breathe as well as others. This is helpful when tuning on a dyno for the absolute maximum horsepower, but it is sometimes difficult to notice any difference when tuning on the street.

Once the engine has been at least roughly tuned, the user can activate the closed loop function, which allows the ECU to make changes to the engine's fuel curve based on the values in the target air/fuel table. It also compares the base fuel table against readings it gets from the oxygen sensor's feedback information.

Another very helpful feature of the ACCEL Gen7 software is that it allows

Oxygen Sensor Placement

Tuning a modern fuel-injected engine is nearly impossible without the use of an oxygen sensor. There are a few points to consider when finding a suitable place to mount the sensor in the exhaust manifold.

First, always try to mount the sensor so that it collects mixture data from as many cylinders as possible. Try to avoid having the sensor only get one cylinder's exhaust whenever possible. On an engine with the cylinders laid out in a V configuration such as a V-6 or V-8, it is most desirable to place the sensor in the exhaust collector where at least half the cylinders come together.

On a small four-cylinder engine using a turbocharger, it is common to place the sensor just before the inlet of the turbo. This a good place to collect exhaust mixture information, however, it is possible to overheat the sensor. Most exhaust gas oxygen sensors can withstand up to about 800 degrees Celsius, but at times, a turbocharged engine can easily exceed this temperature.

Also be sure that there are no openings or cracks in the exhaust system ahead of the oxygen sensor. This can introduce fresh air into the exhaust stream and cause the air/fuel ratios to seem leaner than they are.

Lastly, some modern cars are now using air injection pumps to introduce fresh air into the exhaust stream in order to reduce exhaust emissions. This fresh air can also easily fool the oxygen sensor into thinking the engine's actual air/fuel ratio is leaner than it really is. Be sure to disable any such devices before you begin your tuning.

Always protect your sensor from chemicals such as sealants, and remember that using leaded fuel will drastically shorten the life of your sensor.

Building and Tuning High-Performance Fuel Injection

Chapter 7

Once you are online, the main screen will appear on your laptop. This screen is a useful resource when trying to determine if all the wire connections were made properly and whether or not the sensors are operating correctly. This is called the Dashboard screen.

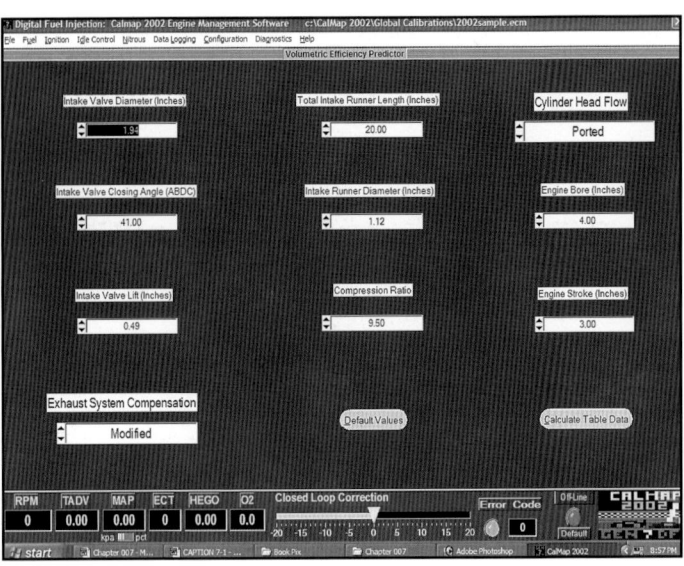

The Volumetric Efficiency Predictor screen you will input information about your engine such as engine bore and stroke, intake valve size, intake runner length, and exhaust configuration, among other things. Once you have entered the correct values the software will generate a base map for the engine.

the user to data-log information with their laptop. The tuner to make changes to the maps, make an actual run, and then download and save the information from the engine sensors to review later on.

I would personally advise any newer tuners to try and take full advantage of this feature. As I stated earlier in the book, when tuning an engine via a laptop, there are many variables occurring, and things happen very quickly. Being able to look over the data logs from a run will allow you to take your time and go over things that you may have missed in the bustle of high-speed tuning. For instance, if you are making a run on a dyno with a very high-powered vehicle, you could easily be looking down at the gauges when the engine goes through a tuned site that causes a momentary lean condition. By the time you look up again, the engines air/fuel ratio could be back to normal.

Having the ability to go back over the data files will allow you to catch these types of errors in the base maps.

Getting Started

Once you have purchased your system and you have fully read the instruction manual, it is time to begin your installation and tuning process. You should always first check to make sure that all the components that your system is supposed to come with are present. You don't want to get halfway through your project and then have to stop and scavenge around for parts you assumed would be there.

Next, I find it beneficial to lay the wiring harness on the ground and follow the wiring diagram to each connector or termination point. Not only will this help you familiarize yourself with the harness, it will give you a head start towards troubleshooting any problems later on.

Once you are satisfied that the harness is complete and that it is the correct harness for your application, you may begin to install it onto your engine. Begin by finding a suitable mounting place for the ECU. Try to keep it in a place that is as free of moisture and dust as possible, and avoid having it next to a source of direct heat such as any of the exhaust components.

Once you have mounted the computer, find a suitable location for the wire harness to pass through the firewall.

Make sure your kit from ACCEL comes with all the parts necessary for the installation. Also be sure that the parts you receive are for your application. You wouldn't want to open up your kit for a small-block Ford, like the one shown here, and find parts for a Dodge engine!

Find a suitable place to mount the ECU. Try to keep it protected from the environment as much as possible. When vibration is a concern, you can mount it on rubber to reduce the chance of failure.

Building and Tuning High-Performance Fuel Injection

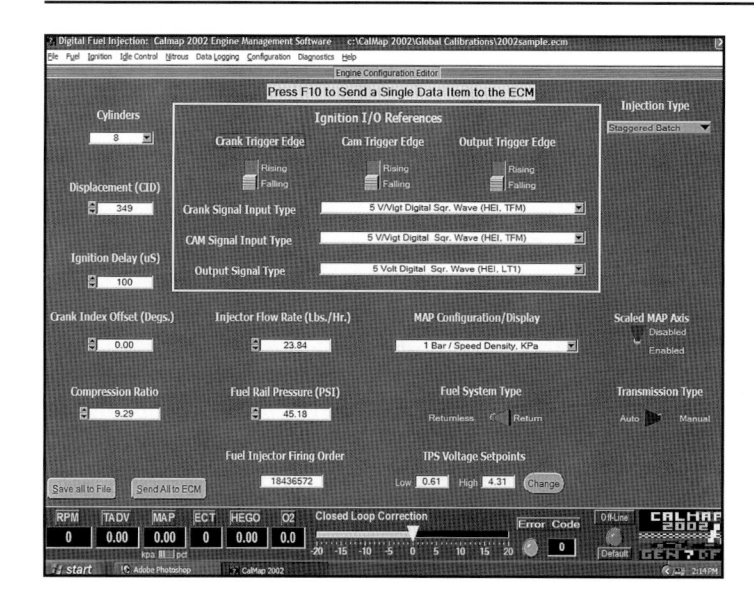

The Configuration Editor screen in the Gen7 software allows the user to access all of the parameters for setting up the engine. Here you can specify what type of ignition system, trigger methods, and load-sensing device the engine will use.

The engine monitor screen allows you to look at all the data from every sensor in real time to try and sort out problems. Use this in conjunction with the data-logging functions to troubleshoot the symptoms of a poor-running engine.

Always use a rubber grommet at any place where the harness might go through a metal wall. This will prevent any wire abrasions and accidental short circuits that might damage the wire harness or other components of the system, including the ECU. Once the harness is routed through the firewall and into the engine compartment, you can begin to install the various sensor and actuator connections.

Normally, I always start with the connectors that are designed to plug in directly to your engine's sensors. I wait until the end to connect any power and ground sources that must be manually crimped or soldered. This allows you the chance to avoid any accidental shorts by connecting the wrong wires to the wrong sensor or actuator. Once all the direct connections are made, you will want to double check the wire diagram to ensure all connections are made properly and in the correct location.

Now you can make the remainder of the connections for ground and main power sources. If the wires in the harness must be terminated, I find it is most reliable to use some solder to fix the required connector to the wires.

Some will say that crimping is a better method, but I feel that the majority of crimping tools that are readily available to the average hot-rod enthusiast are below the minimum quality that I require. Whichever way you choose to connect your wires and fittings, be sure to cover the wire securely to prevent moisture and oxygen from corroding the connection and causing trouble later. I prefer to use heat-shrinkable tubing to cover all my wire connections, however, many people choose standard electricians tape to do this. I do not recommend this method though, because my personal experience has shown that electrical tape will not stand up to the harsh environment of a high-performance vehicle.

When you have finished making all the necessary wire connections, it is time to install the software onto your computer. Do this by inserting the ACCEL Gen7 compact disc that comes in your kit into your laptop's CD drive. Then, install the software into the desired directory and follow the instructions for installation. Once the installation is complete, you will have an ACCEL Gen7 icon on your desktop. Click on this icon to begin using the software.

Once the software is loaded, you will see the launch screen, which will ask you if you would like to edit a file that is already saved, or edit while on-line with the ECU. For this project we will start by going on-line.

Once you are on-line the main screen will appear on your screen. This screen is a useful resource when trying to determine if all the wire connections were made properly and whether the sensors are operating correctly.

Start by checking the values shown in the various gauges. Check to see that the battery voltage is reading at least 12 volts. The air and water temperature gauges should also read close to the actual temperature at the time you are using them. For instance, if it is the dead of summer and you live in Death Valley, it is unlikely that the engine coolant temperature would be –30 degrees! Also move the accelerator pedal and be sure that the TPS percentage value follows the movement of the throttle. If you find gauges that display incorrect sensor readings, now is the time to trace out the harness and test the sensor. Fix any of these problems before you try to start the engine.

The next thing you'll want to check for is that when you crank over the engine, the tachometer on the screen reads the actual RPM. Most engines tend to crank from about 175 to 300 rpm. Again it is unlikely that you would ever see 4,000 rpm while cranking, so if you see this happening, you should recheck everything and find the fault.

Once you have verified that all the sensors are working properly and that

Chapter 7

This small-block Chevrolet 350 engine is using an ACCEL Super-Ram manifold with a complete ACCEL Gen7 engine management system. ACCEL makes fuel-injection kits for many American V-8 engines.

the main screen is displaying the information correctly, it is time to use the ACCEL Gen7 software function that allows you to create a base fuel table to get up and running.

Start by clicking on the "Fuel" tab at the top of your screen. Go to the "Utilities" function and click on "VE Table Estimator". In this screen you will input information about your engine, such as engine bore and stroke size, intake valve size, intake runner length, and exhaust configuration, among other things. Once you have placed the correct values in the tables, click on the "Calculate Table" button at the lower left of your screen. At this point, the software will create an entire base fuel map and ask you if you want to send the information to the ECU. Click on "Yes" to begin downloading the file to your ECU. The software also automatically fills in the sites in the base ignition table.

While on the base fuel screen, you can click on the "3D Graph" button at the lower right-hand side of the screen to see the table in graphical format.

Once you are satisfied with the base map, the software has created you can go to the top of your screen and click on "Configuration". This will allow you access to all of the set-up functions in the software control department. Here you can set limits for engine speed and fan control based on engine temperature, and so forth.

I would recommend turning off any idle-control and closed-loop control functions at this point. Doing so will allow you to tune the base fuel and ignition tables without interference from other sources. You don't want to be making all sorts of changes to your base fuel map trying to get the idle quality correct, only to discover that the IAC solenoid was working against you the entire time and now you have to go back and redo everything you've already done.

Once you have the engine running and have reached operating temperature with a stable idle, you are ready to begin tuning. Follow the procedure set forth earlier in this book for testing and tuning using a dynamometer or driving on the street. The basic idea is to operate the engine, monitor its current state, and make the desired changes to your map. This is a very good time to take advantage of the data-logging function of the ECU.

To use the data-logging software, go to the "Data Logging" button at the top of the screen. From here you can click on "Configuration". This will bring up a screen that allows you to decide which functions to log, set the sampling rate, and determine whether to trigger the data logging process manually, or automatically. If you choose to start logging automatically, you can input what limits you would like to base this on such as a percentage of throttle position, or at a certain engine RPM.

Once you have set up the logger functions, click on the "Save Configuration" button. This will allow you to make consecutive logging sessions without having to set up the logger each time you wish to use it. This is helpful when tuning, since it allows you log a run, make some quick changes, and quickly return to logging again.

When you wish to view the data, go to the "Analyze Data" button under the "Data Logging" menu. This will bring up a screen where you can view the data graphically and numerically to decide what changes to make to your maps.

Again, use this information to try and get the base fuel table to operate the engine as close as possible to the target air/fuel ratios without the help of the closed-loop control function. This will make life much easier later on when you are ready to use the closed-loop control.

When you are finished tuning the base fuel and ignition maps, you can return to the software and begin to fine-tune all of the other functions in the software such as idle control, closed-loop functions, auxiliary outputs such as nitrous, torque converter lockup, and so forth. Be sure to refer to the owner's manual and the help functions of the software any time you have questions or get confused about how to set up these functions.

The last thing I would recommend, is for you to wait until the next morning so that the engine has had a chance to completely cool down. Then get your laptop on-line and communicating with the ECU. At this point, use the tables under "Starting" in the "Fuel" menu to tune the engine's starting and warm-up fuel requirements. Normally I will try and do this as quickly as possible to avoid missing the opportunity to tune in real time, as the engine will begin warming up as soon as you start it. Once it's warm, you will have to wait until it is completely cool again before you will have another chance to tune these sites.

Once you have finished tuning all the base maps and set up all the parameters to operate any auxiliary outputs you may be using, you will want to be sure to save the maps both to your ECU and to a file on your laptop. This was you will always have a backup file if you should lose one or the other. Having a copy of the engine's calibration on your laptop will also aid you in fine-tuning your engine. I find it nice to be able to sit down at night and stroll through a calibration file off-line and try and find places to improve. If you make changes off-line, be sure to save the changes to a new file to avoid losing the original calibration that was at least good enough to run the engine. Also if you make a mistake, you can always go back to the known good file. Take your time, explore the software, and make gentle changes to your program until you are happy with the performance of your vehicle!

Building and Tuning High-Performance Fuel Injection

CHAPTER 8

AEM
PLUG & PLAY

AEM Plug & Play

COST: Approximately $2,000

FEATURES: This system can use all factory sensors and actuators, and it can be converted to use aftermarket functions like nitrous or boost control.

EASE OF INSTALLATION AND TUNING: Installation is very easy, but the tuning software can be somewhat complex for new users.

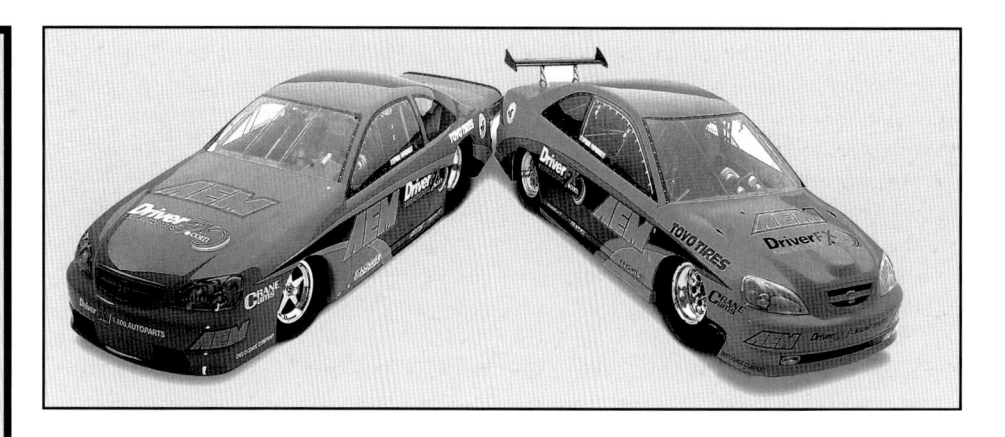

AEM has made a huge splash in the import racing and high-performance community with their offerings of engine management systems for specific vehicles that are "plug and play," meaning the system can plug into the factory wiring with no modifications. AEM is a noted sponsor of import/sport-compact drag racing.

Advanced Engine Management, or AEM, as they are known in the automotive aftermarket industry, has long been a leader in product development and testing for the import performance market.

John Concialdi, the company's president, has been working on high-performance vehicles for most of his life, and has built an amazing variety of different racing and performance engines in his long and illustrious career.

John started AEM as a small one-man shop in Gardena, California, and worked his way up the ladder of recognition through countless hours of hard work and dedication. He used his in-house dynamometer and his small but adequate fabrication room to build and test all sorts of parts for import vehicles. His company's name began to grow very rapidly with the introduction of the AEM cold-air induction kits for numerous makes and models of high-performance street cars.

Before long, John realized that he had found something special in AEM that could serve a very wide marketplace across the world. He then made the decision to team up with some business-savvy partners and formed AEM, Inc. The team picked up shop and moved to their current super-sized facility in Hawthorne, California, with the intention of being a world leader in high-performance technology for the import and sport-compact marketplace.

In order to obtain the most potential from their parts and high-performance add-on kits, AEM began to rely on several aftermarket engine-management systems to allow them complete control over any engine they chose to develop. At that point they realized that however effective these systems might be, they tend to require a much more complex installation than most performance enthusiasts were willing or able to undertake. Systems such as these usually required a fair amount of wiring, soldering, crimping, and bracket fabrication in order to make them correctly operate a given engine.

AEM came up with a concept that

Building and Tuning High-Performance Fuel Injection

Chapter 8

> ### Tire Size and Gear Ratios on the Dyno
>
> Many people often ask me if they should wait to put their car on a chassis dyno until after they have the same size wheel and tire combination on the car that it will normally run.
>
> The answer, quite simply, is no. The size of the tire that is on the car will have little effect on the recorded power output of the car at the wheels.
>
> Other than a very slight difference in parasitic losses, the diameter of the tire will not affect the power output. This can be easily measured by trying several different tire sizes on the same day.
>
> The reason this holds true is because the rolling diameter of the tire acts as another gear ratio for the power that the engine makes to be transferred through. When we measure power on a chassis dyno, we measure the power the engine makes when all of the gearing is calculated out of it. So, if we test in third gear, or fourth gear, we will get the same readings from the dyno.
>
> Since torque is the amount of work we can do, and power is the amount of work we can do in a period of time, it makes sense that gear ratios will cancel out any effects of power changes to the wheels because as we change the amount of torque multiplication to the tires, we also change the tire speed by the same amount.
>
> For example, if we can produce 100 ft-lbs of torque in one rotation of the engine, and we have a 4:1 gear ratio, then the tire would have turned 1/4 of a turn and produced 400 ft-lbs.
>
> Now if we have the same scenario but with a 3:1 gear ratio we would have only generated 300 ft-lbs at the wheel, but the tires would have traveled 1/3 of a rotation. So if we had a tire with a 100-inch circumference we would have traveled 25 inches with the first tire, but more than 33 inches with the second.
>
> In each case, the amount of force available from the engine was the same, so over the period of time we have (1 revolution) the same amount of actual work was done. A taller tire will take more effort to move, but will move farther in one revolution than the same effort applied to a smaller tire. Thus the tire size acts as another gear ratio.
>
> The bottom line is this: Tire sizes and gear ratios will not affect horsepower readings at the wheels.

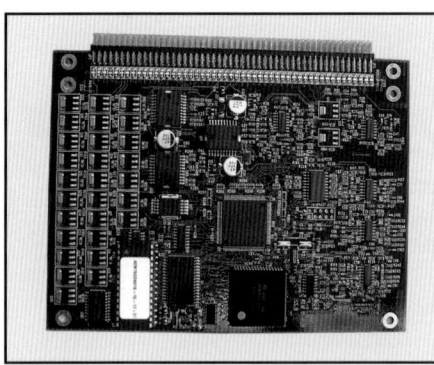

All AEM computers share the same basic design, using a motherboard like the one shown here. It's the adapter boards that make each unit suited for a particular application. Lots of engineering goes into making sure that all of the factory sensors and actuators work properly with the motherboard.

has turned the aftermarket engine management community on its ear. The idea was to produce a totally user-programmable fuel-injection computer that could handle all of the extra power demands of high-performance engines, such as larger injectors, turbochargers, nitrous systems, etc., yet still be able to control all the factory accessories, emission controls, and involve almost no modification to the existing wiring harness or components. Thus, the first Plug & Play engine management system was born!

In order to manage costs and maintain cutting-edge technology, AEM opted not to begin development of their system from scratch, but instead turned to General Engine Management Systems, or GEMS, in England. GEMS, Inc. has been a leader in European performance building and manufacturing racing and high-performance fuel-injection systems for many years. Once a deal was struck between the two companies to allow AEM the licensing rights to GEMSs system, the task of converting the universal units from GEMS into something that would be useful in a plug-and-play environment could begin.

The task begins with finding a suitable make and model of automobile to be covered by a single application, such as model years 1988 though 1995 of Ford Mustangs that use the V-8 engine. They want to figure out just how many models a particular ECU will work for. Once the target model is set, the next task is for the engineers at AEM to completely dissect and decipher the factory wire harness and control strategy. It was important for all of the factory equipment function as normal, and all emissions equipment be left intact and operational. This meant that

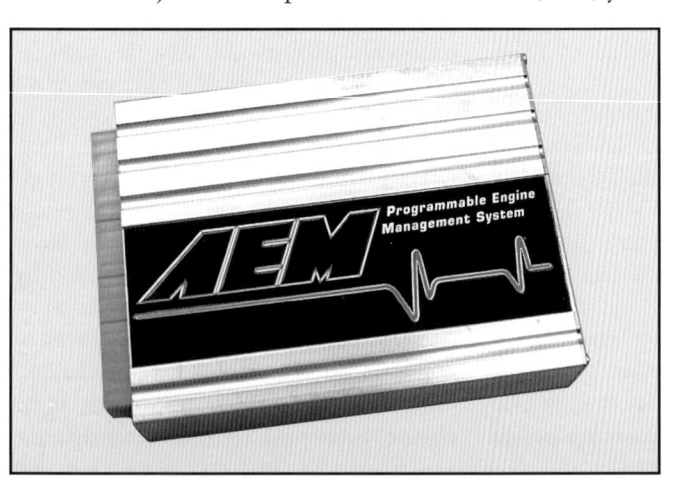

AEM produced the first ever truly plug-and-play engine management systems. These units use all of the factory wiring and sensors, but have all of the same features that most aftermarket systems offer.

AEM Plug & Play

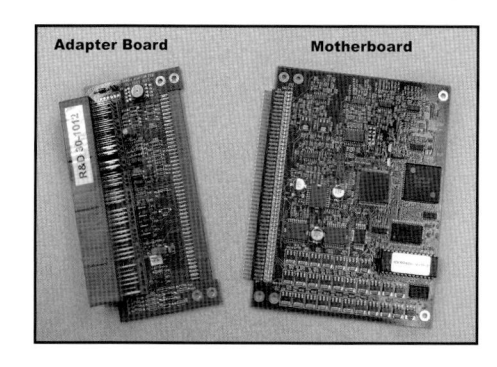

AEM computers are of a modular design consisting of two parts: the motherboard, and the adapter board. This allows AEM to use the same basic layout and ECU functions for every car, and only use a different adapter board to allow changing between makes and models.

the engineers would have to do a lot of research to understand the requirements of these systems. In addition, AEM would need to learn and understand all of the differences in crankshaft and camshaft location trigger patterns that the factory engine sensors use, and then produce a line of code in the software that would allow their motherboard to interpret and understand them. This way, no modification to the factory sensors or wiring would be necessary.

Next, a suitable supply of the connectors required to mate the AEM computers to the factory wire harness was located. Once the connectors were acquired, the process of mating them to the AEM computer could begin. This task required AEM to design what they call an adapter board, which contains all the necessary circuits to mate the AEM motherboard functions to those required to run the vehicle in question.

For this reason, all AEM computers are a modular design consisting of two parts: the motherboard, and the adapter board. This allows them to use the same basic layout and ECU functions for every car, and only use a different adapter board to allow changing between makes and models.

To date, AEM has sixteen different models available, including Honda, Ford, Toyota, and Dodge applications. They are constantly researching more applications and are soon to release several more versions of their systems.

Getting Started

Basically, once the system arrives at your doorstep, it is ready to install. Before you begin, it is highly recommended that you read through the users manual and become familiar with all of the components and procedures you will use. I would also recommend taking a day or two to practice navigating through the calibration software, which should save you a lot of trouble and headaches later on. It is important to remember that even though this system is billed as a "plug-and-play" unit, it often requires a significant amount of actual tuning and calibration before your engine will operate perfectly. AEM offers a well-organized website and technical support group to assist you in getting the most out of your system.

Check to make sure that all of the required components are supplied in your kit when you receive it. A typical AEM computer system includes the ECU, software, data cable, and application-specific instructions in addition to the normal user's manual, which can be found on the supplied compact disk.

Once you have read and understand the users manual and the application-specific instructions, you may begin to install the system in your car. To do this, first locate the original factory ECU. In some cases, you may have to remove some interior kick panels to access it, while in others, the unit may be under the hood. Consult the application-specific instructions provided with your kit or the owner's manual for your vehicle to locate the ECU. Once you have found and removed the factory computer, you can plug in the new AEM unit in its place. Be sure it is mounted securely in your car so it won't move around while you're the vehicle to its limits.

At this point, you can connect the data cable to the ECU and to your laptop computer and download the calibration software to your laptop. Once you have completed the installation, you may open the software and attempt to communicate with the ECU by pressing the "Shift" and "F7" buttons at the same time. The ECU will come online and you may now open up any of the tables and parameters you wish. If

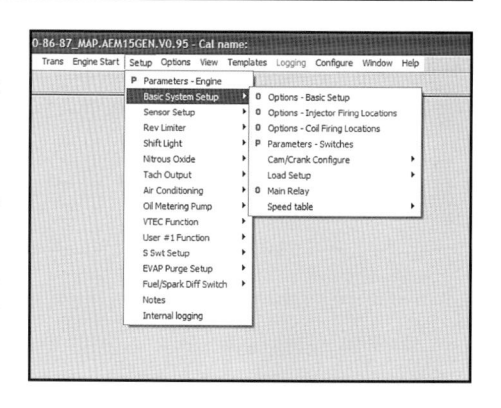

The AEM software set-up page shown here gives you many options for setting up different parameters in the system to match your application. Be sure to set up all the features you would like to use before you begin tuning.

you have already obtained a starting map either directly from AEM, or from another source, now is the time to load it into the ECU. Go to the "File" menu at the top of your screen and select "Open". A list of all the currently available calibration files will be in this directory. Select the one you would like to use and press "Enter". This file will now be loaded into the ECU.

Now you can begin to look at some of the live data displayed on the screen and check to make sure that everything is working properly. Make sure that when the accelerator pedal is depressed the TPS value follows its movements. Also, check out the readings from the various sensors and be sure they are within reasonable limits. You wouldn't want a water temperature reading of 290 degrees if the engine were never started and it was in the middle of January in Maine, just as you wouldn't want it to read 10 degrees of water temperature in Death Valley. If you find problems, now is the time to try and fix them. Because this is a plug-and-play unit that does not require any wiring from the user, you may need to contact AEM for troubleshooting support.

Once your preliminary checks have been completed, you can crank over the engine and attempt to start it up. If the engine starts immediately (as it should), then continue on with the tuning process. If you have trouble getting it started, first check to make sure that the correct maps have been loaded into the

Chapter 8

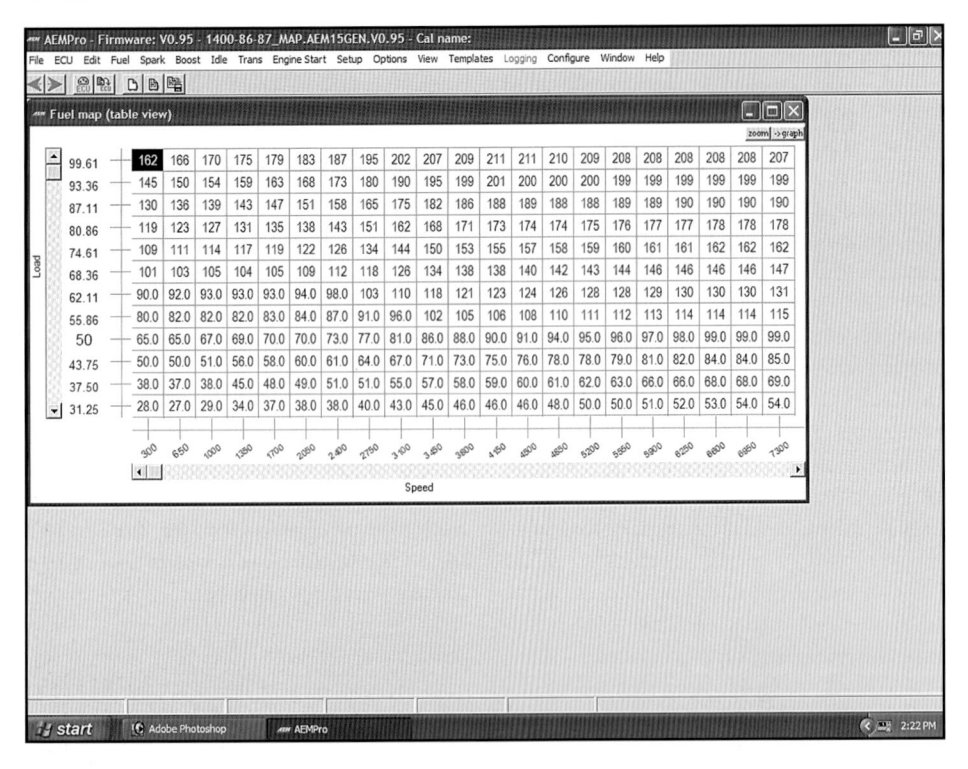

Like many systems, the AEM offer a standard base fuel table. The user can input values to this table in order to tune the base fuel curve. Larger numbers mean more fuel; smaller numbers mean less.

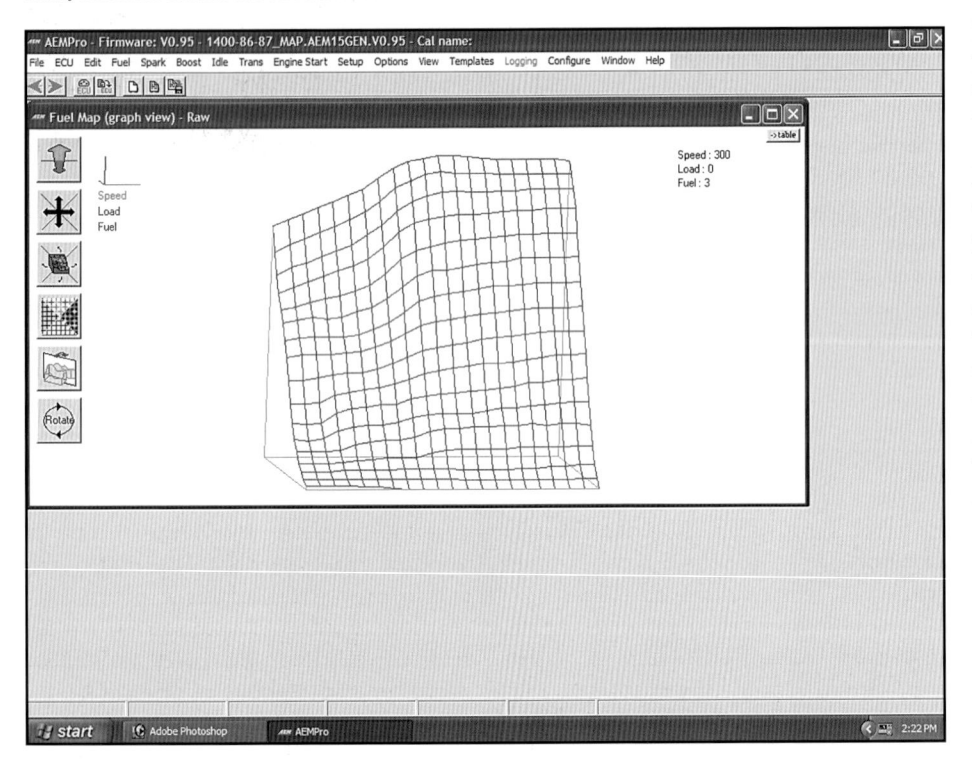

AEM also uses a base fuel graph represented in 3-dimensional form. This is helpful in quickly checking for errors in the base fuel calibration. By visually glancing at this map, it is quite easy to spot trouble areas early and fix them before they become a problem.

ECU, and then watch the live data while cranking and make sure there is an RPM signal present at the ECU. If efforts to troubleshoot the starting problem do not produce positive results, you may need to contact the manufacturer.

Assuming everything has gone smoothly in the start-up procedure, you can begin the process of tuning the vehicle. Start by checking the quality of the engine's idle. It should be smooth, and very near the target numbers set in the idle parameters. If the idle RPM is close to the desired number, but not very smooth, you can attempt to tailor the fuel and ignition timing to get the proper idle quality.

When the engine is idling properly, you may begin to operate the engine under very light loads to tune the fuel and ignition curves. Typically, I like to start out by bringing the engine speed up with gradually more throttle input while the transmission is in neutral. I slowly tailor the fuel map to fit the target air/fuel ratios under all the speed columns with little or no load on the engine. You will find the engine will be happy with considerably more ignition advance at high-speed, low-load conditions than with high-speed, high-load conditions. Keep an eye on the factory knock sensor values, or use an aftermarket knock detection unit such as the ones offered by J&S Electronics in California.

After all the light-load conditions have been tuned, you can move into the tuning of progressively more load sites for all the RPM columns. Do this by either varying the amount of load the dyno places on the vehicle, or if you're tuning on the street, you can use higher or lower gears and a little pressure on the brake pedal to vary the amount of load the engine will see. Use caution when tuning on the street, as the driving conditions can change very rapidly, and safety can be a major concern. It is strongly advised that you have one person drive the vehicle and another actually doing the calibration.

Once you have completed tuning the base fuel and ignition timing maps, you can concentrate on all the auxiliary maps such as starting and warm-up tables, acceleration and deceleration extra fuel tables, boost compensation and etc. Always follow the manufacturer's recommendations for tuning these tables and refer to the user's manual as often as necessary for help.

AEM Plug & Play

Tune your engine on a dyno, like the one shown here, if possible. If you cannot do this, use extreme caution when tuning on the road, as conditions can become unsafe very quickly — not to mention the financial effects a big speeding ticket could bring!

AEM has an entire test lab to actually run each unit and simulate actual engine running conditions. This allows them to verify that each system on the board works properly before they bring it into production.

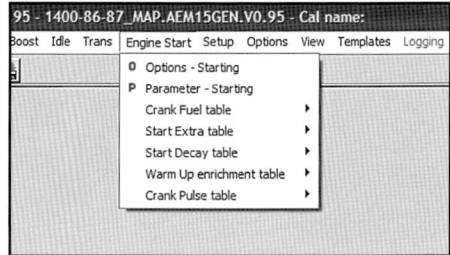

Once you have completed tuning the base fuel and ignition timing maps, you can concentrate on all the auxiliary maps such as starting and warm-up tables, acceleration and deceleration fuel tables, boost compensation, and etc. Always follow the manufacturer's recommendations for tuning these tables and refer to the user's manual as often as necessary for help.

AEM has a massive warehouse to store all of its Plug & Play ECUs awaiting order. Chances are, if they make a part number to fit your application, it will be in stock when you call to place your order.

Using the AEM Plug & Play fuel-injection system has created a way for the average street tuning enthusiast to have a way of controlling all the same variables he would be able to tune with a full stand-alone engine management system without the hassle of wiring it in. This is a great feature of the system, but be aware that because it is so much like a stand-alone fuel-injection system, it will still require all of the same care and attention to detail in tuning as a system you would build yourself.

Take your time, go slowly, don't skip any steps, and the AEM Plug & Play fuel-injection system will let you take lots of satisfaction in the ability to modify your engine tune at will.

Building and Tuning High-Performance Fuel Injection

Chapter 9

Autronic

Autronic is an Australian company well known for their extremely high-quality engine management systems. They currently have two versions: the SMC, shown here, and the SM2. Autronic systems are known for their user friendliness as well as their extreme reliability. Their Auto-Tune software allows users to set parameters for the ECU, which then self-calibrates the engine with no other input from the tuner.

Autronic is a fuel-injection company located in Victoria, Australia. Richard Aubert, a former partner and one of the original founders of MoTeC, started the company on his own in 1987. Since then, the company has remained fairly small, but has been producing some of the finest fuel-injection systems in the world.

When the company's sales began to grow too large for one man to handle, Richard enlisted the help of Ray Hall Turbocharging in Cairns, Australia, to handle worldwide product distribution.

From there, Ray set up distributors for Autronic in dozens of countries all over the world. The reputation for quality and reliability grew quickly and word began to spread that there was a new contender in the high-performance fuel-injection market. One country that was still relatively untapped was the United States. To gain market share here, Ray Hall teamed up with Steve Nichols from Aussie Imports, LLC in Lexington, Kentucky. Steve Nichols took charge of the distribution for Autronic products in the USA, and quickly began building a large base of dealers all over the country to sell and support these units.

Currently, Autronic produces several versions of their ECU. The first is the SMC, which is a compact and sporty version packed with features like fully sequential fuel injection, ignition timing control, boost control, on board datalogging, and a host of other features we will talk about later. Next comes the SM2 model, which is geared mainly at the racing segment with its multiple stages of boost control, two stage rev limiters, anti-lag boost functions, traction control, and flat-shift options. Both of these models are extremely flexible and can be configured to operate nearly any internal combustion engine from 1

Autronic

COST: $1,799 to $2,300

FEATURES: The software and hardware configurations are extremely flexible, so they fit nearly any engine or output task

EASE OF INSTALLATION AND TUNING: The Autronic system requires the user to complete the wire harness, but it has a very nice software interface and is very user friendly.

Autronic systems are all supplied with a user's manual, wire harness, and the necessary sensors. The user needs to connect the harness to the sensors on their particular application.

Even motorcycle enthusiasts are jumping in on the high-performance bandwagon using aftermarket engine management. Autronic's flexibility is well suited to these types of creative projects. Note the hand-held tuning device on the handlebar — making adjustments on the fly in this case isn't a great idea.

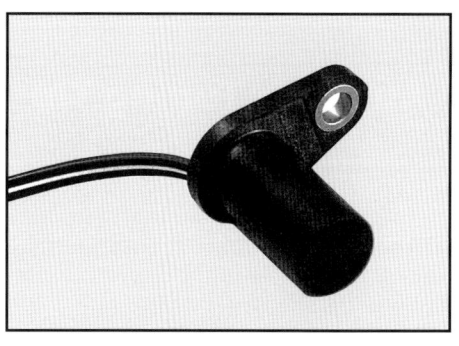

The Autronic systems are only designed to recognize RPM and camshaft position signals from Hall-effect-type sensors. Luckily, most OEM applications use this type of sensor.

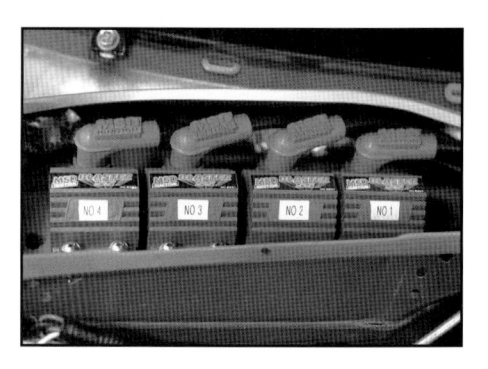

The Autronic ECU can control as many as four ignition outputs at once. This allows full sequential ignition control on four-cylinder engines, or a waste-spark configuration on V-8 engines.

to 16 cylinders in both two-stroke and four-stroke configurations. They even work for rotary engines!

Autronic also produces several plug-and-play units that are designed to directly replace the factory computer with no wiring and fit inside the factory ECU case. These models support the Mitsubishi Evo family, the Subaru Impreza WRX line, and most of the early second-generation DSM series of automobiles (Mitsubishi Eclipse, Eagle Talon, and Plymouth Laser). These units are designed to handle all of the functions the factory ECU controlled, plus give the user full programmability over the fuel, ignition, boost, idle, AC functions, and more. The units also have anti-lag functionality, two-step rev limiters, and flat shift on board. Flat-shift is an option that cuts the ignition system during gear changes, which gives the driver the ability to shift faster and keep the gas pedal flat on the floor.

When you order an ECU from Autronic, the kit includes:

- ECU
- Harness (open ended with no terminations at sensor end)
- Data Cable
- Interface Software
- Water Temp Sensor
- Air Temp Sensor (Autronic specific)
- Fuel Pump Relay

The current Autronic systems are only designed to recognize RPM and camshaft position signals from Hall-effect type sensors. Luckily, most OEM applications use this type of sensor. For vehicles that use older VRT or magnetic sensors, you will need to fabricate new mounts and replace them with the Hall-effect sensors available through Autronic.

The current Autronic ECUs can control as many as four ignition outputs at once, however, they're not equipped with dwell timing to fire ignition coils directly. The output wires must be connected to either an ignitor, such as the units available from Bosch, or to a CDI unit such as MSD, M&W Ignitions, or the awesome Autronic 500R CDI.

The Autronic 500R CDI, or capacitive discharge ignition unit, is by far the most powerful ignition system anywhere in the world. Not only does it have superior firepower to keep the

Autronic produces several plug-and-play versions of their ECU for engine such as the Subaru WRX shown here, and also for Mitsubishi EVO sports cars as well. These systems use the factory harness and all OEM sensors.

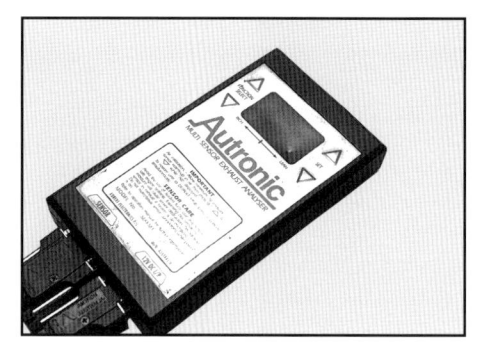

Autronic produces high-quality air/fuel monitors for tuning and for use with their Auto-Tune feature. They have two models. The A model, shown here, uses a Bosch four-wire oxygen sensor.

The Autronic 500R CDI, or capacitive discharge ignition unit, is one of the most powerful ignition systems anywhere in the world. This ignition can provide enough current to meet just about any spark requirement that exists!

Building and Tuning High-Performance Fuel Injection

Chapter 9

Autronic Tuning Tip

One of the most difficult types of engines to tune is one that is turbocharged and uses individual throttle bodies.

When an engine does not have a common plenum from which an ECU can draw a stable manifold pressure signal, it is common to use the throttle position sensor versus engine speed to calculate the load or actual airflow in the engine. This method works quite well for a naturally aspirated engine, but when an engine uses forced induction, it can see many different load conditions when the throttle opening is at or near 100 percent. This makes calibration nearly impossible when using only throttle position and engine speed as load references.

Autronic has found an ingenious way to combat this problem. They start by having the user fill in the desired air/fuel ratios under the target air/fuel ratio table in values of manifold pressure versus engine speed. Then the user selects Throttle/Pressure mapping method in the software and activates the target air/fuel table.

The entire base fuel map is calculated using throttle position and engine speed. The user simply sets the boost pressure at the lowest setting and calibrates the engine to meet the exact air/fuel ratios set in the target air/fuel table either manually, or by using the AutoTune feature.

Once all of the engine speed sites for 100% throttle position have been tuned to meet any one combination of manifold pressure versus engine speed, the software will automatically correct the fuel values for any manifold pressure above or below this manifold pressure any time the ECU sees 100% throttle position at any engine speed!

This incredible method of tuning allows an engine to idle with very strong stability while still maintaining exact precision when calculating fuel mixtures under boost. In this method of calibration, the entire ignition map is done using only MAP versus engine speed. To date, Autronic is the only engine management system I have found that offers such a unique strategy for fueling an engine using both forced induction and individual throttle bodies.

spark plugs lit under any circumstance, but it is the only unit available anywhere that uses twin dump capacitors. Although other units, such as those from MSD and M&W, will get the job done, they simply cannot keep up with the 500R's ability to fire at full energy even at extremely high RPM. This ability is the result of its having double the capacitor storage of the other units. Also, since the 500R was designed specifically for Autronic ECUs, you are virtually guaranteed to have trouble-free operation and compatibility.

Other options that the Autronic systems can be ordered with include:

- IAC Solenoids
- Wideband Oxygen Sensors
- Boost Control Valves
- Air/fuel Monitors

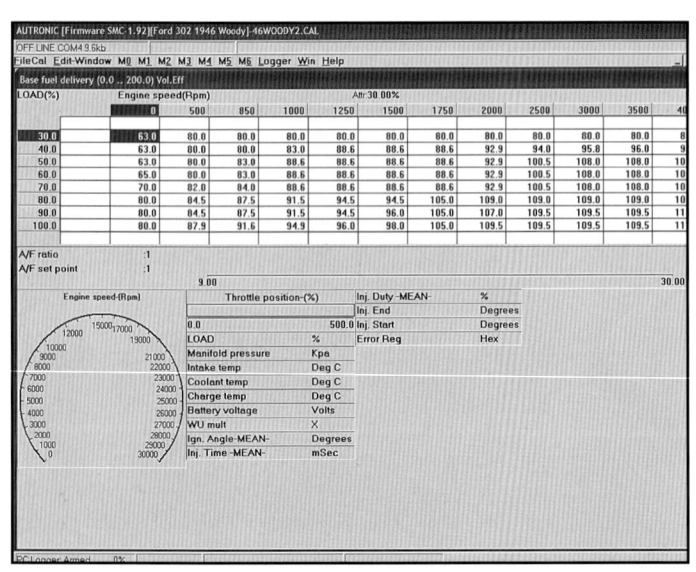

With the Autronic Telemetry system, users can see all of the same data used in the calibration software, as shown here. You can view, change, and data-log information in real time from distances up to two miles away! This can come in handy if you want to tune the engine while someone else drives it (or vice-versa).

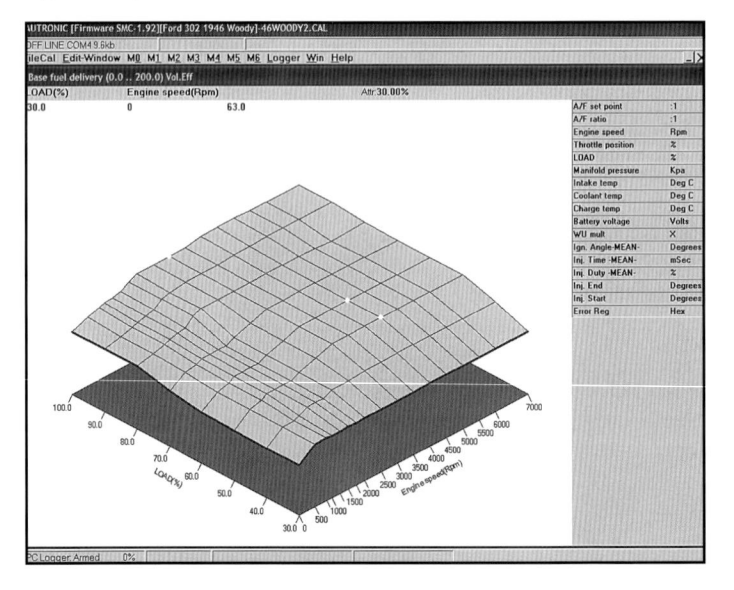

With the Auto-Tune feature, the user can connect the their air/fuel monitor to the ECU and let the software completely tune all aspects of the base fuel tables and graphs!

Building and Tuning High-Performance Fuel Injection

Autronic also manufactures their own Telemetry systems, which allow the user to communicate in real time via radio modems to the ECU even when the vehicle is as much as two miles away! This allows the tuner to monitor, display, and adjust the maps in the computer while the car is off racing around a track somewhere. You can also control the data-logging functions and use all of the benefits in the software package at any time!

The new Autronic SM4 will be released in early 2004. This unit will combine all of the capabilities of both the existing SMC and SM2 units. The SM4 will also have added features such as on-board reluctor interfaces, which will allow the use of magnetic crank, cam, and wheel speed sensors without the need for outside adapters.

The unit will also have user-programmable dwell control built in to give the user more flexibility in choosing ignition components. With this feature, the user can control nearly any imaginable factory ignition system without any modification at all.

The SM4 also has the ability to control variable camshaft timing systems like the ones found on many factory high-performance cars such as Porsche, Audi, BMW, Honda, and Toyota. With this control, the user can completely determine all aspects of variable valve timing.

The new SM4 will also come with the ability to control 2-, 3-, 4-, 5-, and 6-wire factory idle air control valves to give the user complete control over the factory equipment.

Future upgrades to the system will include the ability to utilize the highest technology currently available in knock detection and control called ion sensing. This will give the ECU the ability to completely self-calibrate both the fuel and ignition tables making, this the first and only ECU to have the ability to tune the engine with no user input whatsoever!

One of the other great products that Autronic manufactures is their high-speed air/fuel monitor. They produce two models: the A model, which uses a Bosch four-wire oxygen sensor, and the B model, which can use the same Bosch sensor or the high-speed UEGO sensor for the ultimate in accuracy and speed. For vehicles with a lot of horsepower that use the flat-shift feature, it is recommended to use the faster B-model unit.

Both of these units are designed to constantly monitor and control the temperature of the oxygen sensor and make corrections to the output voltage signal to ensure the highest standards of accuracy. These units are so accurate that they are used testing laboratories and even in production units for General Motors and Ford!

The Autronic ECUs can be connected directly to a standard four-wire oxygen sensor for basic monitoring of air/fuel ratios, or to the air/fuel meter for extreme accuracy while tuning.

One of the best selling features of the Autronic systems is their proprietary software called AutoTune. With this software, the user can connect the Autronic air/fuel monitor directly to the ECU, then activate the AutoTune function and operate the engine as normal. The software will gather information about the engine from various sensors, compare the target air-fuel ratio maps to the actual measured air/fuel ratio, and actually tune the base fuel map in real time, with no input from the operator on the keyboard whatsoever. This can be done at any time whether the engine is at idle, or even under full power! Using this feature will allow even a novice tuner to completely tune an engine in about twenty minutes!

When you order your system, be sure to tell your dealer what functions you want to use, as well as what make and model of engine you will be using. Certain features of the Autronic system require a special chip version or software setting that is not always included in the base kit. Your dealer will be happy to advise you when a change is necessary and will be able to assist you in making the change. Autronic also manufactures a dwell board that can be added to the motherboard of your ECU in order to control some types of factory ignition coils directly. Ask your dealer for details about whether or not your coil types are supported.

Tuning the base maps in this system is extremely easy, because all of the scales for the base fuel and ignition maps are completely user definable. The tables can be configured with as many as 16 load sites and 32 RPM sites, for a maximum of 512 possible sites.

The Autronic system allows the user to define the load value as a function of the MAP, throttle position, mass airflow, exhaust backpressure, or a combination of MAP and throttle position signals. Using any one of these methods, the tuner can custom-tailor the calibration to match the engine's exact requirements. The Autronic is suitable for use on naturally aspirated, turbocharged, supercharged, nitrous-injected, and individual throttle-body engines.

The Autronic system also allows the user unlimited access to its on-board data-logging system, which can be configured completely by the tuner to monitor any number of 65 available channels. The tuner also has the ability to select how often the data is sampled from once every five seconds to as often as fifty samples per second! The data can be saved and stored on file to be displayed later on the screen for analyzing the tune up or troubleshooting a problem. It is also very helpful to use the data-logging feature for tuning, as the Autronic software has some very unique tuning functions built into it such as the mixture tables and the "Math" key functions.

Autronic also manufactures a dwell board that can be added to the motherboard of your ECU in order to control some types of factory ignition coils directly, like these Chevrolet LS1 coils.

Chapter 9

Once you have logged data from a running engine, you can display it on the data-logging screen and bring up the "Mixture Table" menu. This table looks at the recorded data and finds places in the base fuel table where the recorded values did not match the values in the target air/fuel ratio tables. The tuner can then double click on those values and the software will automatically make the required changes to the base fuel table to correct the mixture! When you are tuning an engine you can also use the "Math Key" function to make corrections automatically to the base fuel table. Once you are in the base fuel map, simply highlight any tuning site and press the "M" key on your keyboard. A menu box will appear on your screen showing what the target air/fuel ratio for that site was meant to be and then ask you to input what the actual ratio was. Once you do this and click on "OK", the software will automatically make the required changes to the base fuel table for you.

Tuning an engine using these functions is very quick and easy even for a fairly novice tuner. The easiest way to do this is to data-log a few high-power runs while the Autronic air/fuel monitor is connected. Then go back and look at the data-logs and use either the "Math" function, or the "Mixture Table" function to make the required changes to the base fuel curve. Even very-high-powered engines can be tuned in a matter of minutes using this feature.

Using the Autronic system makes calibration so easy it's actually fun! Even complex tuning for an engine like this Corvette ZR-1 engine with four overhead camshafts is a breeze.

Getting Started

Once you have received your system and you have fully read the instruction manual, it is time to begin your installation and tuning process. First, you should always check to make sure that all the components your system is supposed to come with are present. You don't want to get halfway through your project and then have to stop and scavenge around for parts you assumed would be there.

Next, I find it beneficial to lay the wiring harness on the ground and follow the wiring diagram to each connector or termination point. Not only will this help you familiarize yourself with the harness, it will give you a head start towards troubleshooting any problems later.

Once you are satisfied that the harness is complete and that it is the correct harness for your application, you may begin to install it onto your engine. Begin by finding a suitable mounting place for the ECU. Try to keep it in a place that is free of moisture and dust as much as possible, and avoid having it next to a source of direct heat such as any of the exhaust components.

Once you have mounted the computer, find a suitable location for the wire harness to pass through the firewall. Always use a rubber grommet at any place where the harness might go through a metal wall. This will prevent any wire abrasions and accidental short circuits that might damage the wire harness or other components of the system, including the ECU.

With the Autronic ECU, you will need to terminate all of the connections in the harness. The Autronic harness is a universal harness that can be custom fit to almost any engine. While for some this is a good thing, others may find it to be quite a daunting task. Just be patient, follow the wiring diagrams and the instructions in the user's manual exactly and you'll have no trouble at all. I prefer to solder all my connections and use heat-shrinkable tubing to cover any exposed joints or wires. There are other acceptable methods, but I prefer this because it is fairly easy and very reliable.

When you have finished making all of the connections it is time to begin setting up the software to let the ECU know what type of engine it will be controlling and what sensors it will be gathering information from.

Follow along while I walk you through the set-up process.

Insert the disk into your laptop and download the software. Once this is done, you will have an icon on your desktop. Click on this icon to bring up the software.

First, go to the menu at the top of your screen labeled "M1". Under M1, go to the "Base Settings" menu. Here you will be asked to fill in answers to some basic questions about your setup such as the engine's compression ratio. The most important value in this menu is the "Overall Fuel Calibration Multiplier". This value sets the scale for the base fuel map. Since the numeric values in the base fuel map range from 0 to 200, there must be a way to scale the map such that it can control a wide range of injector sizes. The numbers 0-200 are arbitrary units that represent a quantity of fuel. A value of 100 would produce more fuel on a 72-lb/hr injector than it would with a 30-lb/hr injector. This number also allows very easy adjustment later if you wish to change the injector size used on the engine. Instead of having to recalibrate the entire map, you can simply adjust the Overall Fuel Calibration Multiplier to suit your new injectors.

Once you finish here, continue down to the next set-up menu under

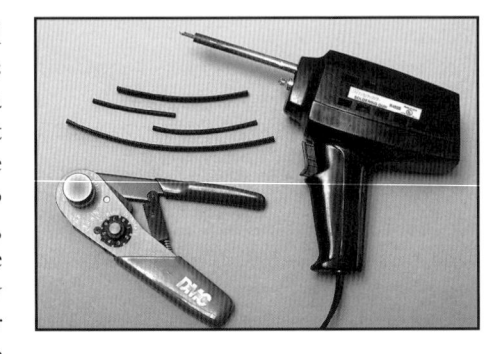

Producing a high-quality wire harness requires some specialized tools such as these wire crimpers, soldering iron, and heat-shrink tubing. Always be sure that your connections are securely fastened and protected from weather.

Building and Tuning High-Performance Fuel Injection

Autronic

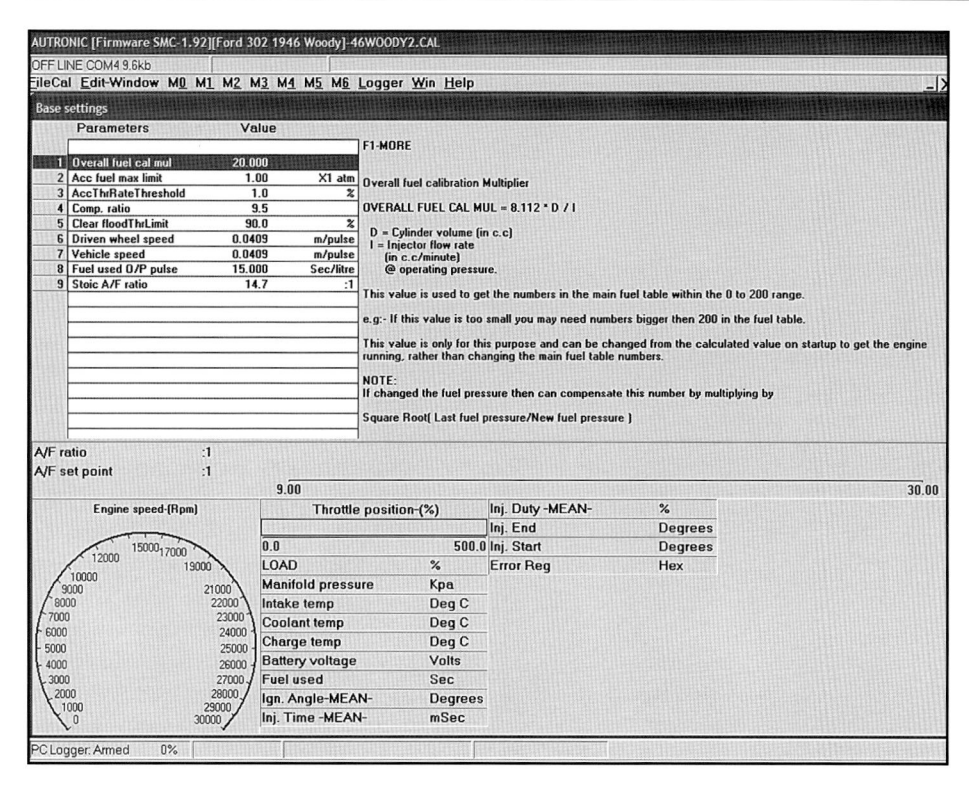

First, go to the menu at the top of your screen labeled "M1". Under M1, go to the "Base Settings" menu. Here you will be asked to fill in answers to some basic questions about your setup such as the engine's compression ratio.

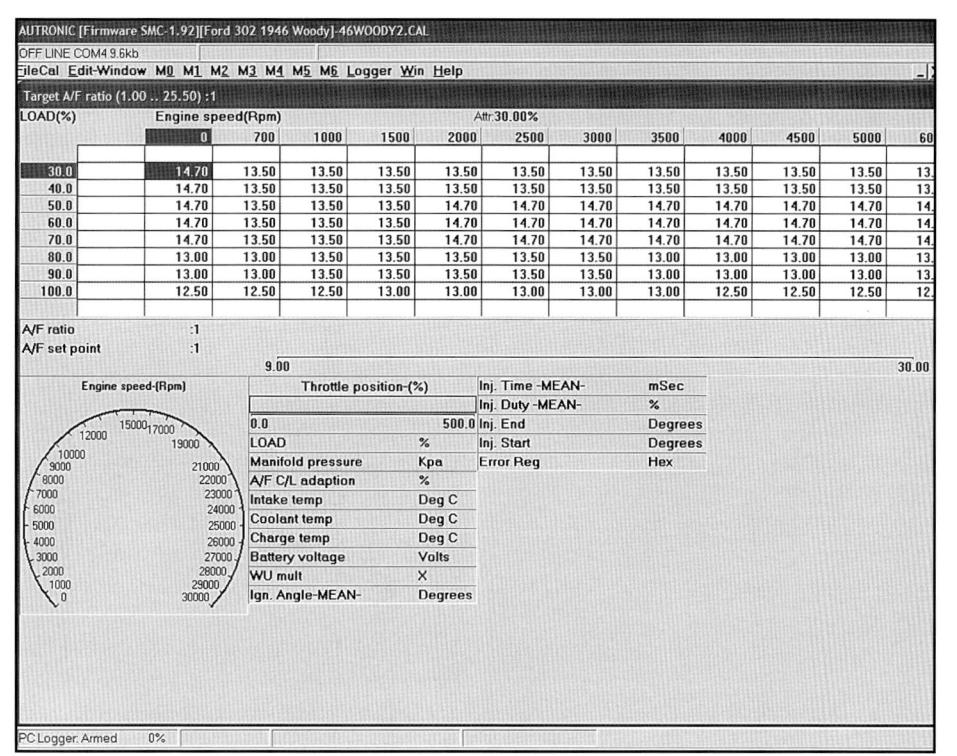

Once you have finished setting up all of those parameters, move on to menu "M2". Here you will find the base fuel and ignition maps, along with maps for trimming the individual cylinder fuel mixtures and the target air/fuel ratio map. Set up this map first with the values you want to engine to operate at for different RPM and load sites.

"M1" to "Engine Set-Up". Here is where you really get down to the nitty-gritty of the calibration. You will be asked how many cylinders the engine has, whether it is a two-stroke or four-stroke engine, and how many ignition coils the engine has. You will also need to tell the compute how to trigger the coils and what type of signal the RPM and camshaft triggers will need to look for. In addition, you will tell the computer whether you have directly connected an oxygen sensor, or if it will receive corrected data from the Autronic air/fuel monitor. Also, the software will need to know what the cylinder pulse offset number is. This number represents the number of degrees before TDC the signal from the RPM sensor happens. Typically this value should be around 60 degrees before TDC. This allows the ECU enough time to calculate injection and ignition values and implement them. For example, if the offset number is 60 degrees, and the base timing map calls for 30 degrees of ignition advance, then the ECU waits until it sees the pulse from the RPM sensor, counts the next 30 degrees, and fires the ignition 30 degrees before TDC. Be sure to follow the user's manual carefully here and if you get confused you can always refer to the "Help" menus in the software.

Once you have finished setting up all of those parameters, move on to menu "M2". Here you will find the base fuel and ignition maps, along with maps for trimming the individual cylinder fuel mixtures and the target air/fuel ratio map. Set up this air/fuel ratio map first with the values you want to engine to operate at for different RPM and load sites. If you would like to add more sites you can use the "Insert" button on your laptop, which will bring up a prompt menu asking what row or column you would like to add. You can also delete rows or columns by using the "Delete" button. If you would simply like to edit an existing row or column, just hit the "E" key on your laptop to bring up a prompt that will allow you to change it to whatever you like. The same rules apply to the software for any map.

Building and Tuning High-Performance Fuel Injection 75

Chapter 9

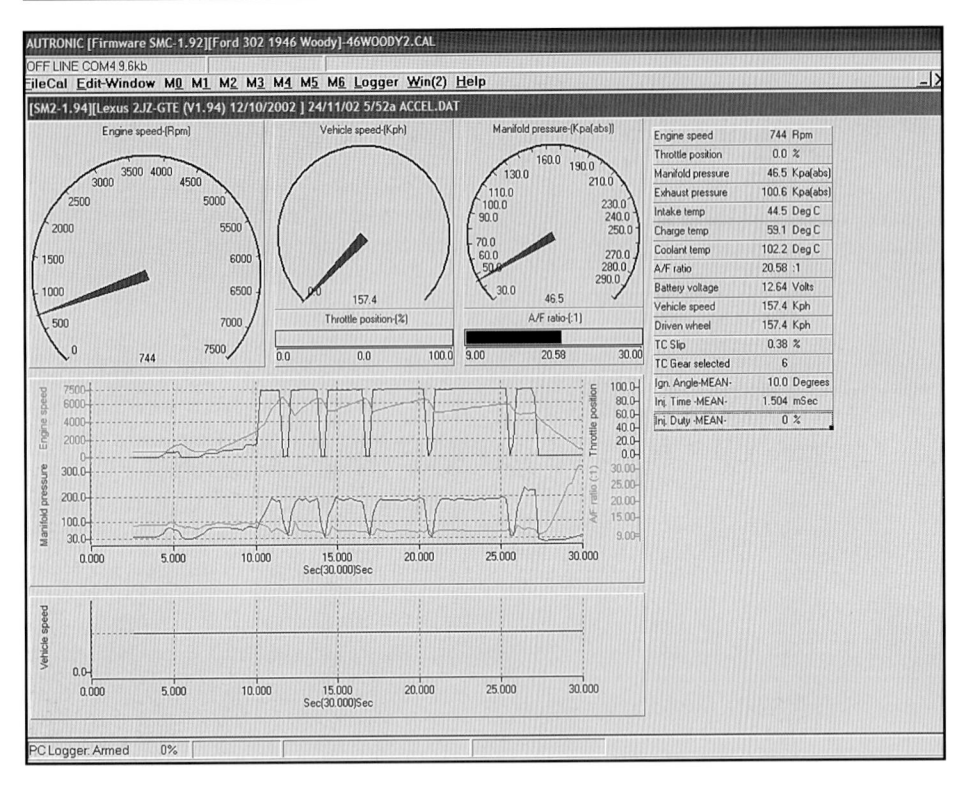

Autronic software has a neat feature as shown here called "Virtual Drive". This allows the user to replay a data-log file in real time, or play it as slow or fast as they like. You can also set the type of display to use, such as gauges on a dashboard, or strip charts and graphs!

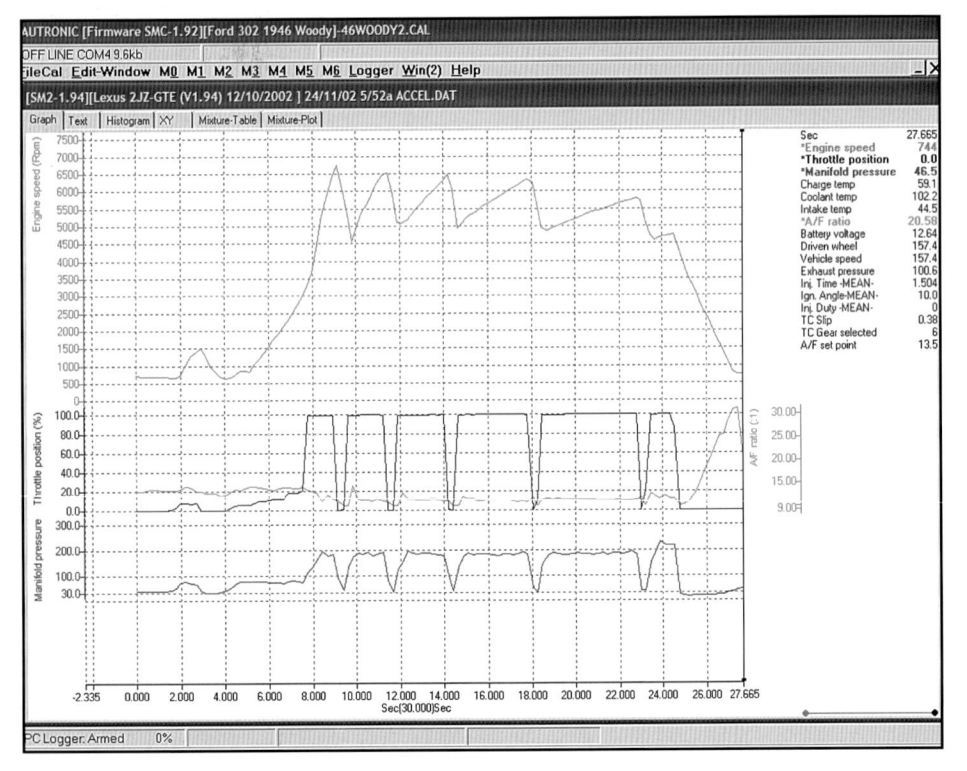

Here is a screen shot of an Autronic data log. You can record data and lay it out however you choose. You can even set all of the scales and parameters for how the data is displayed.

Once you have completed the software set-up functions, it is time to plug the data cable provided with the system into the serial port at the back of your laptop. Once it's plugged in, press the "F3" key or find the option to communicate to the ECU under the "File" menu at the top of the screen.

Pressing the "F4" key will download all the data into the ECU, and pressing the "F2" key will allow you to save the information to a file and give it a permanent file name.

Now that you are online, you can use the live data being displayed on the main screen. Now is a good time to check that all the sensors are operating correctly. Again, be sure that the air, water, and pressure sensors all give readings that appear normal. Move the throttle and be sure the value on the screen matches the movement you've made with the pedal.

Now crank the engine and check for the proper RPM signal and be sure there are no errors reported by the computer. Trace out any errors and correct the problem before going any further.

From here you can begin to input values into the base fuel and ignition tables. My advice would be to use the guidelines set forth in the user's manual and be conservative until you get a bit of experience. Once you begin to tune the base fuel and ignition maps, remember to use the data-logging feature and take advantage of the powerful tuning tools that it has to offer. Gradually add in the extra features you wish to use as you become more familiar with the software and gain confidence in your ability. If you are tuning a high-powered engine, try to tune all the idle and light-load or part-throttle positions first. This will minimize the amount of tuning you'll need to do later, while giving you the confidence you'll need to tune accurately while the beast is roaring!

In any case, try to use as many of the helpful features and functions of this powerful ECU as possible, and enjoy the ride when you are all finished!

Building and Tuning High-Performance Fuel Injection

CHAPTER 10

EDELBROCK PRO-FLO AND ADVANCED PROGRAMMABLE FUEL-INJECTION SYSTEMS

Edelbrock Pro-Flo

COST: Approximately $2,000

FEATURES: This setup only suits a narrow variety of engines (small- and big-block Chevys and small-block Fords).

EASE OF INSTALLATION AND TUNING: This system is extremely easy to install, very simple to get up and running, and requires no laptop for tuning.

Edelbrock has been around since the 1950s and has continuously been a leader in performance technology and parts manufacturing. Edelbrock has also entered the fuel-injection arena with its new Pro-Flo multi-port fuel-injection system. This has been a great selling system that has worked well for them, but now they have really taken things to the next level with their new Advanced Programmable Fuel-Injection System for small- and big-block Chevrolet engines. It will be available in the spring of 2004.

PRO-FLO

Edelbrock currently makes two models of their Pro-Flo system: the Performer, and the Performer RPM. They offer complete kits for big- and small-block Chevy and Ford engines, and kits for Chrysler engines are almost ready for release. The Pro-Flo kits are designed for non-emission engines, and

Edelbrock was one of the first companies to offer complete fuel-injection kits for Chevy engines that included every part needed for installation, including the intake manifold and fuel system. They also allow the user the ability to tune without a laptop computer. Edelbrock's latest offerings from MotoTron look to hold great things for the future of Edelbrock fuel injection.

include everything you need to convert a carbureted engine to powerful multi-point fuel injection.

Using a speed-density system for control over fuel and spark, Edelbrock EFI systems give you total

Building and Tuning High-Performance Fuel Injection

Chapter 10

Setting Advance

Whether you are tuning an engine on an engine dyno or a chassis dyno, you should always make sure that it gets tuned to the proper amount of ignition timing. The best way to do this is to use a steady-state holding pattern on the dyno and hold the engine to a specific RPM. Then load the engine to whatever site you wish to tune and record the instantaneous power readings. When you make a change to add or subtract ignition timing, you will normally see a corresponding change in power output.

Using an on-board or aftermarket knock sensor to check for detonation is the easiest way to find the maximum allowable ignition advance. However, if you do not have access to one, there is another way to get pretty close. Advance the timing until maximum power is reached (this is the point where power begins to fall off when more timing is added). From there, back off the ignition advance one or two degrees and set it there.

Once you have made a few hard pulls on the engine at this setting, shut it off and remove the spark plugs. Inspect them for obvious signs of detonation or erosion. Pay careful attention to the J-shaped ground strap. You will notice that somewhere on the strap it begins to change color.

Ideally, when the proper timing is set, there will be enough heat in the combustion chamber to make the color at about the center of the strap look almost rainbow-like. If it changes more out towards the end of the strap, then there is not enough heat, and more advance is needed. Conversely, if the color change is near the bottom where the strap joins the plug, then take some ignition advance out in order to start the burn later and transfer more heat out the exhaust!

Edelbrock currently makes two models of their Pro-Flo system: the Performer and the Performer RPM. Their current offerings suit the entire Chevrolet line of big- and small-block engines and Ford small-block engines with some Chrysler applications coming soon!

Designed for non-emission engines, these high-performance EFI systems include everything you need to convert a carbureted engine to powerful multi-point fuel injection.

engine control — without a laptop computer. The result is excellent throttle response throughout the RPM range, great fuel economy, incredible horsepower, smooth engine operation, and improved cold starting. Using speed and density also simplifies the installation by deleting all of the necessary plumbing and bracketry used in a mass airflow system.

All of their manifold assemblies, air valves, and electronics for the Pro-Flo system are built by Magneti Marelli Powertrain USA, a major QS9000-certified OEM supplier. Components are matched and tested as a set, and then serial numbers are added for quality control.

All of Edelbrock's manifold assemblies, air valves, and electronics are built by Magneti Marelli Powertrain USA, a major QS9000-certified OEM supplier. Components are matched and tested as a set, and then serial numbers are added for quality control.

Edelbrock EFI systems are shipped without the calibration chip that is necessary to operate the ECU. The user must fill out the camshaft specs on the provided postage-paid card and Edelbrock will send the appropriate chip, free of charge, via second day air. The chip must be installed inside the ECU.

Edelbrock Pro-Flo EFI systems use an exclusive digital Calibration Module. This user-friendly computer allows you to make adjustments at any time right from the driver's seat. You have complete control of the fuel curve, spark advance, and idle speed without a laptop computer. In fact, the fuel and spark curves are infinitely adjustable using a three-dimensional look-up table, with millions of combinations available.

Edelbrock EFI systems are shipped without the calibration chip that is nec-

Edelbrock Pro-Flo and Advanced Programmable Fuel-Injection

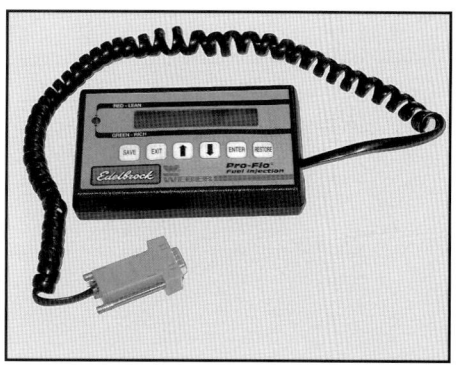

Edelbrock EFI systems are very easy to install. The intake manifold and all related parts come preassembled. Installation is done is if one were merely replacing the stock intake manifold. The ECU and related parts simply plug in their respective locations.

You can save your custom calibrations using the hand-held Calibration Module in one of the three storage areas to be used at start up or selected at any time. These calibrations include fuel and spark curves. For example, you can save separate towing, race, and economy calibrations and instantly select the appropriate one depending on the situation.

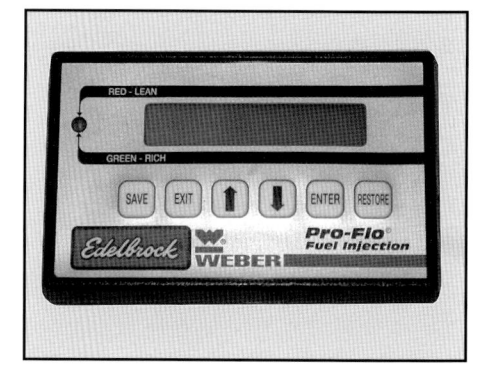

The "Restore" key allows you to go back to previous settings, or use the "Baseline" function to go back to factory settings. I like this feature because in other brands of fuel-injection systems, a laptop is needed to download and upload various calibrations, only storing one at a time.

Performer RPM EFI systems for Chevys and Fords use this aluminum CNC-machined air valve to deliver 1,000 cfm of airflow through its 4-barrel progressive-linkage design. These systems are designed to work on engines that make less than 600 hp and are not using forced induction. There is also a 2-barrel air valve that delivers 750 cfm and comes with the Performer EFI system for small-block Chevys. That system delivers up to 350 hp in a broad power range — from idle all the way to 5,500 rpm.

essary to operate the ECU. If the cam is any brand other than Edelbrock, check with manufacturer for compatibility with EFI (lobe separation angle must be at least 112° or cam must maintain at least 10 inches of manifold vacuum @ 1,000 rpm). Then, fill out the camshaft specs on the provided postage-paid card and Edelbrock will send you the appropriate chip, free of charge, via second-day air (US only).

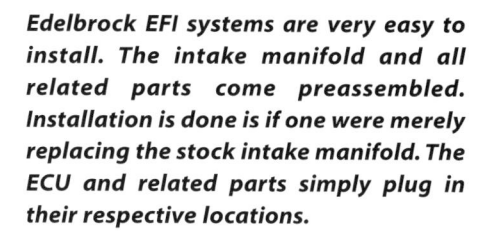

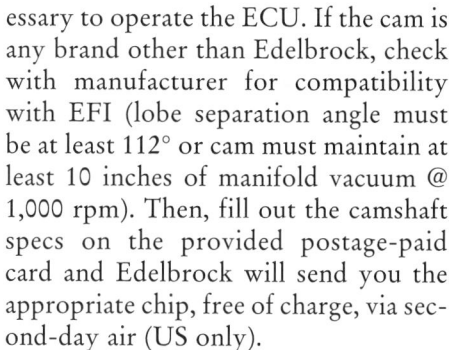

The chip installs into the system computer in minutes. Additional chips are available for a nominal charge if you decide to change your cam. Edelbrock has chips for most cam profiles. This system allows you to get the engine up and running very quickly, and normally it will need only a very small amount of tuning — if any!

Once the engine is up and running, you can interface the ECU with the Calibration Module to make changes to the stock maps and custom tune the engine to your own liking. The hand-held module even has a set of LED lights for a visual representation of the air/fuel ratio that you can watch while tuning.

You can save your custom calibrations, including fuel and spark curves, using the Calibration Module. These calibrations can be saved in one of the three storage areas to be used at startup or selected at any time. For example, you can save separate towing, race, and economy calibrations and instantly select the appropriate one depending on the occasion. A "Restore" key allows you to go back to previous settings or use the "Baseline" function to go back to factory settings. I like this feature because in other brands of fuel-injection systems, a laptop is needed to download and upload various calibrations since the ECU only stores one at a time. This system is very simple to operate, and the display guides you through all of the different functions.

Other features include: an automatic idle RPM control, vacuum readings, built-in tachometer function, water temperature display, air temperature display, and spark timing indicated in degrees. Although the unit doesn't have any sort of data-logging function, these live data displays will aid you in the tuning process.

The ECU is equipped with a Motorola 68HC11 microprocessor and 32 kilobytes of ROM (read-only memory). The Edelbrock System Computer is very similar to the computer used for years by General Motors in their Tuned Port Injection engines, as well as some others. It's a well-proven system that provides the brains for the Edelbrock Pro-Flo EFI systems.

Performer RPM EFI systems for Chevy and Ford engines have an aluminum, CNC-machined air valve that delivers a total of 1,000 cfm of airflow with its 4-barrel, progressive-linkage design. The Performer EFI system for small-block Chevys has a 2-barrel air valve that delivers 750 cfm. This system delivers up to 350 hp in a broad power range — from idle to 5,500 rpm. It's ideal for anyone who wants more power with a mild cam profile and a stock rotat-

Chapter 10

Every Edelbrock system comes with installation instructions that include photos and detailed step-by-step information. The owner's manual includes sections that explain fuel-injection fundamentals, how to operate the Calibration Module, and more.

In order to get an RPM signal, the kit comes with all the necessary parts and hardware to modify your existing distributor to be compatible with the ECU. The kit is easy to install and requires very few tools or special skills. The procedure for installation is outlined in the manual and is very easy to follow.

Edelbrock's newest offering includes complete user-programmable fuel-injection systems manufactured by MotoTron. These systems include all the components necessary to calibrate an engine by using a laptop computer.

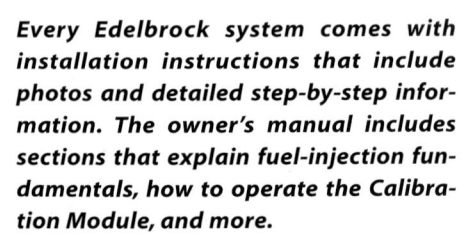

ing assembly. Both types of air valves are assembled by Magneti Marelli Powertrain USA, a major supplier of stock throttle bodies to car manufacturers. Each air valve includes a throttle position sensor that is preset at the factory.

Every Edelbrock Pro-Flo EFI system is complete with intake manifold assembly. All these components are also installed and ready to go:

- Fuel Injectors
- Fuel Rails
- Idle Air Control Valve
- Throttle Position Sensor
- Fuel Pressure Regulator
- PCV Port
- Coolant Temperature Sensor
- Air Temp Sensor
- MAP Sensor
- Barometric Pressure Sensor

Every assembly is pressure tested at the factory, then matched to a specific Calibration Module and ECM with a serial number. Every Edelbrock system comes with installation instructions that include photos and detailed step-by-step information. The owner's manual includes sections that explain fuel-injection fundamentals, how to operate the Calibration Module, and more. These books, along with their expert technical staff, give you all the information you need to install and operate Edelbrock Pro-Flo systems.

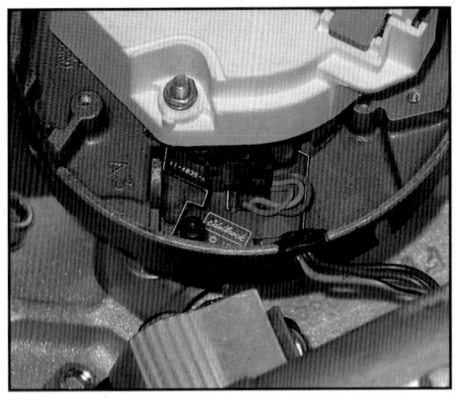

The systems come complete with stock-style connectors on the wiring harness. The kit comes with a plug-and-play harness that fits exactly in the correct location for the engine you have. Every Edelbrock wiring harness is visually inspected and computer tested at the factory and set up especially for the Edelbrock EFI system.

MotoTron has been a leader in powertrain control and engine management systems for years. They have supplied some very high-quality systems to several OEMs and even marine companies such as Mercury Marine. Shown here is one of their ECUs running an engine while submerged in water!

In order to get an RPM signal, the kit comes with all the necessary parts and hardware to modify your existing distributor to be compatible with the ECU.

The kit also comes with the required parts and hardware to install a high-pressure electric fuel pump into your vehicle. Since most V-8 hot-rod engines originally came with a low-pressure mechanical fuel pump, it is necessary to upgrade the fuel system, and Edelbrock has thought of everything!

Edelbrock also makes some conversion kits for late-model vehicles that originally used a throttle-body-injection (TBI) system. These units are a direct replacement and will convert your TBI system to a full multi-point fuel-injection setup. Check with their hotline or an Edelbrock catalog for the latest in product offerings and specifications.

MotoTron

For their newest offering, Edelbrock has turned to MotoTron. MotoTron is a fuel injection and powertrain control system manufacturer located in Wisconsin. The company has been a leader in powertrain control and engine management systems for years and has supplied very high-quality systems to several OEMs, even marine companies such as Mercury Marine.

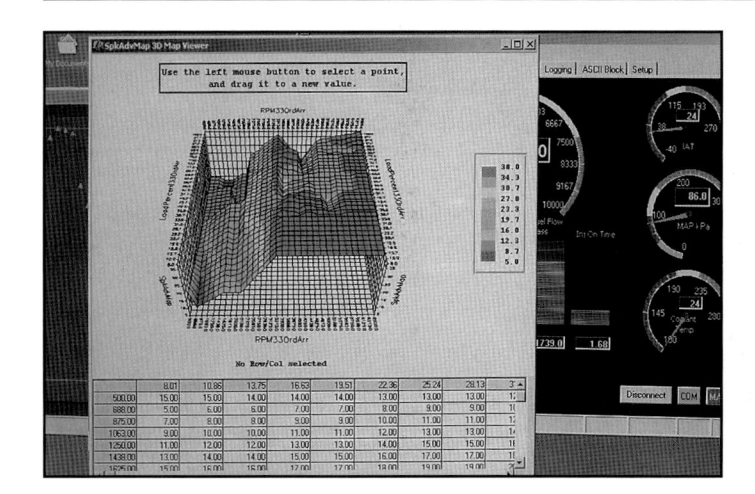

Edelbrock Pro-Flo and Advanced Programmable Fuel-Injection

MotoTron has developed a very unique method of calibrating engines that uses highly sophisticated mathematical modeling to calculate the engine's status. This method takes into account the thermodynamic and mechanical properties of an engine and creates a real-time model of the how air moves through the engine and gets converted into heat energy.

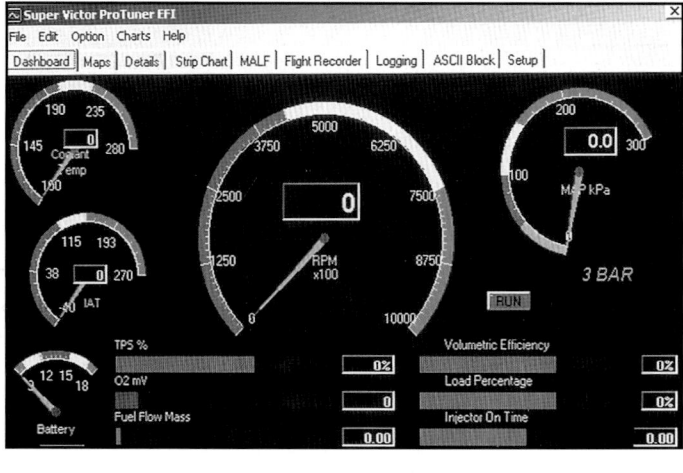

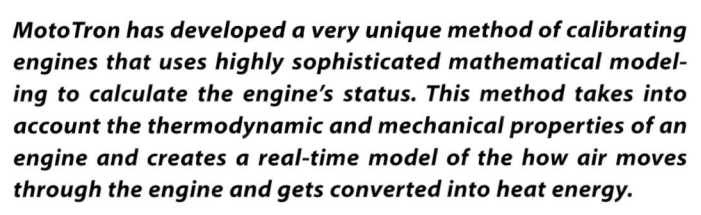

The result of the partnership between Edelbrock and MotoTron is a low-cost system that includes all the necessary parts to build a first-rate engine management system, just the way Edelbrock has in the past with their Pro-Flo systems. The exciting part is — the new systems also allow the user a lot more programmability through the use of a laptop computer.

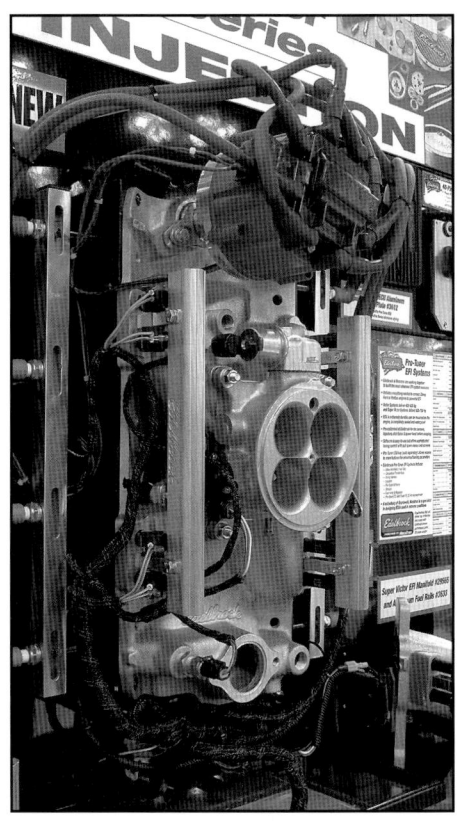

MotoTron has developed several systems for Edelbrock to control small- and big-block Chevy engines. The kits include all of the components shown here to completely install and tune the system. Simply bolt on the manifold and sensors, and plug in the harness, and the system is ready to go!

MotoTron has developed a very unique method of calibrating engines, which uses highly sophisticated mathematical modeling to calculate the engine's status. This method takes into account the thermodynamic and mechanical properties of an engine and creates a real-time model of how air moves through the engine and gets converted into heat energy. This system, although very complex, allows the software engineers to create a system that is so capable of controlling an engine, that they can virtually guarantee perfect engine operation over a wide range of outside conditions, even with varying temperature, altitude, and barometric pressure.

I once heard a story about how engines tested by MotoTron for Mercury Marine were operated at full throttle on a dyno for fifty hours non-stop! Not only did the engines run perfectly, but the MotoTron system was able to maintain the same level of engine performance from beginning to end by using its high-tech, model-based mapping techniques.

Edelbrock has commissioned MotoTron to build some models of their ECUs to be used in kit form on big- and small-block Chevy engines. The result is a low-cost system that includes all the necessary parts to build a first-rate engine management system just the way they have in the past with their Pro-Flo systems, but also allow the user a lot more programmability through the use of a laptop computer. The main benefit to a system like this is that with the extra flexibility of calibration, the user can more extensively modify the engine with radical camshafts, cylinder heads, and higher compression — without the need to order new EPROM chips. They can simply plug in their laptop and make the required changes in real time!

These systems come with venerable Edelbrock intake manifolds that have been recast to include mounting locations for injectors and sensors. The units make use of readily available GM-style sensors and injectors. The kit includes all of the necessary sensors, plus the entire fuel and spark system! Currently Edelbrock has only produced units for Chevrolet engines, but Ford, Chrysler, and possibly Honda engines are sure to follow soon!

Getting Started

Once you have received your system and you have fully read the instruction manual, it is time to begin your installation and tuning process.

You should always first check to make sure that all the components your system is supposed to come with are present. You don't want to get halfway

Chapter 10

Currently Edelbrock has only produced units for Chevrolet engines, but Ford, Chrysler, and possibly Honda engines are sure to follow. All systems will be complete with the parts necessary to install and tune them and will also include start-up maps to help get you going!

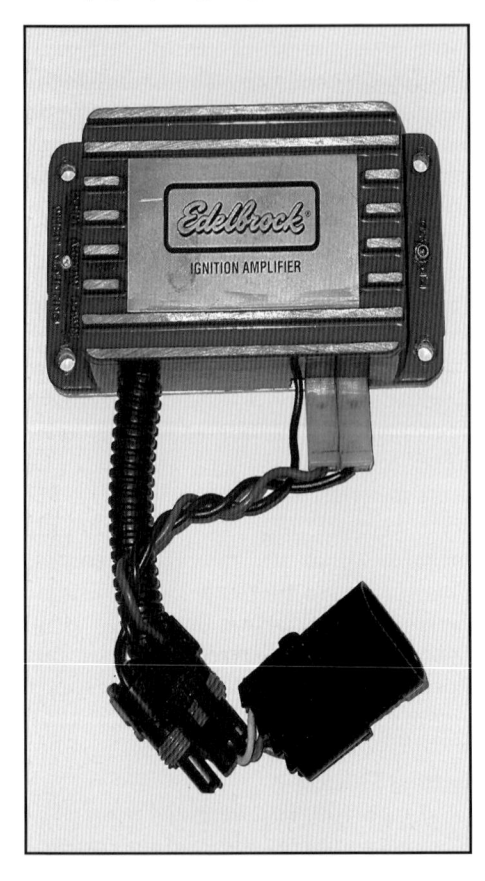

The system also comes with its own ignition amplifier. This unit plugs directly into the wiring harness and amplifies the ignition signal that goes from the ECU to the ignition coil(s).

through your project and then have to stop and scavenge around for parts you assumed would be there.

Next, I find it beneficial to lay the wiring harness on the ground and follow the wiring diagram to each connector or termination point. Not only will this help you familiarize yourself with the harness, it will give you a head start towards troubleshooting any problems later. Once you are satisfied that the harness is complete and that it is the correct harness for your application, you may begin to install it onto your engine.

Begin by finding a suitable mounting place for the ECU. Try to keep it in a place that is free of moisture and dust as much as possible, and avoid having it next to a source of direct heat such as any of the exhaust components.

Once you have mounted the computer, find a suitable location for the wire harness to pass through the firewall. Always use a rubber grommet at any place where the harness might go through a metal wall. This will prevent any wire abrasions and accidental short circuits that might damage the wire harness or other components of the system, including the ECU.

At this point you will want to follow the instructions in the owners manual for installing the fuel pump and modifying the distributor. All of the manuals I have worked with have been very easy to understand and clearly outlined the procedure for installation.

Once everything is connected, remove the backing plate on the ECU that covers the EPROM socket and install the chip sent to you from Edelbrock. Make sure that it snaps in securely, and then replace the aluminum cover. Plug the wire harness into the ECU and mount it in place.

At this point you are ready to fire up the engine and use the Calibration Module for some basic tuning. Follow the instructions on the handheld display and they will lead you through the various maps to make and save your changes.

With this system, you can make changes to any of 24 points in the fuel curve based on manifold vacuum and RPM, and you can also make changes to the spark advance tables in the same fashion. Also, the Calibration Module gives you the ability to make global changes by moving the entire fuel or ignition map up or down by a percentage of the total. You can also alter the warm-up tables and acceleration-enrichment tables to suit your application. When you are done, store the changes in one of the three available memory slots, and enjoy driving the car.

Unfortunately, the Pro-Flo system doesn't come with much flexibility in terms of changing the type of engine, or using any type of forced induction. However, the fair pricing, ease of installation, and reliability make it a good value for a first-time fuel-injection user. If you like the Edelbrock family of products and want the added flexibility to tune your own EFI system, then the new programmable systems are for you!

One of the things I really liked about the Edelbrock Pro-Flo injection system was that it was extremely easy to install and it fired right up and ran perfectly the very first time. I'm certain that the newest offerings from MotoTron and Edelbrock will be even better! Follow the instructions carefully and I'm sure you'll have a similar experience.

Building and Tuning High-Performance Fuel Injection

Chapter 11

EFI Technology

EFI Technology

COST: Approximately $2,000–$25,000

FEATURES: This system can be custom tailored to do anything the user requires for any application.

EASE OF INSTALLATION AND TUNING: The custom wire loom is easy to install, but the tuning software is not for beginners.

EFI Technology is a fuel-injection company that has long been noted for its commitment to quality and customer support. Their systems can be found on racecars all throughout the upper echelons of professional auto racing, in classes such as Championship Auto Racing Teams (CART), Indy Racing League (IRL), Indy Lights, American LeMans Series (ALMS), World Challenge, and many others.

The company was started in 1986 by Graham Western, and has since

EFI Technology is known as a leader in the fuel-injection industry, serving many professional race teams in all venues of auto racing. They have a well-deserved reputation as being one of the best.

Building and Tuning High-Performance Fuel Injection

EFI Technology is a fuel-injection company that has long been noted for its commitment to quality and customer support. Their systems can be found on race cars all throughout the upper echelons of professional auto racing in categories such as CART, IRL, Indy Lights, ALMS, World Challenge, and many others. This is a look at the EFI Technology ECU that gets the job done.

With virtually no advertising other than word of mouth, EFI Technology has made their way into the winner's circle time and again. They are one of the only fuel-injection companies who perform every aspect of production and design in-house. Everything from assembling the circuit boards (as shown here), to building the wire harness is done in their shop!

The 1.1 ECU has up to four high-impedance injector drivers, up to four ignition outputs, and eight analog inputs for measurement of various sensors. Of course, these are all in addition to the TPS, water temperature, battery voltage, intake air temp, air-box temp, oil pressure, and oxygen sensor information already being recorded and used for calibration by this little box!

remained an American-owned-and-operated business. Graham started working on some of the earliest digital fuel-injection systems just shortly after graduating college with a degree in electronic engineering. These systems were developed for use on Cosworth racing engines. Before long, nearly every professional race team was using some derivative of the Cosworth system that he helped produce. When Graham felt the need to grow and spread his wings, he started EFI Technology and has never looked back.

Currently the company employs about twenty people in their workshop in southern California. With virtually no advertising other than word of mouth, their fuel-injection systems have made their way into the winner's circle time and again. They are one of the only fuel-injection companies who perform every aspect of production and design in-house. Everything from assembling the circuit boards, to building the wire harness is done in their shop!

Their biggest customer is presently the world's most prolific tuner of Japanese engines: Mugen. EFI Technology supplies nearly 25 percent of its ECUs to the Japanese firm.

EFI Technology offers many different models of their ECU. No matter what the project, they have an engine management system to fit your application.

EFI Technology offers several models of their ECU ranging from the very cost-effective 1.0 model, which is geared toward the racer with cost effectiveness and compact size in mind, all the way up to the feature packed 4.0 ECU that is specifically designed to meet the stringent standards and needs of professional race teams. They also offer a comprehensive line of CDI (capacitive discharge ignition) systems, which are designed to interface with any of their ECUs or be used as stand-alone ignition amplifiers.

All EFI Technology ECUs use the same control and calibration software. This makes it very easy to take advantages of the built-in features that exist in even the more cost-effective EFI Technology ECUs. Basically, whether you buy the least expensive or most highly priced ECU they offer, you'll get the same level of product sophistication. The main differences in their ECUs are the amount of inputs and outputs the user has to work with!

ECU 1.1

The 1.1 ECU has up to four high impedance injector drivers, up to four ignition outputs, and eight analog inputs for measurement of various sensors in addition to the TPS, water temp, battery voltage, intake air temp, air box temp, oil pressure, and oxygen sensor information already being recorded and used for calibration! This unit is aimed squarely at the budget-minded racer who still wants high quality. All of the ECUs in the

Technology

EFI Technology offers many accessories to liven up your racing effort such as this lap beacon. This unit allows the ECU to track the car's performance at many different points of the track during a run.

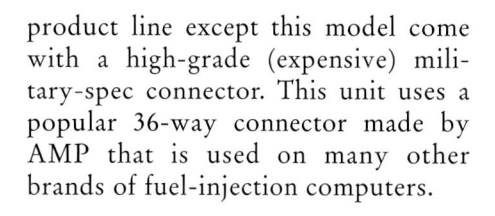

The grandfather of all EFI Technology units is the all-out racing ECU called the 4.0. This unit is designed for all serious race teams with 8-, 10-, or 12-cylinder engines. This is one of the most sophisticated engine management systems available today.

EFI Technology offers a very advanced Telemetry system like the one shown here. These systems allow the user to view and change any and all parameters in the software by a radio modem to relay information between the ECU and a laptop.

product line except this model come with a high-grade (expensive) military-spec connector. This unit uses a popular 36-way connector made by AMP that is used on many other brands of fuel-injection computers.

ECU 1.9

The 1.9 ECU has sequential injection capability with eight injector outputs and four ignition outputs. It carries the ability to accept twenty analog inputs, and four digital inputs for wheel speeds and engine position. It also contains auxiliary output control for idle valve or camshaft control, and closed-loop lambda control! This is the perfect ECU for 8-cylinder engines using sequential fuel injection.

ECU 2.1

The next unit in their lineup is the 2.1 ECU. This unit is extremely powerful because it has sequential injection and ignition capability with up to eight injector drivers, and up to eight ignition drivers. It also has twenty analog inputs, four digital inputs, plus closed loop control, auxiliary output control, and driver-selectable maps for quick testing on the fly or for having more than one operating map for performance or economy! This unit also has an optional upgrade for up to 2 megabytes of onboard data-logging capability and lateral-G measurement for track mapping. This feature can be used to actually create a map-like drawing of the racetrack based on information from the data-logger, and then evaluate the car's performance based on information stored in the logger from other sensors! This is the perfect choice for the race team looking for a complete ECU, data-logger, and telemetry system all in one package!

ECU 4.0

The grandfather of all EFI Technology units is the all-out racing ECU called the 4.0. This unit is designed for all serious race teams with 8-, 10-, or 12-cylinder engines. It has twelve sequential injector outputs, ten coil outputs, four digital inputs for engine-speed or wheel-speed sensors, four switched inputs, four auxiliary control outputs, dual internal lambda amplifiers for oxygen-sensor control, two pulse-width modulated (PWM) outputs for wastegate control, dual K-Type thermocouple inputs for exhaust temperature readings, a DC motor driver for use in drive-by-wire throttle systems, dual-channel knock sensor inputs with knock control feedback, and 2 megabytes of internal data-logging memory! This system is the most sophisticated and highly outfitted unit available almost anywhere. You'd better be serious about competition before ordering up one of these bad-boys on the wife's credit card. The cost is a cool $5,995.00 without the wire harness!

Wire Harness

All of the ECUs offered by EFI Technology come without a wire harness. When you purchase a unit from them, they will send you out a form with a drawing of a wire harness that would fit your ECU. You must then fill in the appropriate lengths for each section of wire as needed to fit your engine, and then return your sheet to them for harness manufacture. Their pricing for wire harness manufacturing is $1,250.00 for a 4-cylinder, $1,350.00 for a 6-cylinder, and $1,450.00 for an 8-cylinder engine. All of their wire harnesses are built in-house using the finest quality components and durable DR-25 heat-shrinkable tubing.

Software

As I mentioned before, all of the units can be calibrated and controlled with the same software package. This

Building and Tuning High-Performance Fuel Injection

Chapter 11

software allows the user full control over all engine functions, data-logging, auxiliary outputs, traction control, shift-cut, boost control, idle control, and on and on. The software is extremely user configurable and can be custom-designed to perform almost any function exactly how the user would like.

The base fuel and ignition tables are user-selectable for load and RPM sites, and can sense engine load as a function of either MAP value or TPS. There are a maximum of 40 programmable RPM sites and 20 programmable load sites, giving the user a total of 800 programmable sites to tune the engine with!

The system also offers total fuel control with target air/fuel ratio maps and fuel pressure detection, which allows compensation based on fuel pressure. The unit can use standard or wide-band lambda sensors for high-load tuning. The data-logging function of the software can be configured to log up to 38 channels at rates of up to 100 Hz for as long as 12 hours!

Getting Started

Getting up and running is fairly easy, since EFI Technology custom builds each of their systems to match the user's requirements. Once you receive your shipment, be sure to check that all the components that you ordered are included. Also, be sure to inspect all the parts to make sure they are the correct ones for your application.

When you have completed your inspection and are satisfied that everything is in order, be sure to read though the entire user manual that you receive either on disk or in printed form. Remember that this system is very complex, and each one is custom-tailored for a specific purpose. Because of this, the software setup and selection of triggers and components can be crucial to optimum performance. Make sure you fully understand the procedures involved before going too far. If you are uncertain about any aspect of the process, be sure to stop and call the technical support line for details.

Now that you are confident that all is in order, and you are sure of your abilities, you can begin installing the

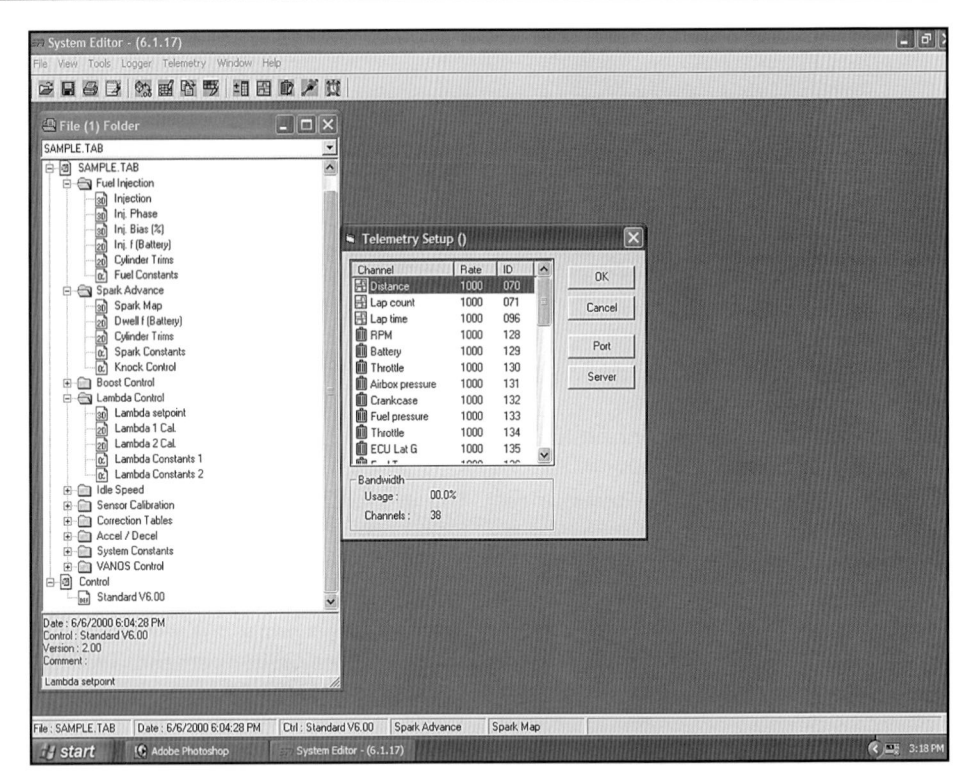

All of the EFI Technology units can be calibrated and controlled with the same software package. This software allows the user full control over all engine functions, data-logging, auxiliary outputs, traction control, shift-cut, boost control, and idle control among many other things!

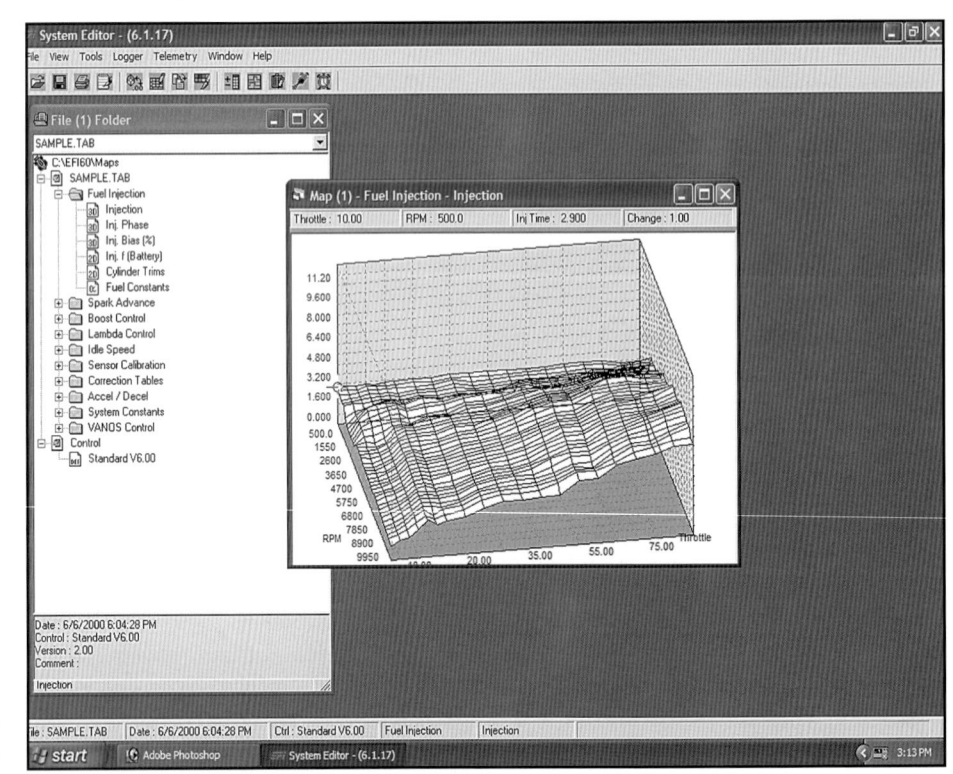

You can use the calibration software to check the live data and find out if any sensor information is out of whack. Fix any problems you find before you begin tuning, this will save you major headaches later on.

Building and Tuning High-Performance Fuel Injection

Technology

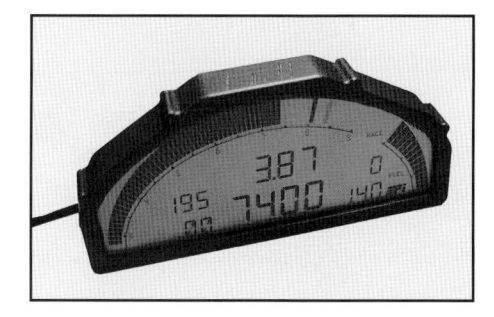

Another one of the great things EFI Technology has to offer is the Virtual Dashboard. Not only does this unit display a lot of useable information, but also it doubles as a stand-alone datalogger. It can collect many channels of data all at once, and it's totally user-programmable!

For many in the upper echelons of racing, EFI Technology serves as the premier engine management system. It can be found on everything from off-road trucks to exotic European road-racing cars like the ones shown here.

As a result of the complexity of their systems, EFI Technology prefers to custom-build each wiring harness that accompanies their ECU. They have all the facilities and materials to do everything in house.

wire harness onto the engine. If you took your time and measured carefully, the harness should virtually drop in place. Just follow the directions and observe the labels on the harness itself and you'll have no trouble at all.

When everything is installed and connected, you can install the data cable and begin to establish communication with the ECU. Once online, you can go through and set up any parameters that were not already configured by EFI Technology for you.

This is a good time to use the live data on the screen to do a complete check of all the sensors to ensure they are working. Look for abnormal readings, such as a throttle position sensor that is reading a 50% opening when the throttle is actually closed. This is just an example of a typical problem you may run into, and is only intended to get your thought process moving in the right direction. Solve any problems you might find with sensors before moving on.

Now that everything is in place, you may attempt to start the engine. Crank it over and make the necessary adjustments to the fuel and ignition tables until it will start and run by itself. From here, follow the tuning guidelines set forth by the manufacturer and those laid out in this manual.

Using a dyno to hold the engine at a steady load will allow you to adjust the spark and fuel parameters in real time and evaluate the effects of the change. Even after you have finished tuning on the dyno, most of the time you will also want to make some minor changes to the software while at the race track. Sometimes a good tuner can create an engine that will compliment the chassis. When a car is not handling well, the calibration can be changed to allow the engine to hit the tires a little softer to help gain a bit more traction. This can be accomplished by taking out a little timing or lowering the boost limit to lower the power output.

Be very careful if you intend to do any real-time calibration with the car on the race track or on the street. The driving conditions can change very quickly and it is very dangerous to drive at high speed and attempt work on a computer at the same time. Always opt for safety over convenience!

When you have completed tuning the engine, you will be a very satisfied customer with one of the most advance fuel-injection systems money can buy! Good Luck!

Building and Tuning High-Performance Fuel Injection

Chapter 12

Electromotive

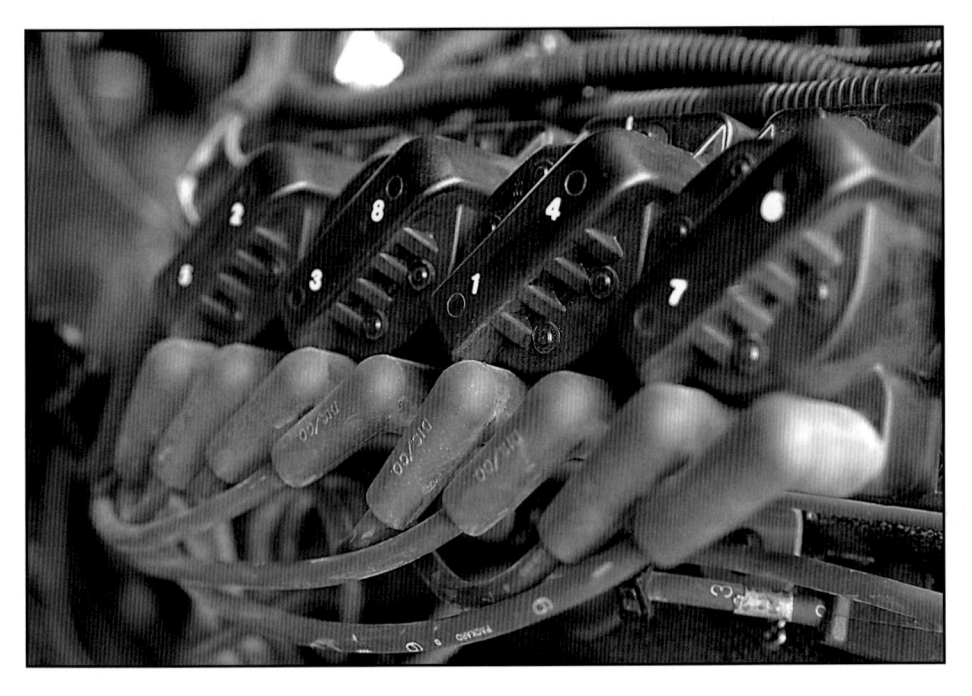

Electromotive fuel-injection systems have been around for quite some time, but what has really set the company apart is the fact that it was the originator of the multiple-coil-pack waste-spark systems like the one shown here.

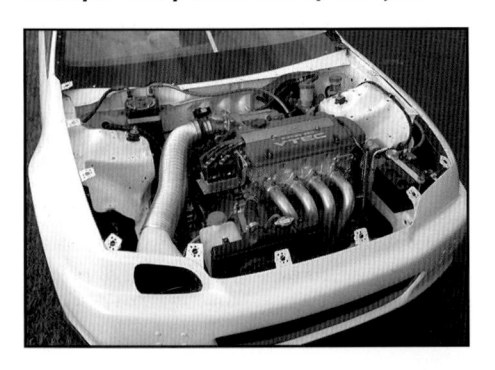

> ### Electromotive
>
> **COST:** Approximately $1,500 to $2,500
>
> **FEATURES:** Electromotive offers coil-on-plug configurations for any engine, but packaging the system is sometimes more of an issue.
>
> **EASE OF INSTALLATION AND TUNING:** The installation is quite straightforward, but the tuning theory is quite different and can be difficult to grasp for many tuners.

In a waste-spark ignition system like this one, cylinders are paired together and one coil fires the two cylinders that oppose each other in the firing order. This way on each revolution of the engine, one cylinder would be at top dead center on the compression stroke, and the other would be at top dead center on the exhaust stroke.

Electromotive has been a leader in fuel-injection system development since it opened in 1987. Not only have they been building universal fuel-injection systems that can be fitted to any make or model of engine, they essentially pioneered the DFI (direct fire ignition) technology. This revolutionary system enabled them to eliminate the spark distributor on an engine and replace it with individual ignition coils that could directly fire each cylinder.

Normally, two cylinders opposing each other in the firing order are paired together, and one coil would provide their spark. This way, on each revolu-

88   **Building and Tuning High-Performance Fuel Injection**

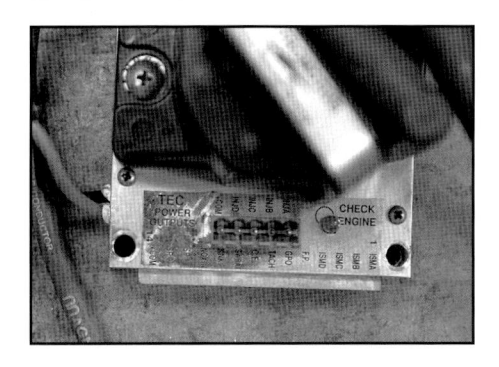

Electromotive

When Electromotive paired their fuel-injection system with their direct-fire ignition system, they created what they call the Total Engine Control unit, or TEC. The TEC is capable of controlling all functions of engine management.

tion of the engine, one cylinder would be at top dead center on the compression stroke, and the other would be at top dead center on the exhaust stroke. Only the cylinder that actually required the ignition event actually uses the spark. This is typically known as a waste-spark configuration.

When Electromotive paired their fuel-injection system with their direct-fire ignition system, they created what they call the Total Engine Control unit, or TEC. The TEC was capable of controlling all functions of engine management from idle control, fuel injection, ignition timing control, and most auxiliary functions such as boost, nitrous, and torque-converter lock-up control.

Since the first Total Engine Control system was introduced to the public, Electromotive has had a very dynamic calibration software program. As new needs arose, Electromotive was quick to provide the software fit those needs.

The earlier software was DOS based, and the currently supported software written for Windows operating systems. The first program was called CAL. This software could control all of the basic functions of the TEC unit.

Second, came Super, which was an updated version of CAL that supported a few more options for basic tuning. Super was available up through 1997.

At that time, Electromotive again raised the bar in technology for aftermarket engine control systems by introducing the first software calibration tool that would allow users the ability to perform full closed-loop tuning.

This software, called PAF (performance air and fuel), gave the tuner the option to define target air/fuel ratios from 10:1 to 21:1 throughout the base calibration tables in order to give the TEC unit control over the fuel correction under all load and speed conditions. A user could now reap the benefits of good power under a load, while maintaining economy at cruise, all in one easy calibration.

Briefly, the TEC units were supplied with an optional software package called PAFZ, which contained algorithms for using mass airflow sensing for calibration to automatically compensate for changes in an engine's volumetric efficiency, rather than the required re-tuning necessary with MAP-based speed-density systems.

Next came the Super Blend software package. This program was introduced to allow easy tuning of engines with individual intake runners and large lift/duration cam profiles used in all-out racing applications. This was achieved by blending TPS voltage and MAP sensor signal voltage, rather than using only TPS as a load input, which proved to be inadequate. The system was also capable of using mass airflow sensors, but did not allow tuning to different air-fuel ratios throughout the load/RPM range.

The last of Electromotive's software offerings to use the DOS-based operating system was PAFBlend. This software calibration tool recognized the street racer's desire to run large lift/duration cams and individual intake runner manifolds, yet not forgo the advantages of PAF air-to-fuel ratio tuning.

Mass airflow sensors pose a limitation to the ultimate power that an engine can produce because of their restriction

Early TEC systems were popular in drag racing segments such as the early to mid 1990s Mustang 5.0-liter crowd.

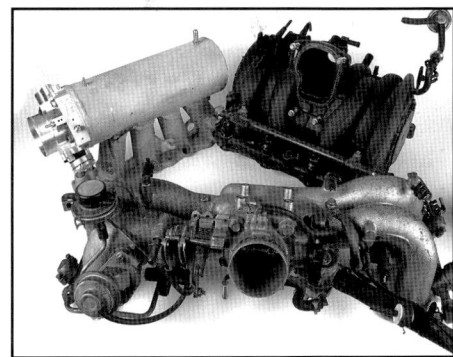

Briefly the TEC units were supplied with an optional software package called PAFZ, which contained algorithms for using mass airflow sensing for calibration. That way, the system could automatically compensate for changes in an engine's volumetric efficiency, rather than require re-tuning like MAP-based speed-density systems.

Building and Tuning High-Performance Fuel Injection

Chapter 12

The last of Electromotive's software offerings to use the DOS-based operating system was PAFBlend, which stands for performance air/fuel with MAP/TPS blending capability. This software calibration tool recognized the desire street/strip crowd to run large lift/duration cams and individual intake runner manifolds, yet not forgo the advantages of PAF air/fuel ratio tuning.

You can always find the latest advancements in TEC offerings on the Accufab Mercury Cougar driven by John Mihovetz. This turbocharged modular V-8 has pushed the Cougar to high six-second quarter-mile times using Electromotive's systems!

to airflow. Because of this, the MAF routines were deleted to accommodate closed-loop tuning and blend routines using MAP based control algorithms.

If you happen to have one of the earlier calibration systems mentioned above, it is important to remember that these systems each had their own EPROM chips inside that were sold under license. If you lose your software, you will need the license number to obtain a new copy through Electromo-

tive's technical support department. Keep this in mind if you intend to sell the unit also, as the new user will need the license number in order to get any access to new software.

The current stable of calibration software packages offers the user the flexibility of Windows-based tuning. The first version called WinTec was based on the older version of PAFBlend. This system was calibrated in much the same way, but allowed the benefits of Windows compatibility.

The latest and greatest offering from Electromotive is the WinTec2 program, which finally allows the user the ability to tune in real time, on the fly. Earlier versions required the user to input values in the calibration tables, then save the file and download it to the TEC unit. The user would then operate the engine and observe the conditions live, or data-log them to a file for analysis at a later time. Once the user decided what changes to the calibration were necessary, he could then input those into the calibration, save the file again,

90   *Building and Tuning High-Performance Fuel Injection*

Electromotive

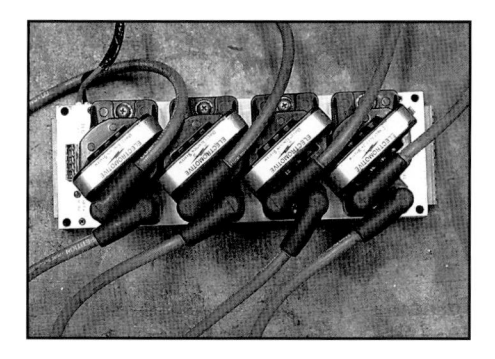

Electromotive's waste-spark configuration makes for a tidy package when mounting the ECU to the chassis. The built-in ECU attaches to the bottom of the coils and is hardly visible.

Today, if you were to order a unit from Electromotive, you would receive the TEC 3 engine management system. This is their latest offering, packed full of options such as the ability to control engines with 1, 2, 3, 4, 6, 8, or 12 cylinders, as well as rotary-style engines. They also have the ability to control a 6-cylinder engine using 2 spark plugs per cylinder.

and reload it into the TEC unit for another try. This was very cumbersome, and often frustrating for tuners. The ability to tune in real time has greatly improved the usefulness and user-friendliness of the TEC system.

Today, if you were to order a unit from Electromotive, you would receive the TEC 3 engine management system. This is their latest offering, which is packed full of options such as the ability to control 1-, 2-, 3-, 4-, 6-, 8-, 12-cylinder and rotary-style engines. They also have the ability to control a 6-cylinder engine using a twin-spark-plug

The TEC 3 also offers dual rev-limiters using their new Triple Smooth Technology, which limits the engine speed in three distinct stages, allowing for an extremely smooth engine speed limiter.

Electromotive coil packs are included with each Electromotive system. They come encased in anodized aluminum for long-lasting good looks. This is a nice little package that contains all of the ignition system in one unit.

Building and Tuning High-Performance Fuel Injection

Chapter 12

Tuning Boost on the Dyno

Tuning an engine with forced induction on a dyno can be a daunting task. Trying to tune an engine that will make lots of boost and a ton of power can be even more challenging. These engines tend to make so much power when they come on to the boost that they often will rip right through the RPM ranges you are trying to tune. This can be very frustrating for a novice tuner.

One thing you can do to help out is to disconnect the tubes that lead from the turbocharger to the intake manifold. This will prevent any boost from reaching the engine, so that you can tune it as you would a naturally aspirated engine. Just operate the dyno so that it will hold you at a constant engine speed while you adjust the load with movement of the throttle and tune all the sites as best you can.

Once you have tuned all the sites for wide-open throttle in a naturally aspirated form, you can connect the boost tubes again and begin tuning the boost sites. If you have an adjustable waste-gate or boost regulator, turn it down as low as it will go and tune the lower boost sites first and gradually work your way up.

When done properly, the shape of the fuel curve under boost should closely match that of the engine while naturally aspirated. It will simply use more fuel, resulting in higher numbers in the map. The reason for this is because the engine's volumetric efficiency for any given engine speed is determined by the combination of cylinder head, camshaft, displacement, etc, and should simply move up or down relative to the amount of boost.

Some ECUs use different values to represent fuel quantities in their base fuel maps, so always be sure to follow the recommended procedure for your particular system!

When you order a kit from Electromotive, you will receive the ECU, a wiring loom for your application, a coolant temperature sensor, an air temperature sensor, a MAP sensor, and an oxygen sensor. You will also receive the software and data cable for communication between the ECU and your laptop. This system is for a Honda engine.

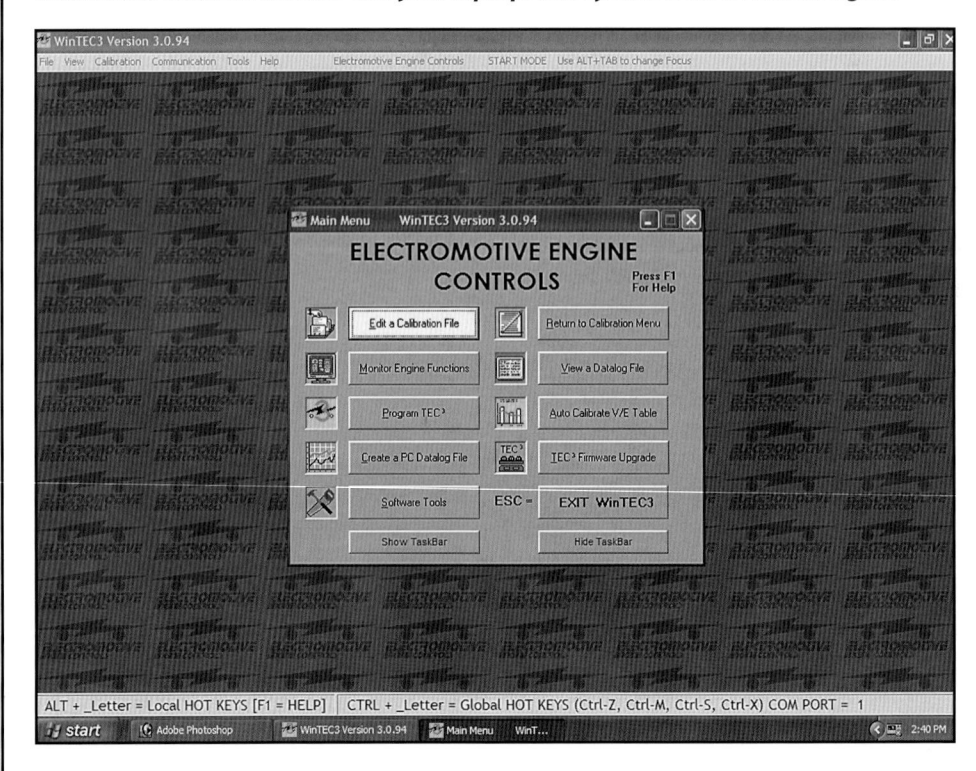

Here is a screen shot of the Electromotive calibration software for Windows operating systems. This is the opening page you will see when you start the software. All other areas can be accessed from this page.

Building and Tuning High-Performance Fuel Injection

Electromotive

option! The units also offer full closed-loop control with target air/fuel ratio tables, boost and nitrous control, and up to four user configurable GPOs, or general-purpose outputs.

The TEC 3 also offers dual rev-limiters using their new Triple Smooth Technology, which limits the engine speed in three distinct stages. This setup makes for one extremely smooth engine speed limiter.

Electromotive also includes the coil packs with all of their systems. This is a nice package containing the whole ignition system in one unit.

When you order a kit from Electromotive, you will receive the ECU, a wiring harness for your application, coolant temperature sensor, air temperature sensor, MAP sensor, and oxygen sensor. You will also receive the software and data cable for communication between the ECU and your laptop. The software will operate with Windows software from Windows 95 and up.

Getting Started

Once you receive the shipment from Electromotive, be sure to first check that everything is included and no parts are missing in the shipment. If you find something that is missing, you can call the Electromotive technical support hotline for assistance.

Begin by finding a suitable location to mount the ECU and the supplied coil-pack ignition system. Normally, I try to keep the ECU inside the vehicle to prevent it from contact with the elements and under-hood temperatures.

Next, follow the instructions outlined within the user's manual for installing the 60-tooth trigger wheel that comes supplied in the kit. Placement of this wheel is critical, as this is what the ECU will use as part of its injection and ignition calculation strategy. If you do not install the wheel correctly, the engine will usually not run at all, but if it does, it will run poorly, and possibly damage your engine.

When you have installed the ECU and ignition system, you can begin to install the sensors on the engine. Be sure to install them in a location that will allow easy access when installing the

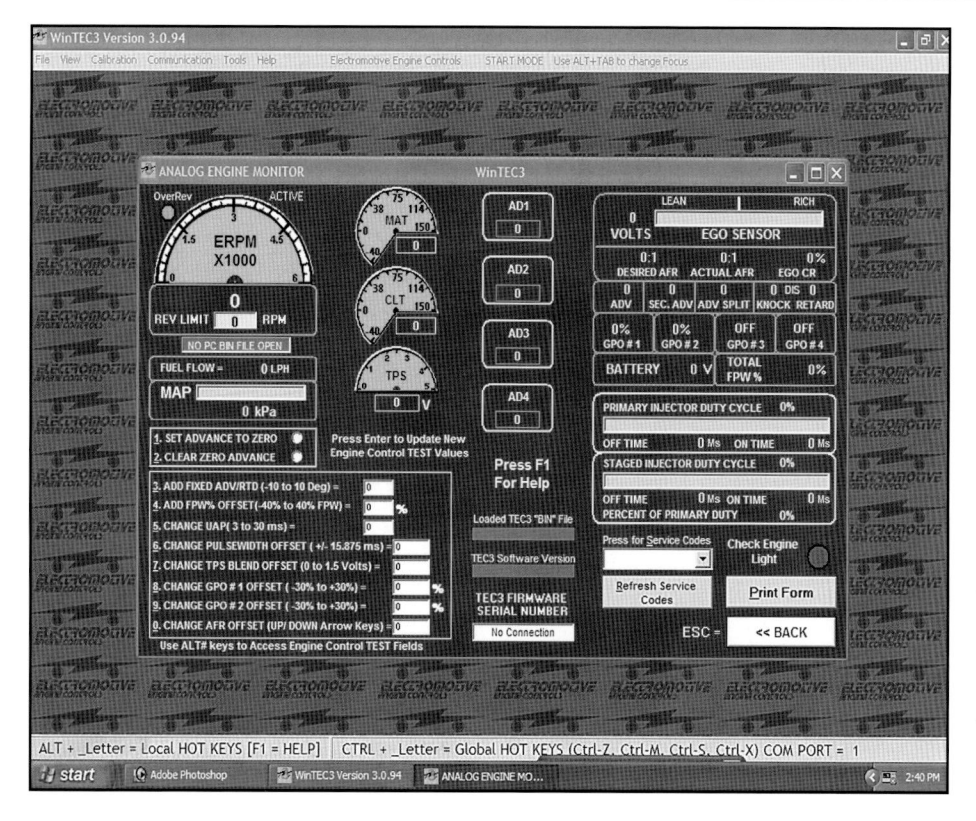

From the Analog Engine Monitor page, you can view all of them important sensor information about the engine. Use the page when you are getting started to find out if everything has been wired up and is working properly.

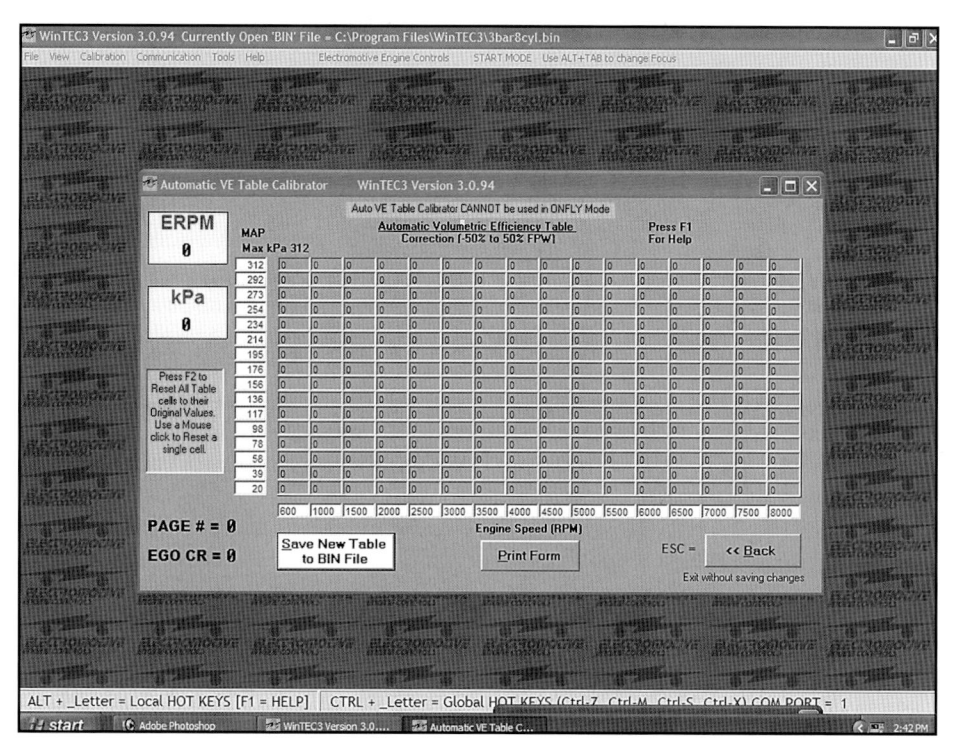

The auto-tuning page in Electromotive's calibration software, shown here, can be used to tune the base fuel tables. Information from the oxygen sensor is used against targets in this table to obtain acceptable air/fuel ratios.

Building and Tuning High-Performance Fuel Injection

Chapter 12

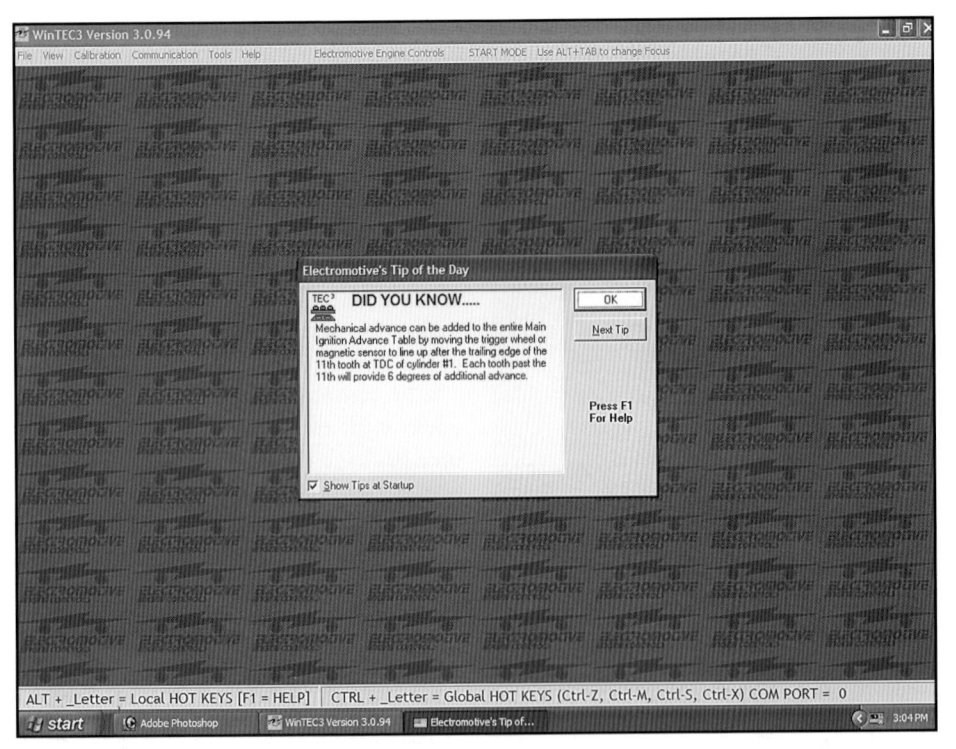

Electromotive has included a neat feature called the "Tip of the Day" into their software package. Each time the software is opened up, a new tip will be displayed — or you could just read them all at once.

wire harness.

Installing the wire harness from Electromotive is fairly easy, because it is already configured for your engine type. Simply follow the instructions in the user's manual and be sure to keep wires away from sources of direct heat. Also be sure to avoid having connections near areas that may be exposed to moisture, as this will cause corrosion of the wiring and poor conductivity. Be sure all ground wires are securely connected to either the chassis or directly on the engine block.

After the system has been completely installed into the vehicle, you may insert the supplied floppy or compact disk into your laptop and load it on your hard drive. Once loaded, open the software and attempt to communicate with the ECU in the vehicle by attaching the data cable to both the laptop and the ECU.

When you have established communication with the ECU, begin by checking the live data screen to ensure that all of the sensors are reading properly. Look for obvious signs of failure, such as a temperature sensor that is way off. A water temperature sensor in an engine that has not been started for some time should read something close to the outside air temperature. If you live in Death Valley and you check the reading in July it should not read 30-degrees Fahrenheit! Now is the time to fix any problems in the wiring harness connections before going any farther with the project. Once you have remedied any problems, you may proceed with the setup and tuning.

WinTec3, Electromotive's latest software program, has a function called Tuning Wizard that will assist you in creating a start-up map that will get the engine up and running so that you can concentrate on tuning instead of troubleshooting. The program uses information from the user about the type of engine, its displacement, camshaft specs, induction and exhaust systems, and injector size to calculate values for the base fuel and ignition tables. Once you have used this function, download this into the ECU and begin to crank the engine over. Watch the screen to ensure a proper RPM signal is being displayed. Once the engine starts, allow it to warm up to full operating temperature before you start to tune any of the sites in the base tables. This will prevent you from making changes to the wrong tables.

When you are ready to being tuning, use the base fuel and ignition tables to program your RPM and load sites to suit your engine combination. The WinTec3 software allows you up to 16 RPM sites and 16 load sites, for a total of 256 programmable sites!

Begin your tuning process as normal by revving up the engine with little or no load on it and use information from the oxygen sensor to change the injector pulse widths to achieve the desired air/fuel ratio. You can also use the closed-loop target air/fuel ratio maps for this function, but I recommend doing it manually at first, until you have a good grasp of how the system operates. Next, tune the light load cells in the map and increase engine speed until you have finished, and then gradually increase the load and repeat the process. I like to tune as many sites as possible before loading the engine heavily to help avoid doing any damage to the engine.

It is always preferable to use an engine or chassis dyno to do your tuning and then finish your fine-tuning on the street while concentrating on driveability and throttle response. Be sure to use caution when tuning on public roads, as conditions can change rapidly and become very dangerous.

Just use common sense in tuning, and be sure to educate yourself as much as possible beforehand by reading the entire user's manual and practicing with the software until you can easily navigate the functions without trouble. You should also take advantage of Electromotive's powerful data-logging features to analyze your tuning efforts. This method will aid in a fast, easy tuning session for your vehicle.

Remember to save your files into the ECU and also to your laptop several times throughout the tuning process to ensure you always have a working backup in case of loss of a good file.

You will find that the Electromotive fuel-injection system has a lot to offer a novice tuner, and you'll be up and running around town in your fuel-injected hot-rod in no time flat.

Chapter 13

F.A.S.T

F.A.S.T.

COST: Approximately $1,800 to $3,200

FEATURES: F.A.S.T. systems have plenty of flexible outputs for extras like nitrous or boost control.

EASE OF INSTILLATION AND TUNING: This system comes with an easy-to-install premade harness, and straightforward software interface.

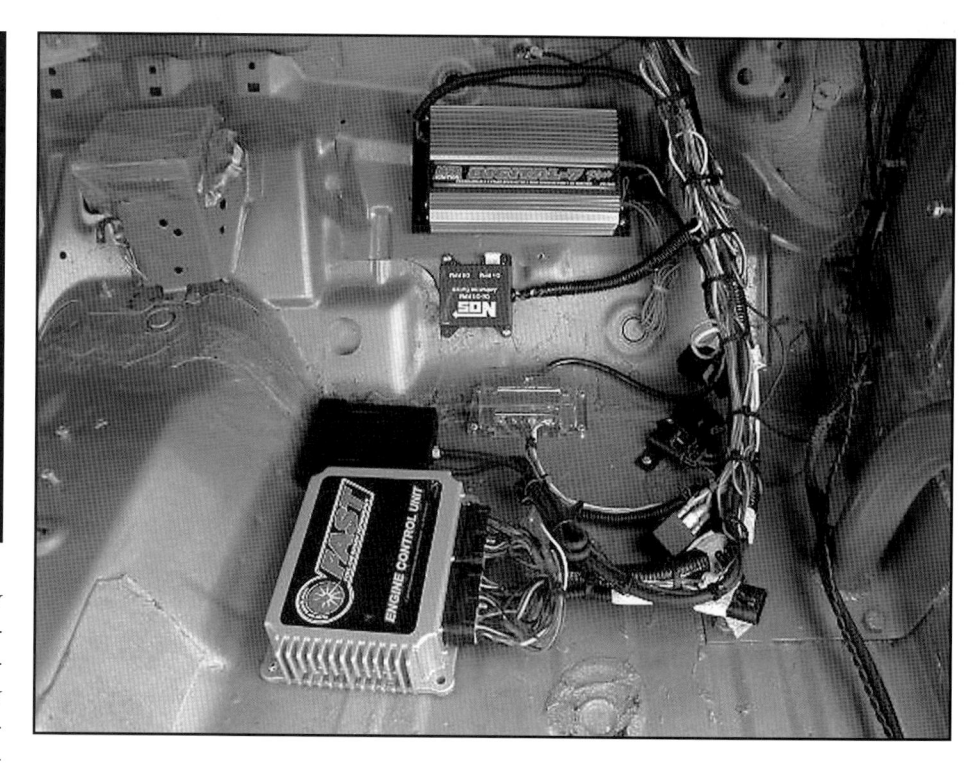

The F.A.S.T. fuel-injection system can be found on many drag cars because of its popularity with import and domestic racers alike. The system is known for its user friendliness.

Fuel Air and Spark Technology (F.A.S.T.) is a fuel-injection manufacturer that has been around the aftermarket scene for quite a while, mostly associated with companies like Speed-Pro and Competition Cams. The company is now owned by Competition Cams in Memphis, Tennessee, which has served in allowing them to increase their market share by combining forces with the aftermarket parts giant.

F.A.S.T sells two basic kits of their fuel-injection system: the Bank-to-Bank System, which fires the injectors every 180 degrees of crankshaft rotation, and the Sequential System, which fires each injector individually in the correct firing order.

F.A.S.T.'s Bank-To-Bank System is the enthusiast's choice for an easy and affordable EFI installation. It is perfect for those who want to upgrade their fuel delivery from carburetion to throttle-body or port-fuel injection. The kit comes with everything you need to install the system, including a premade wire loom with the correct connectors already installed. This type of kit is great for a beginner because most of the problems found later on can usually be traced back to an error made while wiring something incorrectly. With a premade harness, most of those problems can be eliminated.

Building and Tuning High-Performance Fuel Injection

Chapter 13

F.A.S.T. makes ECUs to handle nearly every type of engine available. A very popular application would be something like this big-block Chevrolet engine. F.A.S.T. can fire the eight injectors in bank-to-bank or sequential mode.

F.A.S.T.'s Bank-To-Bank system is also ideal for improving an existing TBI setup or converting to EFI. This system is the right choice for street rods and late-model street machines, both domestic and import, looking for improved reliability and drivability.

The Bank-To-Bank System is also ideal for improving an existing TBI, MPI, or TPI system to sequential operation, or for converting a carbureted engine to EFI. This system is the right choice for street rods and late-model street machines, both domestic and import, looking for improved reliability and driveability. Engines making a lot of power and using several large injectors will benefit the most from this type of system.

The Sequential system is great for all-out racing engines, or for applications where the ultimate flexibility in tuning is necessary. A tuner can fine-tune the engine using very large injectors or radical camshaft profiles much easier with the individual injection strategy of this setup. Using the Sequential System also helps reduce fluctuations in the fuel supply at the fuel rail when using large injectors and firing them at the same time, as you would with the Bank-to-Bank System.

Both systems come complete with the ECU, wire harness, software, communication data cable, and relays to operate the fuel pump. The systems can

The Sequential System is designed for those projects using a radical configuration like this blown alcohol Ford engine. The engine uses eight very large sequentially fired injectors.

Building and Tuning High-Performance Fuel Injection

F.A.S.T

The F.A.S.T. system also has a user-programmable closed-loop table where target air/fuel ratios can be input by the tuner. The system can then be run in closed-loop mode so that the oxygen sensor can correct errors in the base fuel table.

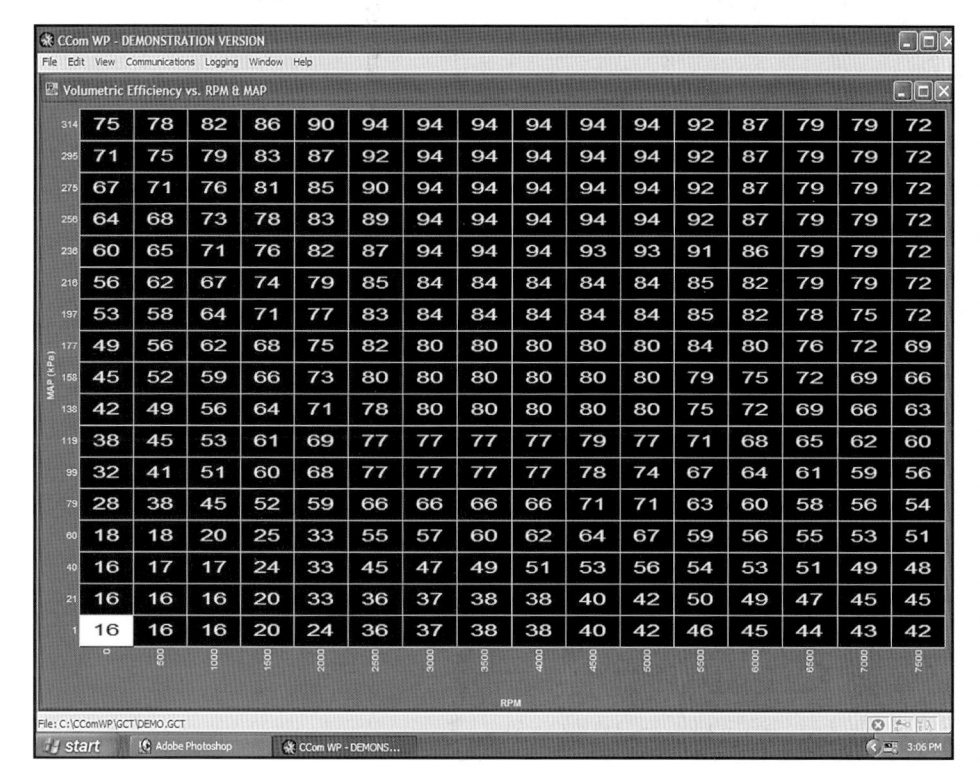

The base fuel and ignition tables are user programmable for both RPM and load sites. There are 16 available inputs for each, giving a total of 256 possible locations for tuning. The user can also copy and paste sections of maps from different calibrations, and use multiplicative functions over selectable areas.

completely control all fuel and ignition events for 4-, 6-, or 8-cylinder engines, and can use either MAP or TPS signals for load sensing. F.A.S.T. has not released a function to date that will allow the use of both methods at once.

The F.A.S.T system also has a user-programmable closed-loop table where target air/fuel ratios can be input by the tuner. The system can then be run in closed-loop mode so that the oxygen sensor can correct errors in the base fuel table. This is a useful feature for a novice tuner since it helps dramatically in getting up and running quickly and avoiding a lot of early frustration. However, it is not ideal to rely solely on the closed-loop table to run the engine. There is no substitute for proper tuning of the base fuel map. It is best to tune the base fuel table as well as possible to avoid problems later in the event of a sensor failure.

The base fuel and ignition tables are user programmable for both RPM and load sites with 16 available inputs for each, giving a total of 256 possible locations for tuning. Users can also copy and paste sections of maps from different calibrations, meaning you can use only the part of someone else's map that works for your project. This is very helpful in getting started if you know someone with a similar project who is willing to let you borrow their already tuned maps. The tables also allow multiplicative functions over selectable areas, meaning you can highlight a large area in one map and multiply the entire area by a percentage. This allows very fast changes to the map overall without the need to visit every site in the map. These functions make for a very easy tuning job with the F.A.S.T. system.

The F.A.S.T. system also has on-board data-logging functions available to aid in tuning and troubleshooting the engine. This system allows the user to record and collect information from every sensor and actuator that the ECU has control over. The user can select which items to log and how often to sample their data. Then the data can be stored for later analysis.

I always recommend taking advantage of the data-logging features a system

Building and Tuning High-Performance Fuel Injection

Chapter 13

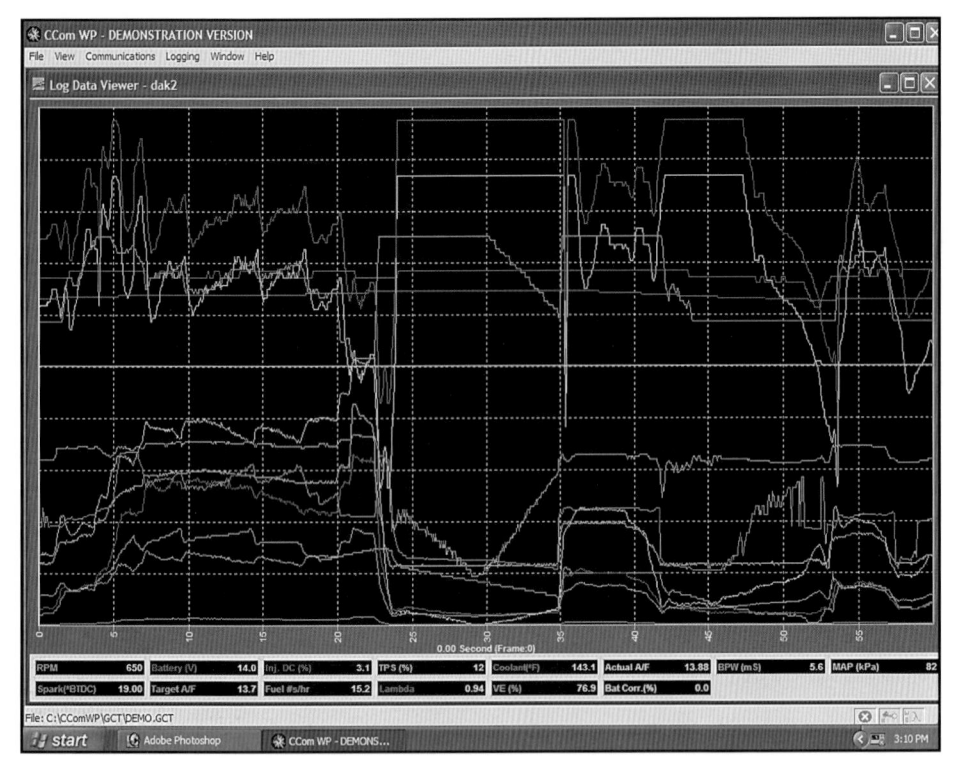

The F.A.S.T. system also has onboard data-logging functions available to aid in tuning and troubleshooting the engine. The system is capable of logging for about 30 minutes when sampling at 10 events per second.

has to offer, as this will definitely make the tuning more efficient. The F.A.S.T. system is capable of logging for about 30 minutes when sampling at 10 events per second. This allows the user more than sufficient time to gather data after making a run and decide what changes to make.

As always, when you receive the shipment, be sure to check that everything has been included. You will normally receive a packing slip that lists all of the items that are supposed to be present. Contact your dealer if there is a missing component or any problems with goods that may have been damaged during shipping.

Once everything is set, be sure to read the entire user's manual and installation instructions before proceeding with the installation. All too many times, I get complaints from people about a problem with their fuel-injection system, only to find out that they skipped an important step that was clearly explained in the user's manual.

When you are ready to begin, find a suitable location to mount the ECU, and make sure it is protected from any harsh environments such as water or extreme heat. Sometimes you can use metal screws to attach the ECU case to the car. Other times it may be advantageous to use rubber mounts to avoid problems caused by vibration.

Route the wire harness through the firewall and into the engine compartment. Lay the harness out and make sure all the connections are present in the harness and that they are the correct length. Make sure any ground connections are made to the chassis or directly to the engine only. Making a ground connection on the body can result in all sorts of problems later.

Once the wiring harness has been installed, the next step is to connect your computer to the ECU. Install the communication cable between the "CCom" connector on your wiring

F.A.S.T. Tuning Tip

According to the technical support team at F.A.S.T., one of the most common pitfalls that tuners seem to encounter while using their systems is cold-starting and idle problems. The technical staff says they find that most customers have an easy time tuning the full-throttle maps because of the wideband Lambda options they have, but many fail to get the optimum performance from their engines at cold-startup and idle conditions. The situation becomes even more difficult when radical camshafts and forced-induction systems are added to the mix.

F.A.S.T. recommends using their IAC (idle air control) option, which allows the user to add an idle air control valve to the system. The IAC allows the computer let extra air into the engine in order to more closely control the idle. This often helps reduce the haunting sensation you get from an engine with a rolling RPM condition as it tries to maintain a steady idle.

Tuning an engine for proper performance during cold running or starting situations can be difficult and sometimes require a lot of time and effort to get it right. To make things worse, each type of engine configuration reacts differently to these conditions. As a result, F.A.S.T. is very particular about sending potential customers to specific dealers. F.A.S.T. has nearly 70 dealers in the USA, and most specialize in a particular type of engine setup. By using a dealer with experience in your engine type, you can often draw on their knowledge and experience to get yourself up and running much easier. Most even offer base calibrations for specific engines to get customers up and running quickly. Ask your dealer before placing your order if they will be able to supply you with information about your project, or to recommend someone better suited to the task!

98   Building and Tuning High-Performance Fuel Injection

The F.A.S.T. system's external data logger is an extra option to add more memory to the logging program and allow you to sample data over a longer period of time. The EDIS, or electronic distributor, shown here, is an adapter to allow engines to run multiple ignition coils with no distributor!

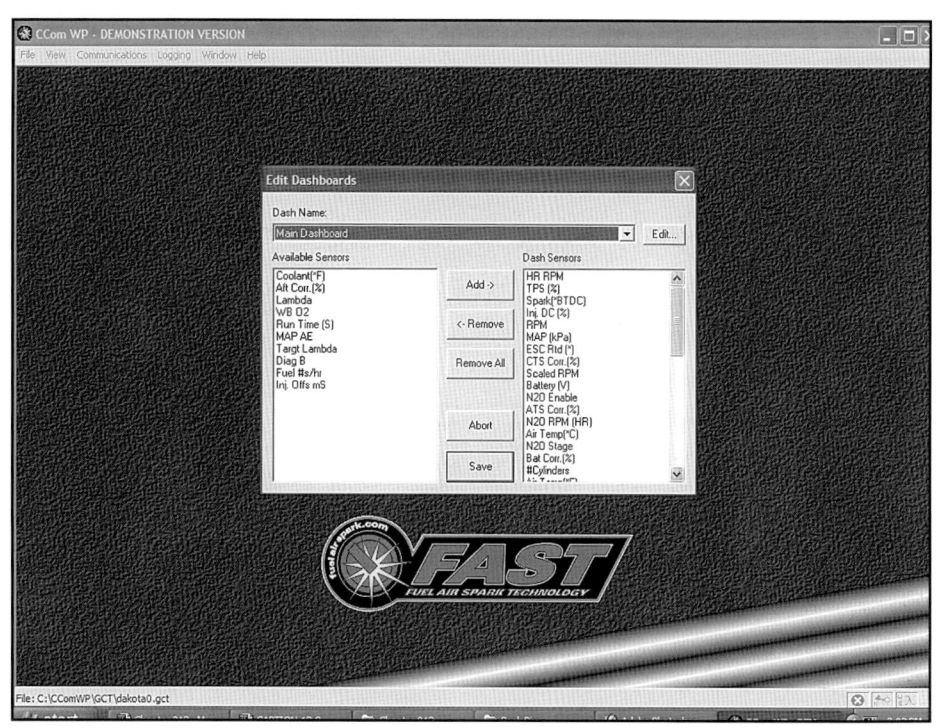

When in the on-line mode, the F.A.S.T. software offers a Dashboard that will display the real-time data from engine sensors. The Dashboard is user-configurable and is set up via the screen shown here called "Dashboard Set-Up".

harness and a 9-pin serial port on your computer. Newer laptop computers may not have a 9-pin serial port. Typically, all new laptops are coming with USB ports only. This problem can be easily solved by a trip to the local Radio Shack where you can find a USB to serial port adapter that plugs into your laptop's USB port and allows you to connect a serial plug on the other end.

There are a few parameters to set up before attempting to establish communication between the computer and the ECU. From the CCom WP pull-down menus, select "Communications" and then select "Setup". On the tab labeled "General", make sure the "Direct Connection" radio button is selected. Next, select the tab labeled "COM Port" and select the appropriate COM port for your computer. This will be "COM1" for most systems. Click "OK" when finished and press the "F2" key. If your computer and ECU are communicating properly, you should see a progress bar in the lower right corner of the screen and the word "Online" should appear in the lower left corner after the progress bar fills in. Refer to the Frequently Asked Questions section of the owner's manual on RS-232 communication if you are unable to make your computer communicate with the ECU.

From the factory, the ECU comes loaded with a calibration file that should be sufficient to get most engines started. However, before attempting to start your car, there are a few parameters that must be set.

These include:

- *Crankshaft Reference Angle:*
  This is set in the "Global Setup Parameters" screen, which can be reached by pressing the "F5" key or through the pull-down menus by selecting "View", and then "System Configuration".

- *Engine Firing Order:*
  This can be accessed through the pull-down menus by selecting "View", and then "System Configuration".

- *Engine Displacement, MAP Sensor Type, Number of Cylinders, and Injector Flow Rate:*
  These can be accessed through the pull-down menus by selecting "View", "System Configuration", and then "Fuel Calc Parameters".

While the computer is connected and online, press the "F9" key to display the main dashboard. You should be able to read the following dashboard parameters with the engine not running and the ignition on.

The TPS reading at an idle should be relatively low, and should increase as you open the throttle. The MAP sensor should read approximately 100 kPa, depending on your actual altitude and barometric pressure. The air and coolant temperature sensors should read the approximate outside temperature, assuming the engine hasn't been run for some time. Battery voltage should be approximately 12 volts. An RPM signal should be present when cranking the vehicle. If you do not see an RPM signal when cranking the vehicle, refer to the owner's manual's Frequently Asked Questions section on RPM signal troubleshooting.

IGNITION SETUP

In order for the ECU to properly control ignition timing, the crankshaft reference angle, as well as the actual

Chapter 13

ignition timing on the engine itself, must be set to the proper value. This value should be the same for both because this serves as a reference point the ECU will use for controlling ignition timing. Different types of ignition systems use different reference angles. The reference angle is the amount of degrees BTDC where the sensor can be triggered each time.

Magnetic Pickup Distributor or Crank Trigger Ignition

If you are using a magnetic-pickup distributor or crank-trigger ignition, set the crankshaft reference angle to 50 degrees. Roll the motor over to 50 degrees BTDC on the number-1 cylinder.

With this type of ignition setup, the ECU requires a 10-degree margin between the reference angle and the highest amount of advance you will run. This means that with a 50-degree reference angle, you can run up to 40 degrees of timing. If you want to run more than 40 degrees of timing, you need to set the reference angle higher than 50.

If you are using a crank trigger:

Center the pickup on one of the magnets in the trigger wheel. Now, roll the motor to wherever you plan to run your ignition timing at the RPM where your engine produces the most torque (30 degrees, as an example). Rotate the distributor until the rotor tip is directly lined up with the number-1 spark plug terminal.

If you are using the pickup in your distributor:

With the motor still at 50 BTDC, remove the cap and rotor and center one of the reluctor tabs with the magnetic pickup in the distributor. If you have an adjustable-phase rotor, roll the motor over by hand to wherever you plan to run your ignition timing at the RPM where your engine produces the most torque (30 degrees, for example). Adjust the rotor position (without rotating the distributor housing) until the rotor tip is directly lined up with the number-1 spark-plug terminal. If you do not have an adjustable-phase rotor, you may

In order for the ECU to properly control ignition timing, the crankshaft reference angle and the actual ignition timing on the engine itself must be set to the proper value. The value should be the same for both, because it serves as a reference point that the ECU will use for controlling ignition timing.

100 Building and Tuning High-Performance Fuel Injection

The correct crankshaft reference angle for F.A.S.T. EFI systems with the Northstar DIS system may vary. To determine the proper reference angle for your system, disconnect the bypass wire (Pin C4-D on the coil pack/module assembly) and crank the engine. Observe the ignition timing with a timing light during cranking. The observed timing value should be used as your crank reference angle.

need to reposition the reluctor wheel on the distributor shaft so that your rotor phase can be optimized without changing the 50-degree crank reference angle.

GM HEI (High Energy Ignition)

This ignition system typically uses a 6-degree crank reference angle. Disconnect the bypass wire (pin "C" on HEI distributors with the coil in the cap, pin "B" on distributors with external coil) and crank the engine. Adjust the distributor until spark advance is measured at 6 degrees during cranking.

Buick DIS

This ignition system uses a fixed crank reference angle of 10 degrees. No calibration or modification of any ignition components is necessary.

GM Optispark Ignition

This ignition system uses a fixed crank reference angle of 6 degrees. No calibration or modification of any ignition components is necessary.

GM Northstar DIS

The correct crankshaft reference angle for F.A.S.T. EFI systems with the Northstar DIS system may vary. To determine the proper reference angle for your system, disconnect the bypass wire (pin "C4-D" on the coil

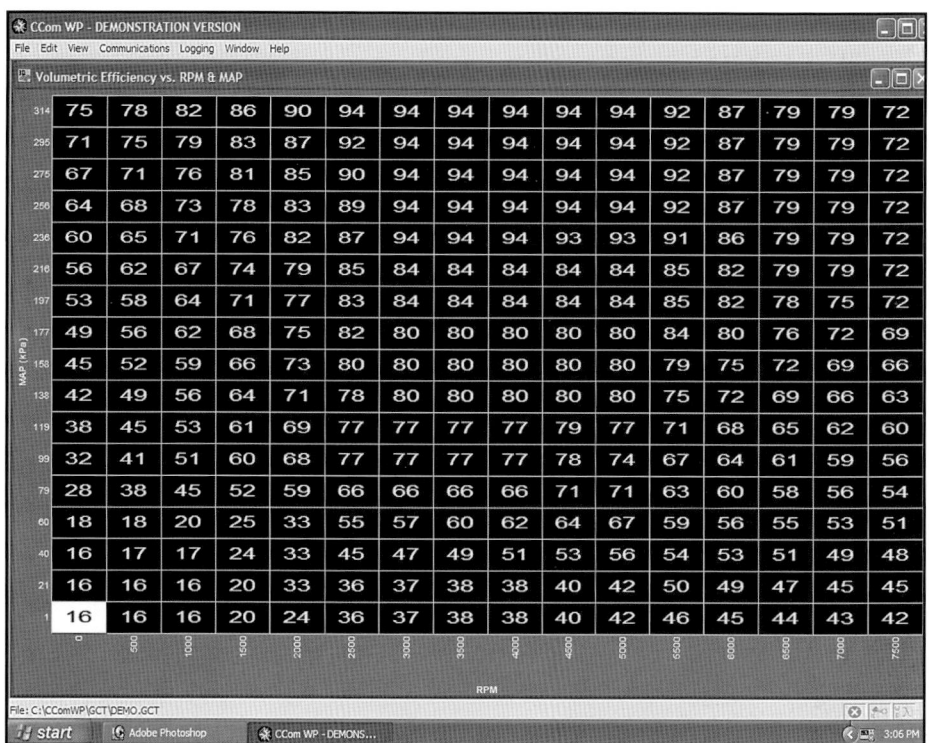

Start by tuning the idle and no-load sites by free-revving the engine and watching the oxygen sensor output. Make changes as necessary to get the oxygen sensor output information to match the desired target set in the target air/fuel tables.

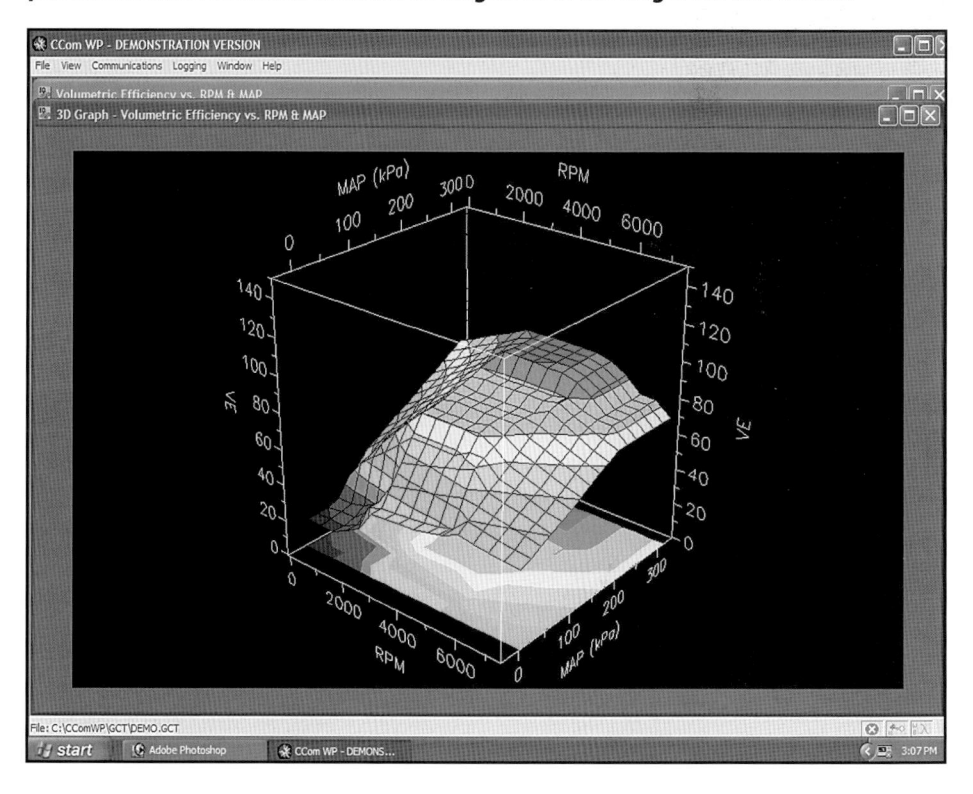

Once you have finished tuning the no-load sites, you can begin tuning the medium-load sites by progressively adding more load as you complete the lightly loaded spots in the map. It is always best to use a dyno to tune, but be sure to be very careful if you must tune on the road.

Building and Tuning High-Performance Fuel Injection 101

The F.A.S.T. system is capable of using most original equipment such as sensors, injectors, relays, and ignition coils like on this big-block Ford engine. Even if you have a unique setup, the F.A.S.T. engineers will work with you to develop a way to control it.

pack/module assembly) and crank the engine. Observe the ignition timing during cranking with a timing light. The observed timing value should be used as your crank reference angle.

Ford TFI (Thick Film Ignition)

This ignition system typically uses a 10-degree crank reference angle. Disconnect the SPOUT (spark output) wire and adjust the distributor until spark advance is measured at 10 degrees with a timing light.

Ford EDIS (Electronic Distributorless Ignition System)

This ignition system uses a fixed crank reference angle of 10 degrees. No calibration or modification of any ignition components is necessary.

TUNING THE ENGINE

Now that everything has been set up properly, you may run the engine and start the calibration process. Be sure to let the engine warm up to operating temperature before you begin tuning.

Start by tuning the idle and no-load sites by free-revving the engine and watching the oxygen sensor output. Make changes as necessary to get the oxygen sensor output information to match the target air/fuel tables. You may do this with the closed-loop control turned on, but usually I recommend tuning with it off. If you choose to use the closed-loop control, then just keep making changes to the base fuel table until the closed-loop correction amount is as low as possible.

Once you have finished tuning the no-load sites, you can begin tuning the medium-load sites and progressively add more load as you complete the lightly loaded spots in the map. Remember that many other things are happening inside the engine while you are tuning, so it is very important to remain aware of things like coolant temperature and oil pressure. You may need to stop several times during tuning to let the engine cool, or just to observe everything and ensure the engine is operating normally.

It is always best to use a dyno to tune as you can safely control the engine speed and load while tuning. It is also very helpful to be able to assess the engine's performance by using the dyno to record and play back the engine's power and torque output. This makes it easy to evaluate the benefit of making any particular change.

Tuning an engine without a dyno can be done, but I would advise you to use extreme caution when tuning on the road, as conditions can change very rapidly and become dangerous. Also remember that the speed and safety laws on public roads still apply when you are tuning.

Tuning with the F.A.S.T. system can be very easy and lots of fun as a result of all the time their engineers have spent making the interface software very flexible and user-friendly. The system is capable of using most original equipment such as sensors, injectors, relays, and ignition coils. Even if you have a unique setup, the F.A.S.T. engineers will work with you to develop a way to control your configuration.

All the engines that I have tuned using the F.A.S.T. system have run very well and been fairly easy to calibrate. If you take your time, read all the instructions, and practice off-line with the calibration software, you will very likely have the same experience!

Chapter 14

Haltech

Haltech

COST: Approximately $1,500 to $2,500

FEATURES: The Haltech system is very flexible. It can accept a wide variety of sensors and command many different outputs

EASE OF INSTALLATION AND TUNING: The user can choose to either connect their wire harness, or use the universal premade unit. The software is very easy to understand.

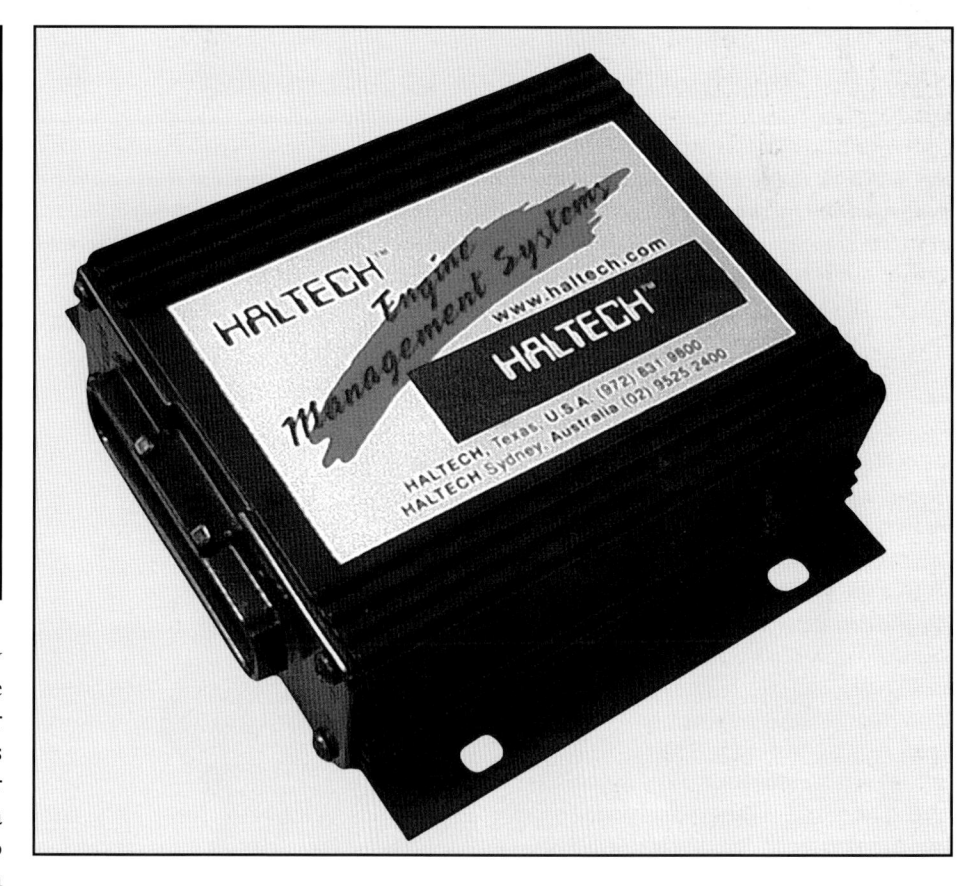

Haltech is an Australian manufacturer of aftermarket fuel-injection systems. It has become well known for its extremely easy-to-use tuning software.

Haltech is an Australian company that was started in 1986 by Steve Mitchell with the backing of his father Bill Mitchell. The original intention was to develop diagnostic equipment for electronic fuel-injection systems, but a request by *Modern Motor* magazine to solve the problem of supplying fuel to a supercharged Ford project car led to the development of a supplementary fuel-injection computer. This project opened their eyes to a brand new market place where the need for a user-programmable fuel-injection system existed. This realization lead them to develop the world's first real-time programmable engine management system, meaning that the ECU could be programmed while the engine was running.

Screwdriver-adjustable engine management systems had been available before the first Haltech ECU. There were systems such as the English Zytek, which were very good systems, but they were expensive and weren't programmable in real time. These ECUs could be adjusted by simply turning a screw on the side of them to deliver more or less fuel to suit the engine's requirements.

The first system, the F2, was followed by the F3 model, which was produced by the thousands, and there are many of both models still running today. Later, the F7 model was produced originally for motorcycles and rotary engines, but curious customers soon found innovative ways to adapt these systems to their V-8 and V-6 engines with good results. This spawned a whole series of fuel-only computers to follow the F7, consisting of the F7A, F7B, F7C, F9, F9A, to the F10 that we have today.

Then came the E5 fuel-injection computer, which was a big development over the F-series model above, which only controlled fuel. The E5 did not, however, control any of the ancillary devices like the later E6 series. The E5 eventually led to the development of the E6, E6A, and E6S fuel-injection and ignition-timing computers, which in turn gave rise to the current E6X model computer. The E6 series began a whole new era of engine management, because it controlled not only the fuel and ignition, but also the idle speed and many ancillary devices such as air conditioning, nitrous, and VTEC.

The unit that we are most concerned about in this book is the E6X. This unit is capable of firing 4 injectors sequentially, up to 8 injectors semi-sequentially, or 8 injectors using batch firing. The unit can also handle staged injector combinations on a 4-cylinder engine, which is a process of using 2 injectors per cylinder and having only 1 injector work for low-speed and low-power situations, and then turn on both of them when the fuel demand gets higher. This allowed the user to avoid the poor idle and low-speed running characteristics of using one very large injector.

The E6X also has up to 4 ignition outputs available for using 4 sequentially firing individual coils, which means it can provide spark for up to 8 cylinders in a waste-spark configuration. The unit can also be configured to control 10 or 12 cylinders and rotary type engines using spilt spark timing.

Haltech was the first fuel-injection manufacturer to develop a system that could be programmed by the user in real time, similar to their E6X version shown here. Several other companies had already built systems that could be adjusted with a screwdriver, but Haltech was the first to use on-line programming with a computer.

The unit that we are most concerned about for this purpose will be the E6X. This unit is capable of firing four injectors sequentially, up to eight injectors semi-sequentially, or use batch firing. The unit can also handle staged injector combinations on a four-cylinder engine.

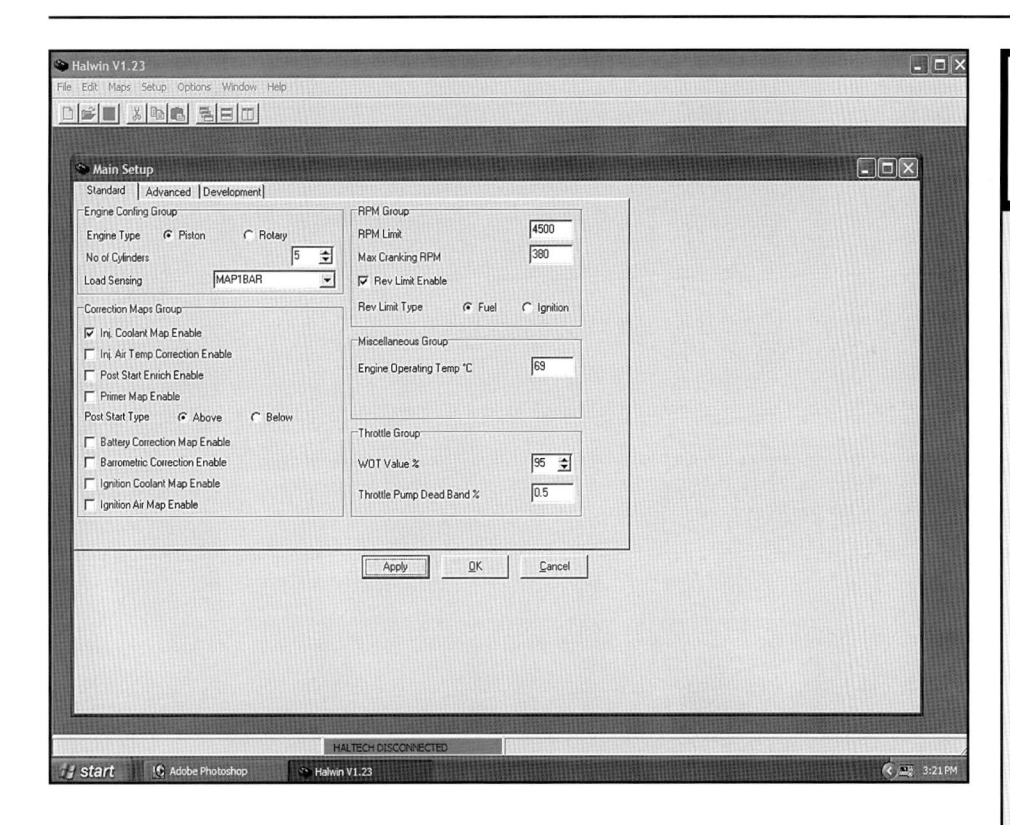

The user can also select between using speed and load breakpoints every 500 or 1,000 rpm. There are a total of 16 engine speed ranges with 32 load sites per range giving the user 512 possible tuning sites to work with.

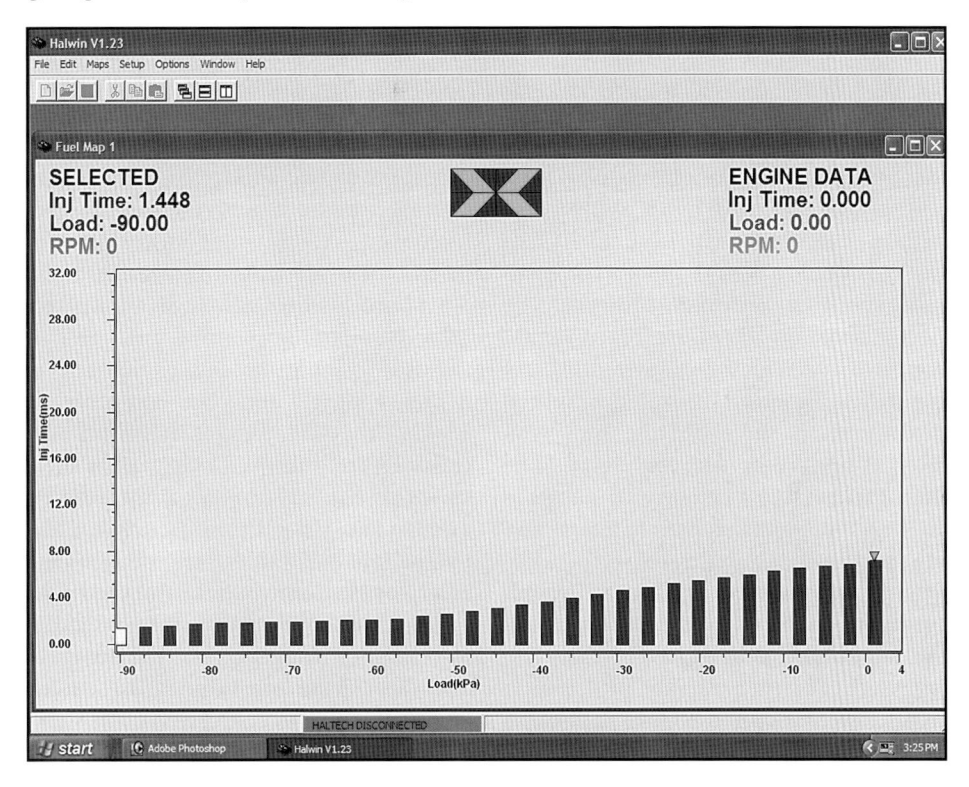

Instead of using a grid for base fuel calibration as most other manufacturers do, Haltech has taken a slightly different approach. They use one screen for each engine speed range, with the engine load points for that particular RPM traveling across the page horizontally.

Haltech Tuning Tip

One of the most common mistakes people make when tuning a Haltech E6X engine management system is to forget that the most fuel is going to be consumed by the engine at the point where the engine load is highest at the engine speed where peak torque occurs. An engine will always use the most oxygen, therefore the most amount of fuel, at peak torque. At any other engine speed, the engine will naturally consume an amount of air and fuel proportional to the load on the engine. In other words, more load means more air and fuel, and less load means less air and fuel.

Since the calibration feature of the Haltech software uses a single page to display all of the load sites for a given RPM range, it is common to see the injector pulse width increase across the load sites on any given RPM range. The airflow across the engine doesn't usually change drastically over a small change in engine speed, so it is also common to see the same pulse-width request for RPM sites that are close to each other.

This method is actually very simple, and sometimes it's almost too simple! What often happens is that people get carried away in making sure that each increasing load site gets more fuel. This can actually lead to a fuel curve that gets progressively richer as the engine speed climbs above the point of peak torque.

When you are tuning an engine using this software, be aware that the injector pulse width should always match the desired air/fuel ratio for any given speed and load point. Doing this will prevent a rich condition at high engine speeds.

Building and Tuning High-Performance Fuel Injection

Chapter 14

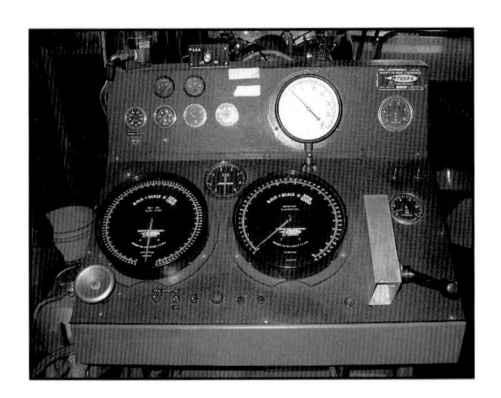

Try to tune all the load sites within a given engine speed range, and then move to the next engine speed. This setup is actually very easy to tune — as long as the engine can be held at a constant RPM, like it would be on this dyno.

The E6X can be programmed by the user to sense engine load as a function of engine speed versus either manifold pressure or throttle position. The Haltech software does not offer any blend-type function that allows the use of both manifold pressure and throttle position for calculating the engine's load.

The user can also select between using speed and load break points every 500 or 1,000 rpm. There are a total of 16 engine speed ranges with 32 load sites per range, giving the user 512 possible tuning sites to work with.

Instead of using a grid-style table for base fuel calibration as most other manufacturers do, Haltech has taken a slightly different approach. They use one screen for each engine speed range, with the engine load points for that particular RPM traveling across the page horizontally. As the user builds load for a given engine speed, by increasing the throttle angle, the site in the table being used moves to the right, and the user can then tune that load site.

When engine speed changes, the user must scroll to the screen for the new engine speed and continue tuning each of the load sites for that engine speed. Once all the fuel tuning is finished, the ignition tables are laid out in the same way. Just try to tune all the load sites within a given engine speed range, and then move to the next engine speed. This is actually very easy as long as the engine can be held at a constant

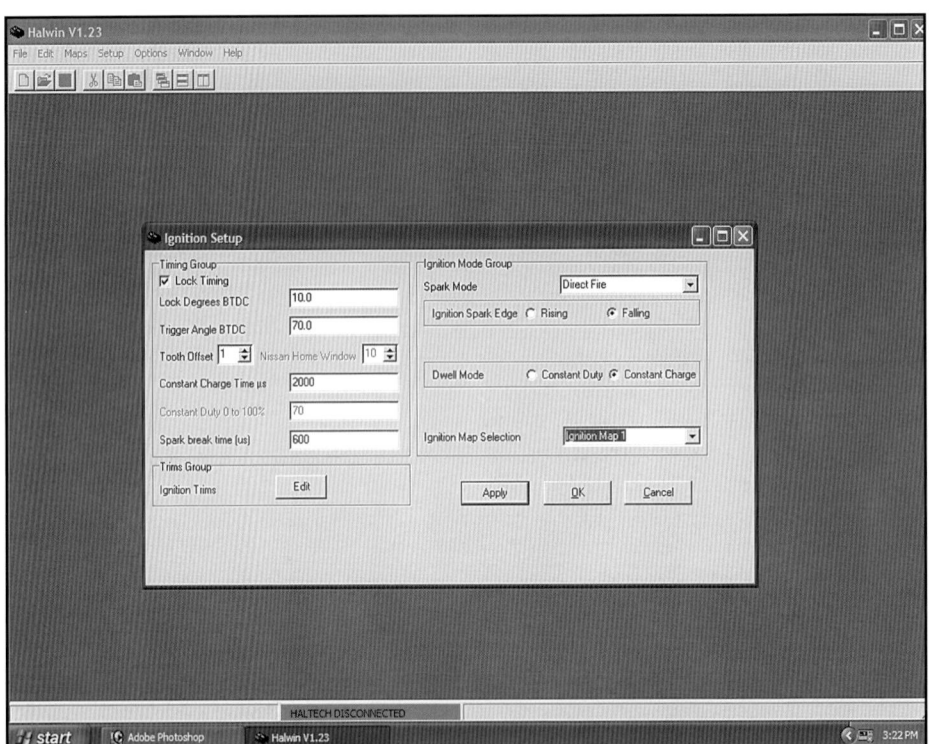

Haltech's E6X offers an automated ignition mapping feature that allows the user to input the amount of initial timing and advance to have under light load and full load conditions. That way, the software can calculate the proper timing curve for the engine.

RPM. This can be easy on a dyno, but tuning on the road can be quite difficult because the engine speeds change so quickly.

One good thing about the E6X is its ability to recognize most any trigger pattern and waveform. Like all ECUs, the E6X needs a digital signal in order to recognize a trigger event. However, the E6X has an on-board analog-to-digital converter, or reluctor adapter, so that a standard magnetic sensor can be wired directly to the unit and the ECU can convert and recognize the signal. The unit also has the flexibility to decipher all sorts of multi-tooth triggers and missing-tooth configurations in addition to the traditional standard trigger pattern of a sensor, which produces only the same amount of signals as there are cylinders. This is a very helpful option that saves time when wiring and fabricating new sensor mounts for aftermarket sensors. Haltech also offers the wiring harness as either a generic 4-, 6-, or 8-cylinder terminated harness, or as a flying-lead harness where the engine side of the wiring must be custom-fin-

ished by the user. If you choose to order the flying-lead harness, be sure that you have all of the correct connectors to hook up you sensors and actuators. Finding a unique connector that you are missing can be a time-consuming and frustrating task when you are already halfway through your installation.

Haltech's E6X offers an automated ignition-mapping feature that allows the user to input the desired amount of initial timing, and the amount of advance they want under light-load and full-load conditions. The software then uses this information to automatically calculate the proper timing curve for the engine. These values are determined solely by the user though, and the ECU creates the timing map values based on information supplied by the user. It does not have the ability to detect engine knock and correct it in a closed-loop manner. Be sure that the ECU is supplying the required amount of timing before going too far.

Haltech also does not offer any auto-mapping features that utilize wideband oxygen sensors or target air-

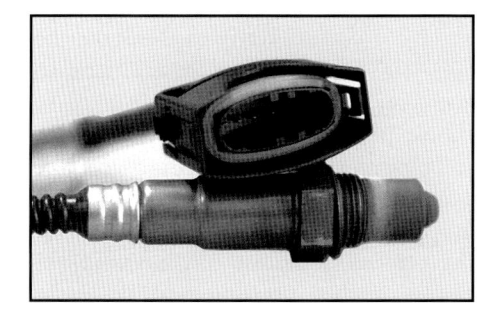

While a four-wire wide-band oxygen sensor such as this one from Bosch can be used with the E6 series ECU, it cannot be used with any sort of automatic mapping function. All fuel-curve tuning must be done manually.

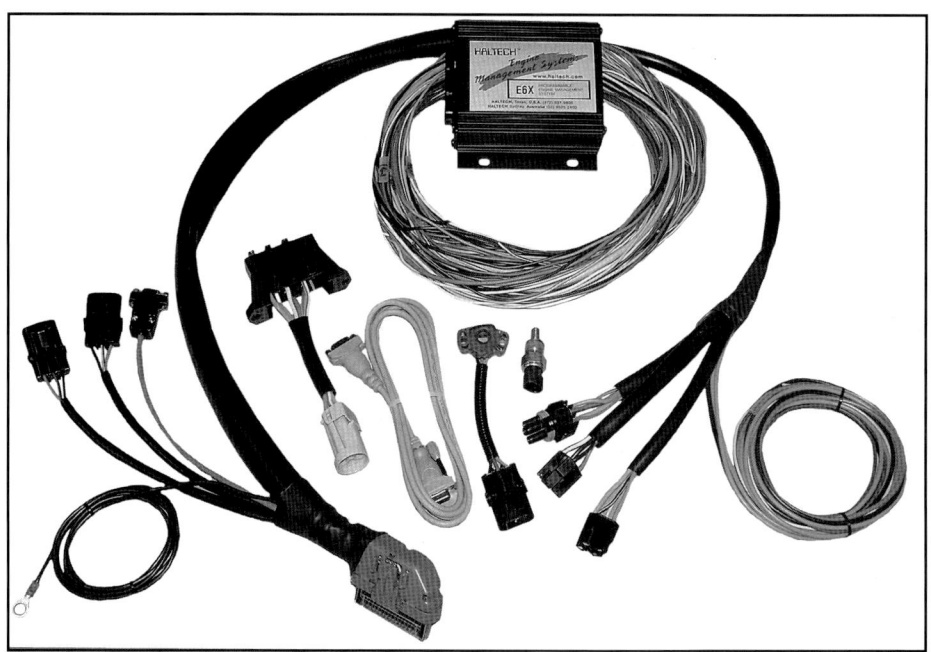

All E6X kits include an ECU, wiring harness, fuse block, fuel pump relays, intake air temperature sensors, coolant temperature sensors, throttle position sensors, data cable, software, and user's manual.

fuel ratio tables. All the tuning necessary to set up proper fuel maps must be done manually.

All E6X kits include an ECU, wiring harness, fuse block, fuel pump relays, intake air temperature sensor, coolant temperature sensor, throttle position sensor, data cable, software, and user's manual. As an additional option, you could include a 1-, 2-, or 3-bar MAP sensor, idle air control valve, boost control solenoid, oxygen sensor, and ignition coil packs.

Once you have received your shipment from Haltech, be sure to inspect the kit and account for all the items that were supposed to be included. There is normally a packing slip to inform you of all the items that were intended to be shipped. If there is any problem with the shipment, contact your dealer immediately. Be sure to thoroughly read the owner's manual and installation instructions before you being any part of the installation. Understanding the information in the manual will prevent many easily avoidable errors later on.

When you are ready to begin, start by finding a suitable location to mount the ECU. I prefer to keep them inside the vehicle in an effort to avoid any moisture or unnecessary heat from the engine compartment. You can use metal screws to mount the unit directly to the vehicle or you may choose to use a rubber mount to isolate it from harsh vibrations. Be sure to use a rubber grommet anywhere the wire harness passes through the firewall to avoid abrasion

Find a suitable location to mount your ECU and ignition system. The coil packs shown in this photo are next to the valve cover under the hood. This is an acceptable location for them, but most ECUs are happier inside the car.

and possible failure of the harness.

Lay the harness out on the engine and be sure all the connections reach the intended location. If you are completing the flying lead harness yourself, be sure that all the connections are secure and protected from the element to avoid corrosion.

Building and Tuning High-Performance Fuel Injection

Chapter 14

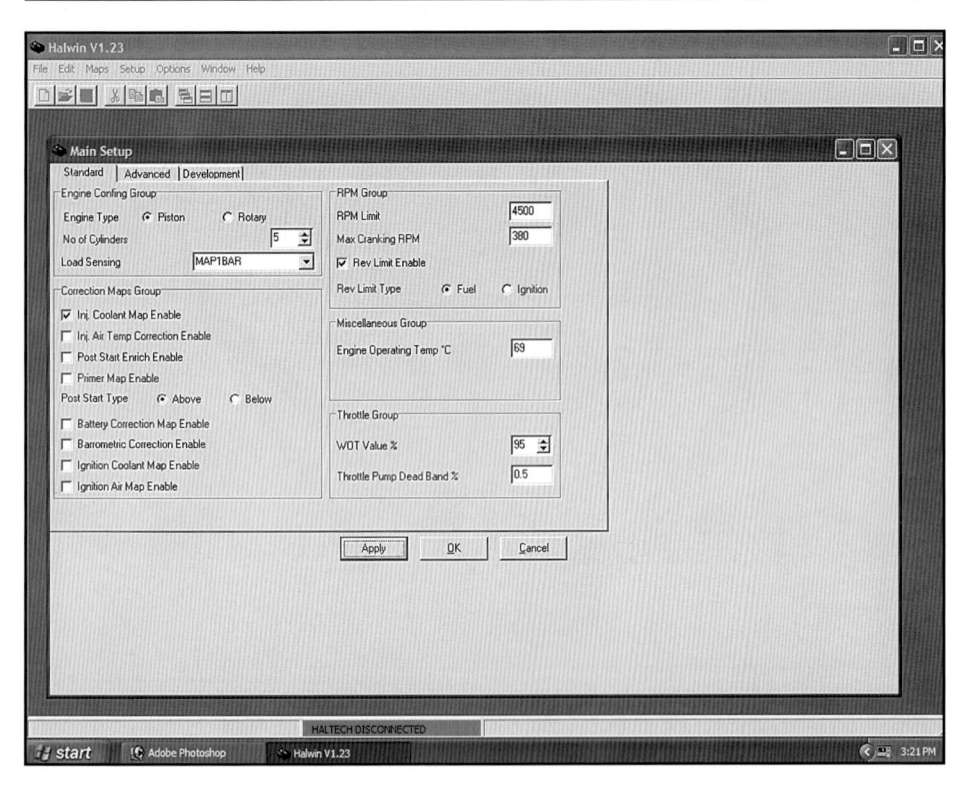

Now you are ready to check out the live data. Click on the "Maps" icon to give you a selection of tuning maps to choose from. Choose "Fuel" from the list and pick an RPM to start from. When the page comes up, you will be able to monitor the live engine data on the bottom of the screen. Look for obvious signs of trouble, such as a throttle position sensor that starts out at 100 percent and goes down as you depress the gas pedal, or a coolant temperature sensor that reads –30 degrees in the summertime.

After you are certain that everything in the wiring and live-data settings are correct, you will want to crank the engine over. Once the engine has started, allow it to warm up fully to operating temperature before you make any changes to the base fuel and ignition maps. This will prevent you from having to redo any changes you've made when all of the warm-up corrections to the maps have timed out.

The best way to tune the E6X is to place the engine under a constant load at a given engine speed by using either a chassis dyno or an engine dyno. Then tune all of the load sites within that engine speed range to the desired air/fuel ratio before moving to the next engine speed. Repeat this procedure until all of the sites you plan to use in real operation have been tuned. Be sure to use caution in tuning, as lean mixtures could cause engine damage.

Also be aware that engines will tend to overheat more when a car is operated on a chassis dyno due to the lack of wind to cool the radiator. You may have to tune in 4- or 5-minute sessions to avoid engine damage from overheating. Once all the fuel mixture sites have been tuned to your satisfaction, you can concentrate on tuning the ignition sites in much the same manner as the fuel sites.

Hold the engine speed constant and tune all of the load sites for maximum power, and then reduce the advance by one or two degrees to provide a margin of safety against pinging or detonation. As always, pay close attention to the instructions in the user's manual and practice navigating the software ahead of time to make your experience with the Haltech E6X a fun and rewarding time.

When you have established communication with the ECU, click on the "Setup" icon at the top of your screen to begin the set-up procedure. Follow the guidelines in the user's manual for selecting the proper triggering, injection method, and ignition types your engine will use. At this point, you may also set the type of MAP sensor and the engine speed limiter.

Haltech also offers this nifty little air/fuel ratio monitor called the Haltuner. The unit uses LED lights to indicate a rich or lean condition in the exhaust. This is certainly not the most exact tuning tool, but it is quite useful for quick, on-the-fly tuning.

Once you have made all the proper connections, you can plug the harness into the ECU. Now you can download the supplied software onto your laptop and connect the data cable between the laptop and the ECU.

When you have established communication with the ECU, click on the "Set-Up" icon at the top of your screen to begin the set-up procedure. Follow the guidelines in the user's manual for selecting the proper triggering, injection method, and ignition types that your engine will use. You may also set the type of MAP sensor and the engine speed limiter at this point.

Building and Tuning High-Performance Fuel Injection

Chapter 15

Holley
Commander 950

Holley Commander 950

COST: Approximately $1,500 to $2,500

FEATURES: The Holley system has plenty of user-defined outputs, but they're mainly focused at American vehicles. However, the system is flexible enough to control imports too.

EASE OF INSTALLATION AND TUNING: Holley's premade harness is simple to install, and new wideband tuning option is very functional. Overall the software is a bit cumbersome.

The Commander 950 fuel-injection system is the latest offering from the performance giant Holley Performance Products. While the company has been well known for its performance carburetors, they aim to prove that their quality lives on, and as times change, so will they!

Holley is probably one of the most well recognized names in the high-performance industry. They have long been the leader in performance parts for American V-8 engines, most notably their series of performance 4-barrel carburetors. Holley has always been on the forefront of fuel delivery, and their new Commander 950 engine management system is no exception!

Holley decided that in order to keep up with the demands of late-model hot-rod enthusiasts and the ever-increasing trends from manufacturers to use electronic engine controls, they would need to develop their own line of engine management systems. These systems would need to control not only fuel-injection duties, but also add the capability to control the factory ignition units.

To that end, Holley introduced the Commander 950 complete engine management system. This is a highly capable system aimed squarely at the domestic V-8 marketplace. Though the ECU can be used on any combination of 4-, 6-, or

Building and Tuning High-Performance Fuel Injection

Chapter 15

Holley is one of the most well recognized names in the high-performance industry. They have long been the leader in performance parts for American V-8 engines, most notably their series of high-performance 4-barrel carburetors.

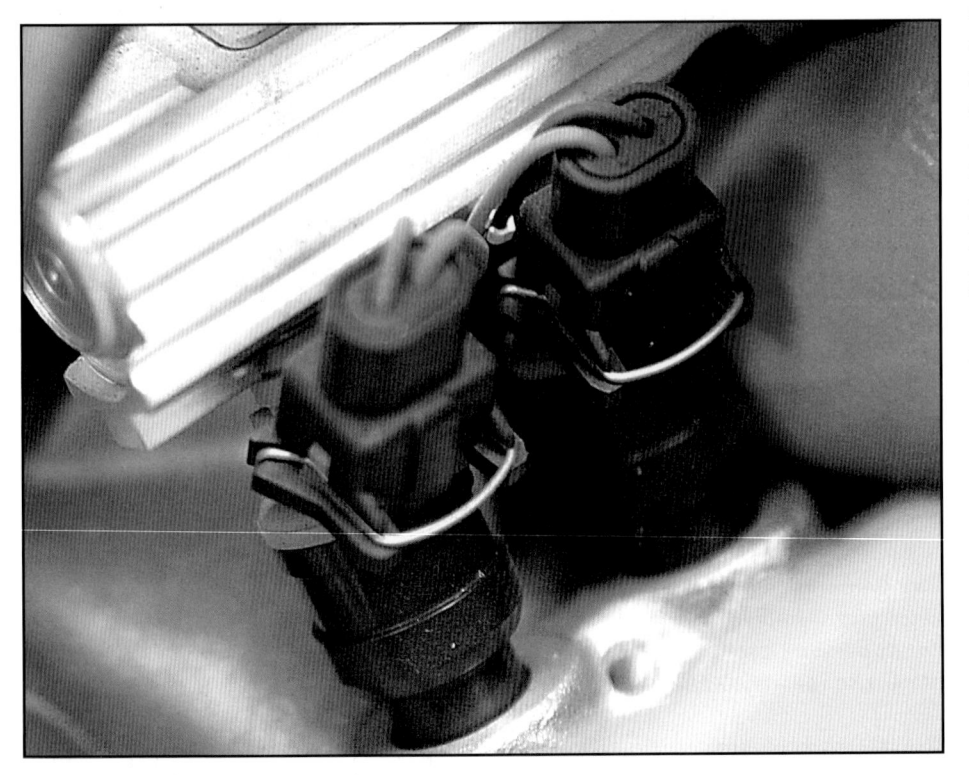

This unit is capable of driving up to eight injectors of either low or high impedance in batch fire, or up to four injectors in a sequential fashion. It can also recognize any 1-, 2-, or 3-bar GM MAP sensor, and it can use almost all GM-style sensors and connections for easy placement into any domestic engine compartment!

The Commander 950 engine management computer system is capable of being used on any of 4-, 6-, or 8-cylinder engine. However, it is mostly found on large-displacement V-8 engines in unique hot rods. It typically fires two injectors at a time, like the ones shown here.

8-cylinder engines, it is mostly found on the larger-displacement V-8 engines in unique hot rods.

This unit is capable of driving up to 8 injectors of either low or high impedance in batch fire, or up to 4 injectors in a sequential fashion. It can also recognize any 1-, 2-, or 3-bar GM MAP sensor, and uses mainly all GM-type sensors and connections for easy placement into any domestic engine compartment. The unit can also be programmed by the user to sense engine load as a function of either MAP or TPS, but it cannot use blend both at the same time, like some of the other units we have talked about.

The Commander 950 ECU also has user programmable digital outputs for controlling things like cooling fans, air conditioning compressors, nitrous solenoids, and just about any other switched function that can be operated via a relay or solenoid!

All Holley Commander 950 units also have on-board data logging, which can aid the user in tuning and troubleshooting. With the use of the optional Race version of the calibration software, the user can set the parameters to be logged, as well as take advantage of some of the closed-loop control features the system has to offer.

The latest addition to the Holley

110   **Building and Tuning High-Performance Fuel Injection**

line of product offerings is the wideband oxygen sensor option, which allows the user the ability to insert target air/fuel ratios in a map and then enable the closed-loop fuel control function to let the ECU make corrections to the base fuel map. This method helps novice tuners get up and running quickly and easily and helps advanced tuners create accurate calibrations by finding out information about how much correction is needed to the base fuel map.

The high-speed oxygen sensor and heater control unit used in the Holley system has been developed by FJO. FJO is a Canadian company that specializes in high-performance tuning equipment and its own line of engine management computers. FJO is widely recognized as a leader in the exhaust analyzer field.

The base version of the calibration software comes ready to install and also offers many base maps for the user to select. These base maps are an easy starting point for all different types of engines, from naturally aspirated big-block Chevys to turbocharged 4-cylinders.

The Holley Commander 950 system can also be ordered with custom wire harness configurations to fit a variety of engines including most GM and Ford crate engines, including LS1, LT1, and ZZ4 Chevrolet configurations and Ford mustang 5.0-liter engines.

The standard version of the calibration software offers the tuner 16 ranges of engine load and 16 ranges of engine speed for a total of 256 possible points to program the fuel and ignition curves. In the Race version of the software, the user can define the breakpoint values between engine speed and load sites. This allows the user to have a fairly coarse calibration in areas where the change in volumetric efficiency is not very great over a corresponding change in engine speed. It also allows the user to make the calibration much more precise in areas where the volumetric efficiency changes rapidly, such as when an engine reaches its powerband.

The Race version of the software also allows the user to set target air/fuel ratio parameters and use feedback information from an oxygen sensor to correct errors in the base fuel calibration. This function allows novice tuners to get up and running quickly and lets racers compensate for changing environments without expensive and time-consuming retuning.

The Commander 950 ECU also has user programmable digital outputs for using on things like the RPM-referenced shift light attached to left-hand side of this tachometer. The user tells the ECU when to turn on the light, so the driver knows when to change gears.

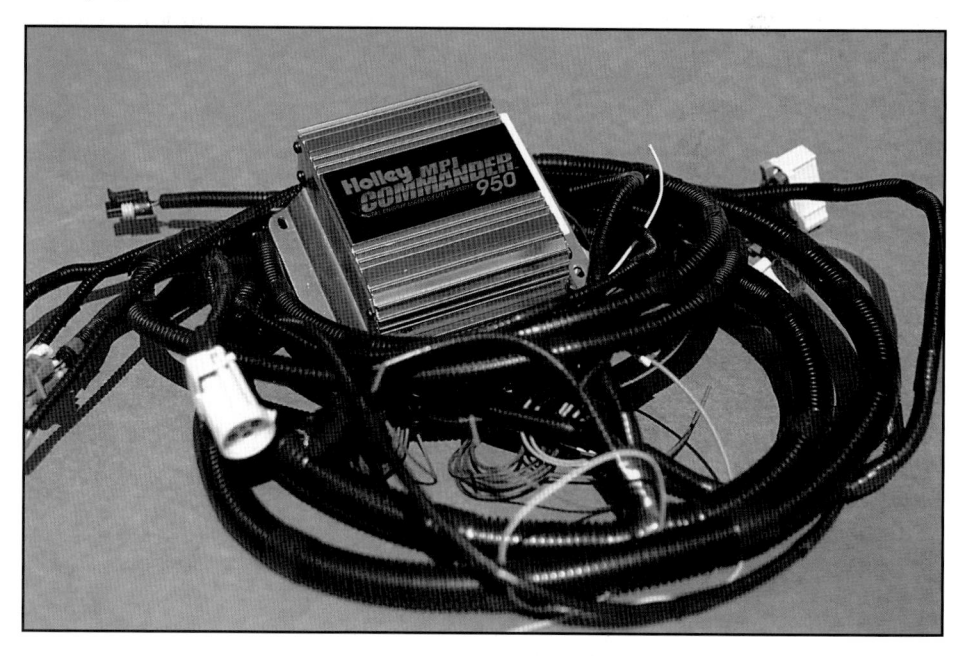

The Holley Commander 950 system can be ordered with custom wire harnesses to fit a variety of engines including most GM and Ford crate engines. Chevy LS1's, LT1's, ZZ4's, and Ford 5.0-liter engines are some of the most popular applications.

Be sure to inform your dealer when ordering the system about what type of engine you will be using, so that they can supply you with the correct type of wiring harness and sensor package.

Once you have received the unit, be

Chapter 15

The Race version of the software allows the user to set target air/fuel ratio parameters and use feedback information from an oxygen sensor to correct errors in the base fuel calibration. Here is a good look at an oxygen sensor located in the exhaust system.

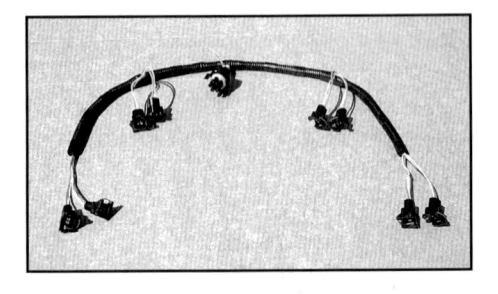

All Holley units come with an injector sub-harness like the one shown here. This allows easy connection of the injectors to the rest of the harness, and to allows the harness to be customized more easily to fit more applications.

The throttle position sensor shown here has a very important role in correctly calibrating the engine. Before starting the engine for the first time, check to ensure it is sending the proper signal to the ECU. If not, the engine may have difficulty starting.

sure to inspect the kit and account for all the items that were supposed to be shipped. If there is any problem with the shipment, contact your dealer immediately. Be sure to thoroughly read the owner's manual and installation instructions before you being any part of the installation. It is also a good idea to begin practicing navigating your way through the calibration software a few days before actually starting the project.

When you are ready to begin, start by finding a suitable location to mount the ECU. I prefer to keep them inside the vehicle in an effort to avoid any moisture or unnecessary heat from the engine compartment. Be sure to use a rubber grommet anywhere the wire harness passes through the firewall to avoid abrasion and possible failure of the harness. It is also a smart thing to try and keep the unit away from any source of electronic noise such as an ignition system to prevent any interference with the operation of the unit.

If you have ordered the correct harness for you installation, it should be an easy task to connect all of the fittings (which all come labeled for easy identification) to their respective sensors. If you have ordered a blank harness, be sure to make all of the crimp connections securely, or use some solder if wires must be joined together. Always protect any connections or bare wire from the outside elements to avoid corrosion.

Once the harness and ECU have been installed in the vehicle, you may download the software to your laptop and attempt to communicate with the ECU. If your engine configuration is close to any of the engines that Holley has provided start-up maps for, it is a good idea to use one and load it to the ECU now.

When you have established communication with the Commander 950, the first thing to check for is that all of the sensors in the live data screen are operating properly. Look for anything out of the ordinary such as a throttle position sensor reading backwards, or a faulty air or water temperature sensor reading.

Before cranking the engine, it is necessary to go into the set-up menu and ensure all of the settings are correct for your engine. Check to make sure that the number of cylinders matches and also that the correct MAP sensor is being used. You can also set up the type of injectors you are using and the type of ignition system you will have on the engine.

After you have verified the correct settings in the set-up screen and checked that all the sensors are reading

Holley Commander 950

The Holley Commander 950 has an elaborate idle control function that allows the user to input idle speed values based on engine temperature, battery voltage, and throttle position to control how far open the IAC valve is at any time.

When using the Race version of the software, the tuner can use information from the optional GM knock sensor for tuning the ignition curves to avoid detonation. This is a very helpful feature for the all-out race engine.

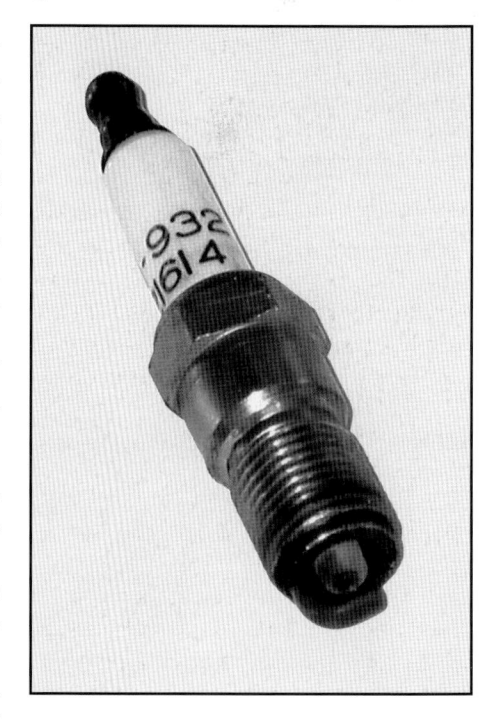

You can always look to the spark plugs for an idea of how well the tuning is going. If an engine is experiencing detonation, there will be tiny deposits of black or shiny aluminum on the center electrode. In severe cases, the entire J-shaped electrode will be missing!

correctly, you can begin to crank over the engine using the starter and check for the correct engine speed reading on the live data screen. Once the engine starts, be sure to let it warm up fully to operating temperature before making any changes to the base fuel tables.

The Holley Commander 950 has an elaborate idle control function that allows the user to input idle speed values based on engine temperature, battery voltage, and throttle position. Always make sure to adjust these functions according to the user's manual if you are having trouble establishing a steady idle. With a little work, the engine should idle just as evenly as a new factory engine.

Once the engine has warmed up to operating temperature and you have established a steady idle, you can begin to tune the base fuel and ignition curves for the no-load and light-load sites on the map. This can be done in neutral by free-revving the engine or by lightly driving the vehicle to reach the light-load sites.

I would recommend using a dynamometer for the medium and heavy-load sites. Tune the engine by holding it to a specific engine speed and gradually increasing the load to reach each site in that engine-speed column. Once all those sites are tuned, you can move to the next engine-speed column.

When using the Race version of the software, the tuner can use information from the optional GM knock sensor for tuning the ignition curves to avoid detonation. If you do not have access to a knock sensor or the Race version of the software, tune with caution. Find the maximum power output of the engine and then back the ignition advance down one or two degrees. This should provide a margin of error against harmful detonation.

You can also stop tuning every few minutes or so to have a look at the spark plugs and search for telltale signs of detonation.

Take your time when tuning the Holley Commander 950, and try to take advantage of all it has to offer by thoroughly reading and understanding the installation manual and the software version you will be working with. Holley has stepped up to the plate again with its latest offering, and hopefully your experience with their fuel-management products will reflect that. I have personally tuned dozens of vehicles with this system, and I have found that once you get used to it, the engines run very well and quite reliably. I hope you have the same experience.

Building and Tuning High-Performance Fuel Injection

CHAPTER 16

MoTeC

MoTeC is viewed by many as the king of the hill when it comes to flexibility and reliability in a fuel-injection system. MoTeC's desire to be the industry leader in fuel-injection technology has driven it to stay on top of all the latest technology. Chances are — if you have an engine, MoTeC can control it.

> **MoTeC**
>
> **COST:** Approximately $2,200 to $15,000
>
> **FEATURES:** MoTeC systems provide the ultimate flexibility to control any output function or engine type.
>
> **EASE OF INSTALLATION AND TUNING:** The MoTeC-supplied wire loom always fits perfectly, but special training is necessary in order to properly use the software and realize its potential.

The name MoTeC has become synonymous with high-performance and racing EFI systems. The company, based in Australia, has become known worldwide for their commitment to quality and cutting-edge performance.

MoTeC has concentrated on becoming the industry leader in aftermarket fuel-injection technology. They have kept up with every advancement by the OEM, including variable camshaft technology, variable intake runner control, and the latest in computer-controlled drive-by-wire throttle technology.

In 1987 MoTeC of Australia teamed up with JGM Tooling, Inc. of Hunting-

MoTeC

Many late-model luxury and sports cars are becoming very complex right from the factory with options like the new drive-by-wire, where the throttle is controlled by the ECU. MoTeC is one of the few companies who have kept pace with the OEM.

MoTeC offers four basic units, each of which can be upgraded to perform just about any function one would want. Starting with the M4 and moving up to the M48, M8, and M800-880 series, you can find a system that has just the right features for your project.

At JGM's 10,000-square-foot facility, they can design, build, assemble, and test an engine management system for any type of arrangement you can think of. They also carry an amazing variety of inventory from connectors, to wiring supplies, to ECUs.

ton Beach, California, to reach out to the budding EFI marketplace and capture an audience looking for the ultimate in high-performance engine control.

At JGM, their 10,000-sq-ft facility offers a complete array of services from race car engine management system installations to assisting customers in the simplest of projects. Their engineering staff is constantly researching and developing new processes and hardware, which allows MoTeC to remain on the leading edge of racing technology. JGM is in regular contact with the engineers at MoTeC Australia who are working overtime to make sure they produce the highest quality hardware and software available. They also provide dealer training and certification to those shops wanting to supply their customers with the best in the fuel-injection world.

MoTeC offers four basic units, each of which can be upgraded to perform just about any function one would want. The M4 unit, which is the most basic, offers sequential operations for 4-cylinder engines. The M48 can be used on up to six cylinders in sequential form, or up to twelve cylinders in batch-fire mode. From there you can purchase the M800 or M880 units, which allow up to twelve cylinders to be fired sequentially, and up to six cylinders of direct ignition control or twelve cylinders with waste-spark configuration.

Also, MoTeC recently released new versions of the M800 called the M400

Building and Tuning High-Performance Fuel Injection

Chapter 16

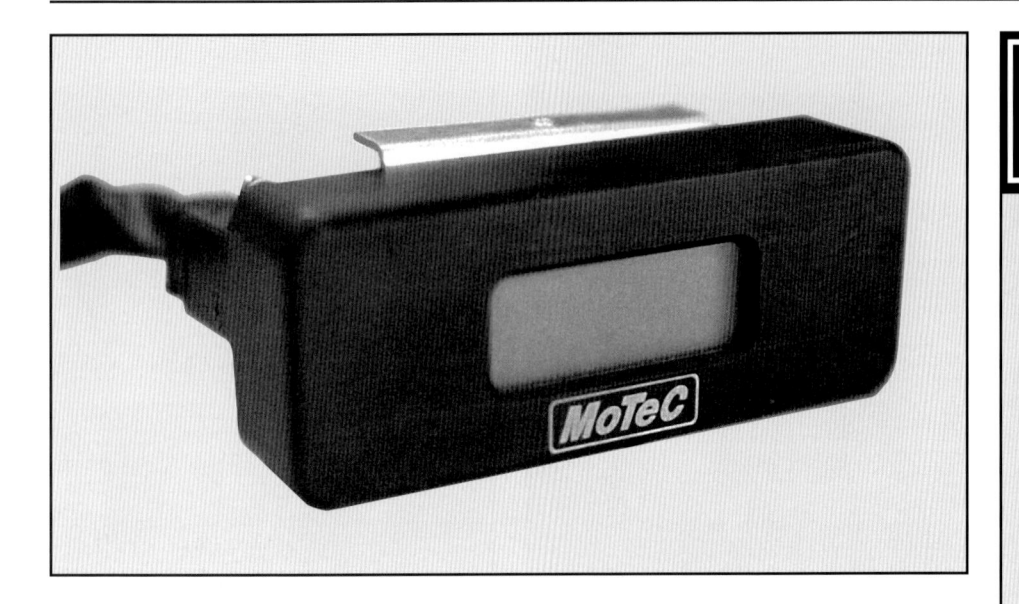

All MoTeC ECUs offer lambda control as an option. The units can use a direct coupling to a narrow-band sensor or this meter called the MoTeC PLM. PLM stands for professional lambda meter.

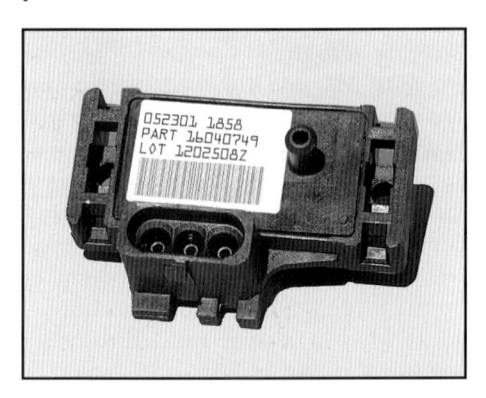

All MoTeC ECUs can use just about any type of sensor for calculating engine load, including MAP, throttle position, Karmann Vortex, or mass airflow sensors. The most common though, is the 1-, 2-, or 3-bar GM MAP sensor shown here.

MoTeC has made their ECUs completely compatible with all OEM sensors for load, engine speed, engine position, engine and atmospheric temperatures and pressures, and any factory wheel speed sensors.

and M600. These units are designed to lower the cost of 4- or 6-cylinder engine management systems that still require the specialized features of the M800, such as variable camshaft position control and the highly sophisticated drive-by-wire control systems.

All M4 and M48 ECUs come complete with the ECU, software, communication cable, semi-custom wiring harness, and six hours of data logging and wideband lambda control. The user can upgrade the logging and wideband control as an option at the time of purchase, or at any later time.

All MoTeC ECUs are capable of fuel and ignition control, boost control, idle control, traction control, launch RPM control, flat-shift, wideband oxygen sensor tuning via target air-fuel maps, and gear detection based on wheel speed versus engine speed.

The MoTeC family of fuel-injection computers can be ordered with a staggering amount of features that could be enough to fill an entire book. The company has done a fantastic job of staying on top of what the industry wants and making features available to suit the needs of the customer.

For instance, the MoTeC fuel-injection systems can use any voltage or frequency device such as MAP sensor, throttle position sensor, MAF sensor,

MoTeC Tuning Tip

MoTeC engine management systems are very complex. The good news is that they have tons of features that can be programmed to suit nearly any imaginable configuration or task. The bad news is that this can sometimes be overwhelming and a bit of a hindrance to productivity for a newcomer to the field.

Jim Munn, owner of JGM, Inc. in Huntington Beach, CA, also known as MoTeC USA, has this advice to offer newbies:

"Get the basics first. Many people do not fully understand how to properly set up an engine management system to accept the correct signals from the existing sensors. The MoTeC units are very flexible and can accept many different types of inputs from all sorts of sensors. However, these inputs must be configured before they will operate correctly. If you are unsure about whether or not your system is set up properly, always get help from your dealer, or directly from the technical staff at MoTeC."

A common mistake that Jim sees is people who have gotten halfway through the tuning process and find that they must change the basic setup and start all over because they didn't do it correctly in the first place. One such area of great importance is the "CRIP" function in the software. CRIP stands for the crankshaft reference index point on the flywheel, which is used to inform the ECU of the exact location of the crankshaft on multi-toothed engines. This value can be set from 0 to 719 degrees to match the engine's trigger pattern. If this is not set correctly at the outset, then all of the calculations for fuel and ignition timing events will be incorrect from the beginning. Be sure to follow all the directions for setting up the CRIP in the manual, or ask for technical assistance to make sure you get it right the first time.

MoTeC

With the MoTeC Ignition Expander shown here, a user can increase the number of ignition output channels that any of MoTeC's ECUs can produce. This allows using an ECU that would only have four outputs in standard form to operate an engine like the Chevrolet LS1, which has eight individual coils!

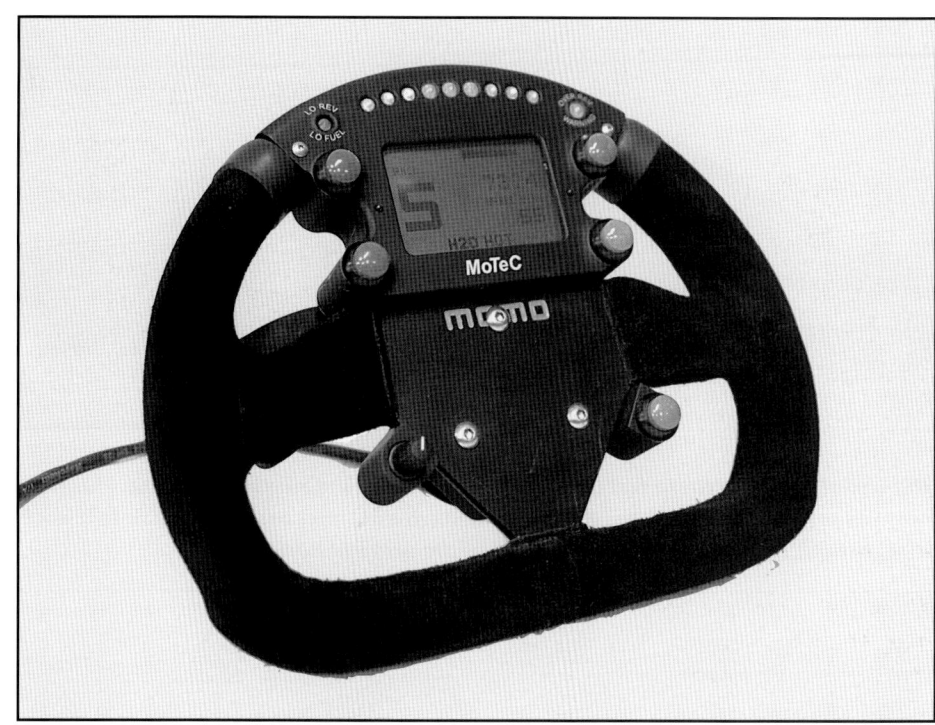

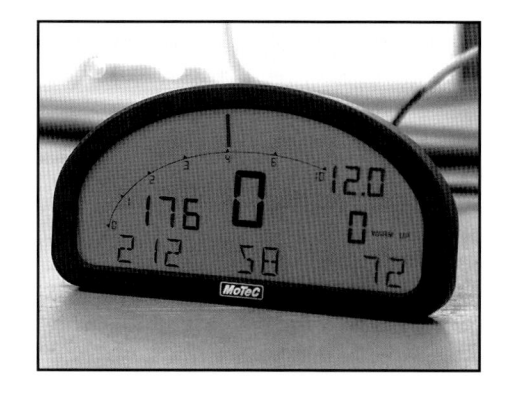

While all the MoTeC ECUs have on-board data-logging capability, they also offer this Dashboard that can function as a stand-alone data-logger! The MoTeC Dashboard can be used in conjunction with any MoTeC ECU, or by itself, to log any function the user wants. It is totally user configurable!

In addition to MoTeC's line of ECUs and data-logging equipment, they also offer a fully programmable steering wheel. This wheel can be configured to control any number of functions, and you can assign tasks to each switch or button. It also has a programmable shift light built in!

Karmann Vortex generators, and any combination of these to sense engine load. A Karmann Vortex generator is a Japanese OEM airflow-measuring device that uses sound and pressure waves to determine airflow.

MoTeC has made their ECUs completely compatible with all OEM sensors for load, engine speed, engine position, engine temperature, wheel speed sensors, and atmospheric temperature and pressure.

As I mentioned earlier, MoTeC has even researched ways to give their units complete control over variable camshaft control systems, and even the latest motor-controlled drive-by-wire systems from Chevrolet, BMW, Audi, Mercedes, Toyota, and Porsche. No other system has proven as capable as the MoTeC family of engine management computers.

The MoTeC calibration software gives the user full control over every aspect of engine tuning and setup. The user can set values for every sensor and actuator on the engine from high to low — even noise filter levels to prevent false signals from being generated and causing errors in the calibration.

On the base fuel and ignition tables, the user can select over a range of 40 engine speed sites and 21 load sites for a total of 840. No other system anywhere in the world offers the user such high resolution. The units also offer fuel-pressure measurement and the ability to manipulate injector pulse width to compensate for changes in fuel pressure, in addition to compensation for changes in battery voltage.

The MoTeC units also offer an amazing array of data-logging functions that can be totally user defined and sampled at rates of between 20 and 200 times per second, depending on the model.

With any system, it is always important to read through the users manual before attempting to use the unit. This is even more important when using the MoTeC ECUs. Since MoTeC computers are so flexible in reading just about any sensor information or trigger pattern available, it is extremely important to understand all of the functions of the unit. It may be necessary for you to contact a dealer in order to make sure you have it set up properly. The ECUs will not function normally if all of the inputs are not configured correctly.

It is also highly important to inform your dealer of the type of engine you will be working on and what functions you will need the ECU to perform. That way, you are sure to get the correct model and wire harness to do the job.

Once you receive the shipment from your MoTeC dealer, inspect the package to make sure everything is in place that

Building and Tuning High-Performance Fuel Injection

Chapter 16

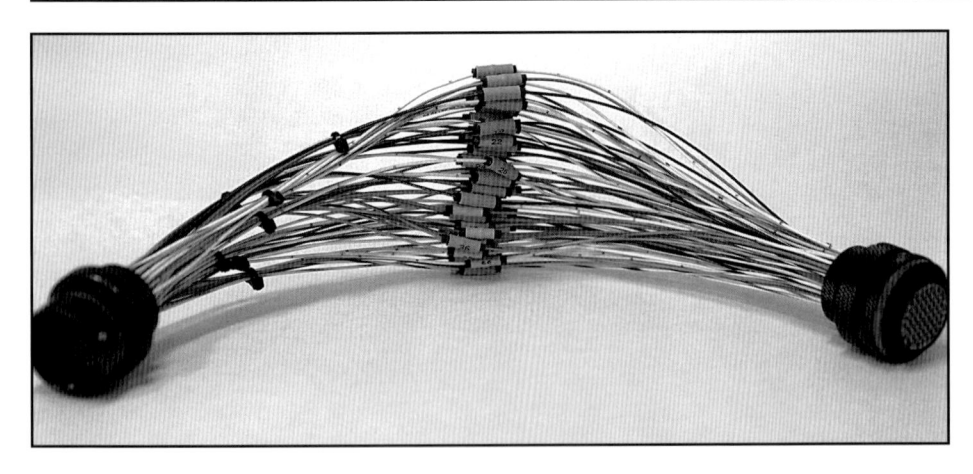

You can also obtain these test harnesses from MoTeC's wiring department. This harness plugs in line between the ECU and main wire harness to allow you to test each wire without compromising the integrity of the original harness!

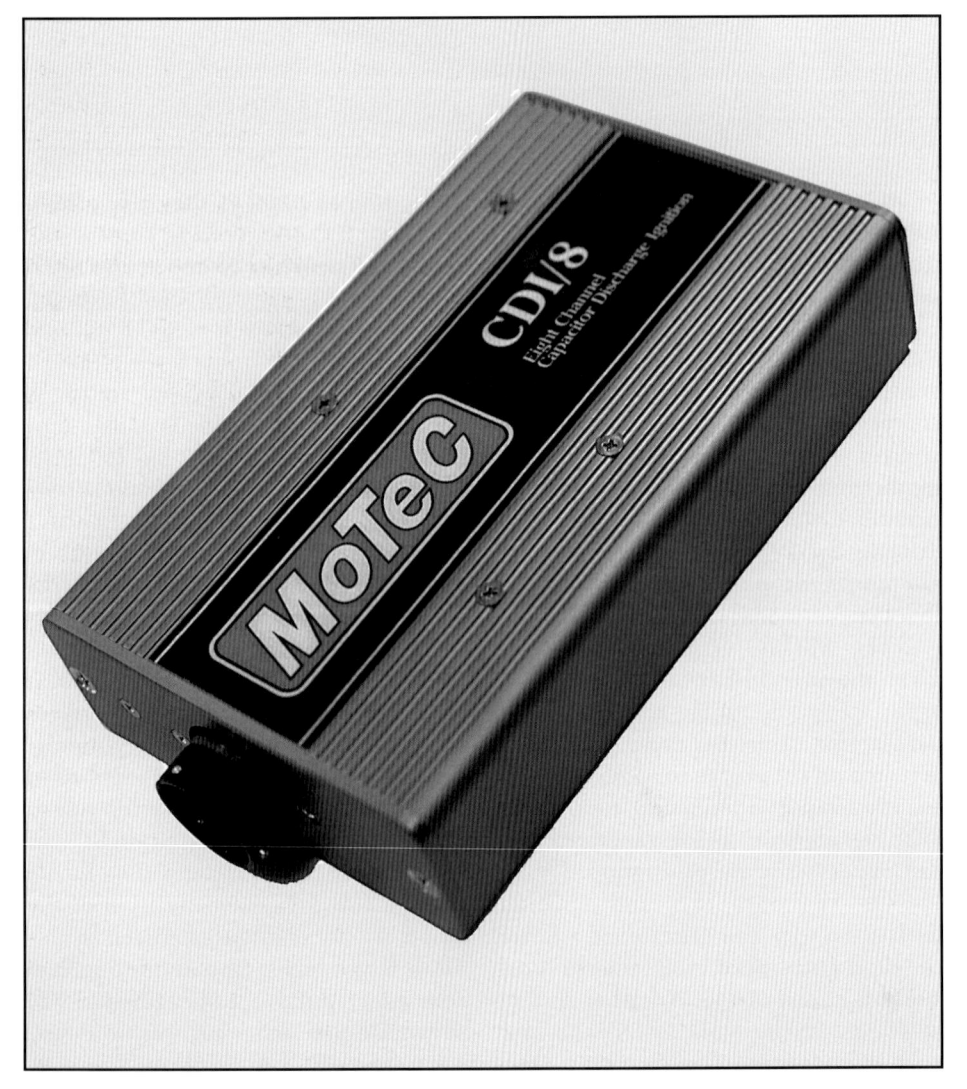

MoTeC also offers this very powerful CDI/8 eight-channel ignition unit. The unit uses capacitors to store energy before discharging a more powerful spark to the ignition coils. The CDI/8 is very popular in applications that require a hot spark to several individual coils.

was ordered. Contact the dealer immediately if there are any problems with missing or incorrect items.

I would strongly recommend spending several days practicing the software navigation process before attempting any part of the installation. Be sure to read through the entire user's manual several times to make sure you understand everything.

When you are comfortable with all of the functions and installation procedures that you will need for the project, you can begin by finding a suitable location for the ECU. MoTeC ECUs are fairly well protected from the elements and can withstand a slightly harsher environment than some other units on the market, but I would still recommend keeping the unit inside the vehicle if at all possible.

Be sure that all power and ground connections are made securely. The grounds should be made directly to the chassis or engine block, not the body of the car. Make sure that anywhere the wire harness passes through the firewall of the car you use a rubber grommet to protect it from abrasion. Once you have fitted the harness to the engine, you may download the software to your laptop and attempt communication.

Open the software and connect the data communication cable between the laptop and the ECU. Once on-line you will be prompted by the software to choose an existing map or start from a new one. If a map in the software library matches closely to your combination, you can choose to start with that as a point of reference.

When configuring the software to match your application, go to the "General Setup" and "Sensor Setup" menus to program the proper injector type, the proper injector scaling for fuel tables, and set the trigger patterns to match your engine. You can also tell the ECU what type of sensor to use for sensing engine load, and set the breakpoints in the base fuel and ignition maps.

The set-up procedure can also be used to set the parameters for auxiliary controls such as VTEC switch points, shift indicator lights, and an array of other uses. Consult your dealer for set up procedures concerning your application.

Use the MoTeC PLM (professional lambda meter) to tune the air/fuel ratios for your engine on a dyno. You can also use the PLM as a stand-alone unit for tuning all types of vehicle. The PLM will work with gasoline, methanol, diesel, and propane fuels.

MoTeC has a test bench that can simulate any input or output function of any one of their ECUs. They use this tool to test every wire harness and ECU that goes out to ensure you can spend time on tuning rather than troubleshooting!

Now that everything has been set in the "General" and "Sensor Setup" tables, you can go to the base fuel or ignition tables, which will also display the live engine data. Check here for any sensor information that may be incorrect, such as faulty air temperature sensors or throttle position sensors that are wired incorrectly. Fix any of these problems before going any further. When you are done checking out all the sensors, you can try to crank the engine over and look for a proper RPM signal. If the RPM signal doesn't seem normal, you may need to go back and check the settings for the trigger patterns. And don't forget to check the connections at the sensor itself!

When everything has been set properly, the engine should start and run normally. You may need to adjust the throttle plate to get it to run on its own. Be sure to let the engine fully warm up before you begin tuning any of the base maps.

The best way to tune the MoTeC unit is to place the engine under a constant load at a given engine speed by using either a chassis dyno or an engine dyno. Then tune all of the load sites within that engine speed range to the desired air/fuel ratio before moving to the next engine speed. Repeat this procedure until all of the sites you plan to use in real operation have been tuned. Be sure to use caution in tuning, as lean mixtures could cause engine damage.

Also be aware that engines will tend to overheat more when a car is operated on a chassis dyno due to the lack of wind to cool the radiator. You may have to tune in 4- or 5-minutes sessions to avoid engine damage from overheating.

Once all the fuel mixture sites have been tuned to your satisfaction, you can concentrate on tuning the ignition sites in much the same manner. Hold the engine speed constant and tune all of the load sites for maximum power, and then reduce the advance by one or two degrees to provide a margin of safety against pinging or detonation.

As always, pay close attention to the instructions in the user's manual and practice navigating the software ahead of time to make your experience with the MoTeC fuel-injection system a fun and rewarding time.

CHAPTER 17

SIMPLE DIGITAL SYSTEMS (SDS)

SDS

COST: Approximately $900 to $1,600

FEATURES: SDS makes simple systems for simple applications, without too many frills.

EASE OF INSTALLATION AND TUNING: The SDS system utilizes an easy-to-use hand-held tuning module, but typically the user must connect their own wire harness.

SDS, or Simple Digital Systems, is committed to building reliable fuel-injection systems for those who want the benefit of electronic engine control without all the complexity of tuning with a laptop, and without all the fancy extras. They like to keep it simple, and they do a good job of that!

SDS has maintained their keep-it-simple attitude towards engine control. The SDS units do not use a laptop for control, and they are not compatible with factory OEM trigger patterns, or idle air control valves. The units do not contain any data-logging capability, and do not use any sort or RS-232 serial cable for computer interface. Most Volkswagen owners agree that keeping it simple is the way to go, at least when it comes to fuel-injection systems.

Simple Digital Systems, or SDS, as it has become known, is now in its tenth year of supplying affordable, easy-to-use fuel-injection systems for the performance market. Their theory is quite simple in that they wanted to build a no-frills system that could be easily installed and even more easily programmed by the end user without a laptop computer. To accomplish this task, the company has built several models of ECUs that can control 4-, 6-, or 8-cylinder engines. They control both fuel and ignition timing and also allow the user to completely tune the engine through the use of a handheld calibration unit.

Building and Tuning High-Performance Fuel Injection

Simple Digital Systems (SDS)

The SDS units are very easy to install and operate. Each one comes with all its own sensors, including a crank-trigger system, which the user will need to mount on the crank pulley.

A custom wire harness is shipped along with the ECU, handheld LCD programmer, intake air temperature sensor, coolant temperature sensor, and optional throttle position and MAP sensors. Other options include knock sensors, oxygen sensors for closed-loop control, fan relays, injectors, fuel pump, and a backlit LCD display unit.

The units are designed to fire injectors in a batch-fire mode; sequential operation is not available with the SDS systems.

The SDS computer can use either throttle position or MAP sensor information as a load reference signal when programming. It is recommended that engines using radical camshafts or individual throttle bodies apply the TPS value as the load signal, while engines using turbochargers or superchargers should use the MAP.

In a time when most engine-management companies are racing towards a feature war where each company strives to bring to market more functions and features than the next guy, SDS has maintained their keep-it-simple attitude towards engine control. The SDS units do not use a laptop for control. They are not compatible with factory OEM trigger patterns, or idle air control valves. The units do not contain any data-logging capability, and do not use any sort or RS-232 serial cable for computer interface. The systems are also not compatible with engines using Siamese intake runners or uneven firing patterns.

The system is aimed at those in the performance market place who have wanted to update their engines to fuel injection in a simple fashion, but did not care to use or learn anything about laptop computer operation. The SDS units are very easy to install and operate. Each one comes with all its own sensors, including a crank trigger system, which the user will need to mount on the crank pulley.

Fuel or Ignition Problem?

When I was young and just starting out tuning engines, an old man said to me: "Ninety percent of all your carburetor problems will be found in the distributor." At the time, I thought he was just a kooky old man. After years of tuning, my own experience seems to have proven him right. Many tuning issues with both carburetors and modern fuel-injection systems are mistakenly blamed on the fuel system.

One thing to watch out for when tuning an engine using a modern fuel-injection system is false information from an oxygen sensor when an engine misfires. When an ignition event fails to happen, or the engine misfires, the oxygen sensor will want to read a leaner mixture that what really exists. This is due to the fact that the oxygen sensor can only read burned hydrocarbons. When the engine misfires, the unburned fuel doesn't get recognized by the sensor, so it seems that there is a large excess of oxygen in the exhaust system.

Many novice tuners immediately begin to add fuel to the base fuel tables in an attempt to correct a lean mixture induced by a misfire. Not only does this not usually correct the problem, it often serves to make matters worse. Having too much fuel can cause a misfire. You can see how the viscous cycle can get started.

Always be sure that the ignition system is in good working order. Visually inspect spark plug gaps and set them according to the manufacturer's recommendations. Also check that the spark plug wires are not burned or melted by the hot exhaust manifolds, or simply worn out.

It is also a good idea to check all the power and ground wires to the ignition system and the high-voltage leads to the ignition coils. While it is certainly possible for an engine to misfire due to a lean mixture, I have found that going back to the basics and thoroughly inspecting the ignition system will almost always rectify the problem.

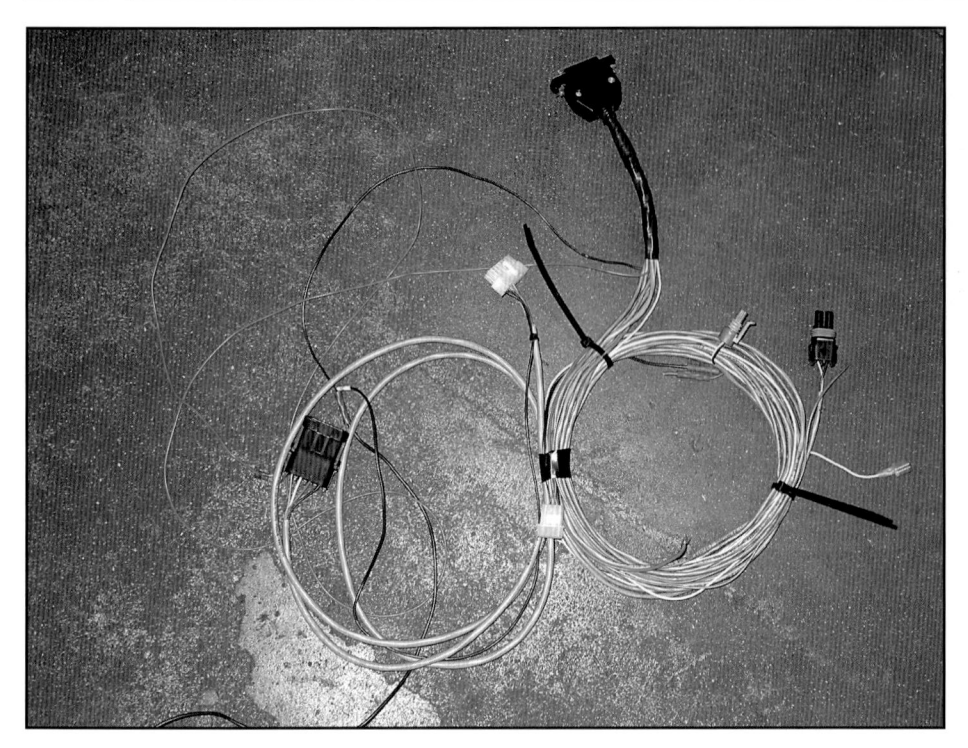

Chapter 17

A custom wire harness is shipped along with the ECU, hand-held LCD programmer, intake air temperature sensor, coolant temperature sensor, and optional throttle position and/or MAP sensor(s).

Tuning the SDS fuel-injection units is quite easy with the hand-held LCD programmer. The unit can be used to scroll through any of a total of 204 programmable points in the RPM and load ranges.

SDS also offers this tuning pod, which allows a very quick adjustment of the fuel curve in real time. Simply dial the knob to add or subtract fuel at any point until the mixture is correct, and then program the current value into the ECU!

different engine loads, and the difference cannot be distinguished by the TPS value alone.

Tuning the SDS fuel-injection units is quite easy with the hand-held LCD programmer display. The unit can be used to scroll through any of a total of 204 programmable points in the speed and load ranges.

The RPM ranges begin at 250 rpm and continue in 250-rpm increments until 9,750 rpm. The unit can be adjusted at each RPM for more or less fuel and ignition timing as the engine requires. The unit has a maximum injector pulse-width capability of 32 milliseconds with a 0.1 millisecond resolution. Ignition timing can be adjusted in 1-degree increments.

It is worthwhile to note here that because the LCD programmer is easier to use than a laptop-programmed fuel-injection system, it does not negate the need for proper tuning. Before you can tune an engine's fuel curve, regardless of the actual method, you must have a broad understanding of what the engine needs in order to perform correctly. The handheld programmer will not solve any tuning issues that the user creates. It still just does whatever you tell it to do. Be sure you understand what changes to make and why to make them, before attempting to tune any engine.

Although the SDS systems can operate in closed-loop mode with the addition of the optional oxygen sensor, they

Engines with radical camshafts or individual throttle bodies tend to generate erratic vacuum-signal pulses to the MAP sensor, which makes low-speed fuel calculations very difficult. Engines using forced induction are not suitable for TPS load calculations because 100% throttle opening could represent many

Simple Digital Systems (SDS)

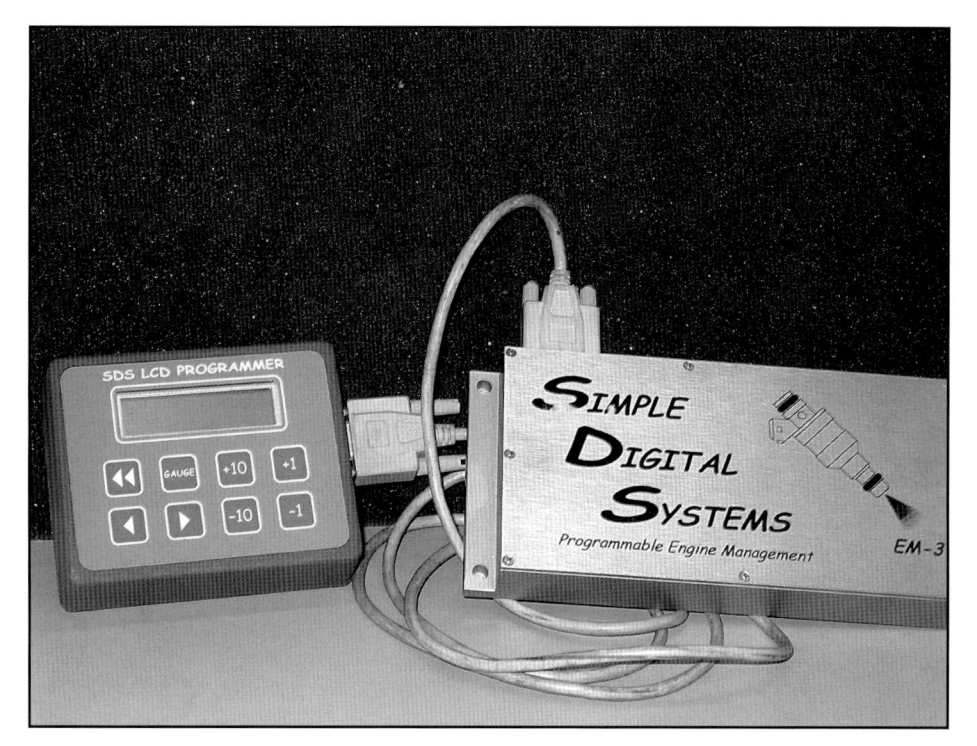

The SDS hand-held module is quick and easy to use. It plugs directly into the ECU with the supplied cable and allows the user to scroll through the fuel and ignition maps and make changes.

The SDS computer can be used on engines up to 3-bar of manifold pressure when accompanied by the correct MAP sensor. However, no blending function of TPS and MAP values is available for engines using radical camshafts and forced induction. It is also adaptable to several different styles of sensors, like the GM model shown here.

Once you have received your SDS fuel-injection system, be sure to check and be sure everything has arrived in the package. All SDS units come with the special ignition coil packs included.

do not actually permanently change the base fuel curve based on values in any target air/fuel ratio tables. The unit simply reads information about the engine's air/fuel mixtures during periods of light load and medium to high engine speeds, such as when cruising on the highway, to add or subtract fuel from the base calibration in order to achieve closer to a stoichiometric air/fuel ratio.

These units also do not have any software ability to create fuel and ignition tables for startup, but they do however come shipped from the factory with a base fuel and ignition map built into them based on information about the engine displacement and injector size. The SDS computer can be used on engines up to 3 bar of manifold pressure when accompanied by the correct MAP sensor. No blending function of TPS and MAP values is available for engines using radical camshafts and forced induction.

Once you have received your SDS fuel-injection system, be sure to check and be sure everything has arrived in the package. Call the technical support line or your dealer immediately if there is any problem.

The first thing you should always do when installing any fuel-injection system is to read the user's manual carefully and make sure you fully understand every aspect of the installation and tuning process. This is a very important step, as continuing from this point without the proper knowledge is sure to cause problems later on.

Building and Tuning High-Performance Fuel Injection

Chapter 17

SDS supplies its wire harness with common connectors like this one from Packard that are commonly referred to as Weather-Pack connectors. These easy-to-find connectors make parts replacement less stressful and keep with the simplicity philosophy of SDS.

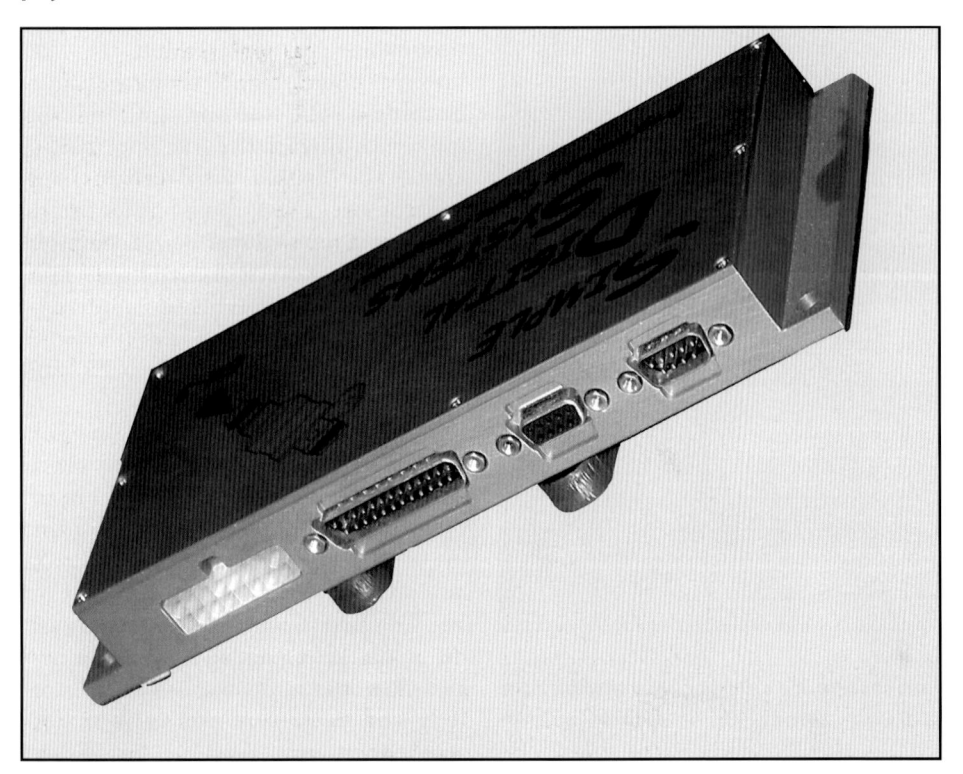

Once the harness has been installed on the engine, it is very easy to plug directly into the ECU. All of the connectors are installed so that they can only fit in one location and cannot be mismatched!

Installing the SDS unit is very simple. Start by following the manufacturer's recommendation for installing the supplied crankshaft position sensor and its magnets. It is this sensor that will give the ECU all the information about the engine speed so it knows when to fire the injectors.

Next, find a good spot to mount the ECU itself. SDS recommends keeping the unit inside the vehicle to protect it from dust, moisture, and vibration. Although SDS uses high-quality components, they realize that a harsh environment can sometimes still get the best of an electronic device. Make sure the unit is mounted securely, it is not a bad idea to use some rubber mounts to further isolate it from vibration.

Once you have mounted the ECU, the next step is to mount all of the sensors that were supplied with the unit. SDS supplies its own sensors to ensure product compatibility. Follow the instructions carefully to avoid any problems later on caused by improper installation or adjustment.

When the ECU and sensors have all been properly installed, you can begin to install the wire harness. SDS normally constructs the wire harness before shipping to ensure proper fitment for your engine. However, because not all engines are exactly alike, it is wise to check for correct location of all the connectors in the harness before going too far. When you are certain everything will fit properly, you can start by connecting the main plugs to the ECU. Route the rest of the wire harness through the firewall to the engine. Be sure and use rubber grommets where any wiring goes through the body of the car to avoid chafing or abrasion to the harness.

After everything is connected and the unit is powered up, you can scroll through the screens on the LCD display to check the condition of all the sensors. Check to make sure everything is in order before you start the car. The TPS value should change evenly from 0 to 100 percent as you depress the accelerator pedal. Also look for abnormal MAP and coolant temperature readings to be sure everything is in order.

Simple Digital Systems (SDS)

It is always best to use a dyno like this one for tuning, but it can be done on the street if you are extremely careful. Be aware that tuning and driving at the same time can be very dangerous, as driving conditions can change very quickly.

This Yamaha Raptor four-wheeler, owned by Jim Behrens of The Dyno Shop in El Monte, California, has been turbocharged and converted to electronic fuel injection with the help of an SDS computer! Hold on tight Jim!

When you are ready to go, crank over the engine and make sure the RPM is correct. If there is a problem with the signals or erratic readings, consult the user's manual and go over the installation procedures. If this doesn't solve the problem, you may need to contact the dealer or technical-support department.

Once the engine is up and running, be sure to let it warm up fully to operating temperature before you tune any sites in the base fuel curves. Tuning with the LCD programmer is very simple and is done by scrolling to the correct RPM range for where the engine is operating, and making an offset change to the fuel or ignition values. Start with the idle and light-load conditions first, and move progressively towards the higher-load points. It is always best to use a dyno for tuning, but this can be done on the street if done carefully. Be aware that tuning and driving at the same time can be very dangerous as driving conditions can change very quickly. Obey all traffic signal and local traffic laws to avoid turning your tuning experience into a legal nightmare.

In the end, you'll find that there are many fuel-injection systems on the market that have tons of features, some of which you may never use or don't even understand. The decision to go with a certain system should be made as the result of a logical thought process and a lot of research. Only then can you make an educated choice, and only then will you find the right kit for you.

If you are looking for a system without all the features that you'll never use, and you aren't too crazy about the prospect of obtaining a laptop computer for tuning, then an SDS system could be for you. Take your time when reading the user's manual to make sure you understand everything and be sure to follow the installation instructions exactly. If you pay attention to what the engine wants and don't get in a hurry when tuning, you'll have your engine up and running smoothly in no time flat, and you won't have to be a computer genius to do it!

Appendix A

EFI Manufacturers

ACCEL DFI
10601 Memphis Ave #12
Cleveland, Ohio 44144
Phone: (216) 688-8300
Fax: (216) 688-8305
www.mrgasket.com

AEM
Advanced Engine Management, Inc.
2205 126th Street, Unit A
Hawthorne, CA 90250
Phone: (310) 484-2322
Fax: (310) 484-0152
www.aempower.com

Autronic
USA Distributor Aussie Imports, LLC
Lexington, KY 40515
Phone: (859) 983-4966
www.aussieimportsllc.com

Edelbrock
2700 California Street
Torrance, CA 90503
Phone: (310) 781-2222
Fax: (310) 320-1187
www.edelbrock.com

EFI Technology
4025 Spencer Street #102
Torrance, CA 90503
Phone: (310) 793-2505
Fax: (310) 793-2514
www.efitechnology.com

Electromotive
9131 Centreville Road
Manassas, VA 20110
Phone: (703) 331-0100
Fax: (703) 331-0161
www.getinjected.com

F.A.S.T.
151 Industrial Drive
Ashland, MS 38603
Phone: (662) 224-3495
www.fuelairspark.com

Haltech
10 Bay Rd. Taren Point
NSW Australia, 2229
Phone: (612) 9525-2400
Fax: (612) 9525-2991
www.haltech.com

Holley
1801 Russellville Rd.
P.O. Box 10360
Bowling Green, KY 42102-7360
Phone: (270) 782-2900
Fax: (270) 745-9590
www.holley.com

MoTeC
5355 Industrial Drive
Huntington Beach, CA 92649
Phone: (714) 897-6804
Fax: (714) 897-8782
www.motec.com

SDS
Racetech, Inc.
1007-55 Ave. NE
Calgary, Alberta, Canada
T2E 6W1
Phone: (403) 274-0154
Fax: (403) 274-0556
www.sdsinjection.com

APPENDIX B

FUN FORMULAS

DISPLACEMENT:

$$(Bore / 2)2 \times Stroke \times 3.14 = Displacement\ (per\ cylinder)\ in\ inches3$$

Example:

$$(3.552/2)\ 2 \times 3.543 \times 3.14 = 35.09\ in3$$

Or

$$Bore2 \times .7854 \times Stroke = Displacement\ (per\ cylinder)\ in\ inches3$$

Example:

$$(3.552)\ 2 \times .7854 \times 3.543 = 35.1\ in3$$

COMPRESSION RATIO:

$$Compression\ Ratio = \frac{V1 + V2 + V3 + V4}{V2 + V3 + V4}$$

V1 = cylinder displacement volume
V2 = deck clearance volume
V3 = head gasket volume
V4 = head chamber volume − piston dome volume (or + piston dish volume)

Example:

$$\frac{37.699 + .188 + .478 + (3.841 - .121)}{.188 + .478 + (3.841 - .121)} = 10.74:$$

Building and Tuning High-Performance Fuel Injection

Appendix B

VOLUMETRIC EFFICIENCY:

$$(VE) = \text{Theoretical Airflow} \div \text{Actual Airflow}$$

$$\text{Theoretical Airflow} = (RPM \div 2) \times (\text{Displacement} \div 1{,}728)$$

Example:

$$\text{Theoretical Airflow} = (7000 \div 2) \times (281 \div 1{,}728)$$

$$3500 \times .1626157 = 570 \text{ cfm}$$

PISTON SPEED:

$$\text{Piston Speed in feet per minute (fpm)} = (\text{Stroke} \times 2 \times RPM) \div 12$$

Example:

$$(3.543 \text{ in} \times 2 \times 7{,}000) \div 12 = 4{,}133.5 \text{ fpm}$$

The maximum recommended piston speed is 3,700 fpm. Max piston speed for special-built race engines with appropriate internal parts is 4,600 fpm. These speeds will keep the tensile stresses on the pistons, rods, and rod bolts below a reasonable recommended limit (check with your parts' manufacturers for their specific recommendations).

INJECTOR SIZING:

$$\text{Engine Power @ Flywheel} \times BSFC / (\text{\# of Cylinders}) = \text{Required lbs per hr}$$

For BSFC use:
Naturally aspirated engines: .4-.5
Supercharged or Turbocharged: .5-.6

Example:

$$(305 \times .5) / 8 = 19.0625 \text{ lbs per hr}$$

This formula assumes 100% duty cycle. To calculate based on an 80% duty cycle, divide the final number by .8.

$$19.0625 \div .8 = 23.83 \text{ lbs per hr}$$

INJECTOR FLOW INCREASE FROM FUEL PRESSURE

When increasing or decreasing the pressure to an injector, the new flow rating of the injector can be found as follows:

$$\text{New Flow} = \sqrt{(\text{New Pressure} / \text{Old Pressure})} \times \text{Old Flow Rate}$$

Example:

$$\text{New Flow} = \sqrt{(60 / 43.5)} \times 19 \text{ lbs per hour}$$
$$\text{New Flow} = 1.174 \times 19 \text{ lbs per hour}$$
$$\text{New Flow} = 22.3 \text{ lbs per hour}$$